Coping with Seasonality and Drought

Coping with Seasonality and Drought

Martha Alter Chen

SAGE PUBLICATIONS
New Delhi Newbury Park London

First published in 1991 by

Sage Publications India Pvt Ltd
32 M-Block Market, Greater Kailash I
New Delhi 110 048

Sage Publications Inc
2455 Teller Road
Newbury Park, California 91320

Sage Publications Ltd
6 Bonhill Street
London EC2A 4PU

Published by Tejeshwar Singh for Sage Publications India Pvt Ltd, phototypeset by Pagewell Photosetters, Pondicherry, and printed by Chaman Enterprises.

Library of Congress Cataloging-in-Publication Data

Chen, Martha Alter.
   Coping with seasonality and drought / Martha Alter Chen.
      p.   cm.
   Includes bibliographical references and index.
   1. Droughts—Economic aspects—India—Maatisar. 2. Water resources development—India—Maatisar. 3. Maatisar (India)—Economic conditions. I. Title.
HC438. M33C46   1991   363.3' 492—dc20   91-13734

ISBN 81–7036–231–8 (India)
            0–8039–9689–6 (U.S.)

Dedicated to the
People of Maatisar
and the
Staff of SEWA

Contents

List of Tables

List of Maps
and Photographs

Abbreviations

CBI	Central Bank of India
CPRs	Common Property Resources
DSP	Deputy Superintendent of Police
GRD	Gram Raksha Dal (Village Protection Force)
HYV	High-yielding Varieties
IRDP	Integrated Rural Development Programme
LFPR	Labour Force Participation Rate
NGO	Non-Government Organisation
PPRs	Private Property Resources
RLE	Rural Labour Enquiry
SBI	State Bank of India
SEWA	Self-Employed Women's Association
TLA	Textile Labour Association

Foreword

There are many who study village life in India. They conduct impressive research on caste and class relations, or on socio-economic factors that impede change. Their research is thorough, well-intentioned and full of convincing arguments backed by weighty statistics. The hard work involved in studying or documenting society often bears fruit in the form of good research papers that are read at conferences, influencing colleagues, bureaucrats or activists. Unfortunately that is where most studies end. On shelves, in computers or in the minds of like-minded people. And life in the village they have studied goes on.

The struggle to meet the basic needs for living is unrelenting. Harsh ecological conditions have made fuel and water scarce, its search often dominating rural women's lives. The summer months are tough, but in years of drought they are ruthless. A village woman also works in the fields—her tasks are invariably tedious, back-breaking, unskilled, and low-paying. Yet her income is crucial to the family. There is not enough work to last the year round.

Marty Chen's study of the village of Maatisar began when the state of Gujarat was suffering a severe drought. The Self-Employed Women's Association (SEWA) was engaged in relief work, providing employment to the villagers. Other than simple surveys and lots of interviews, SEWA had not made an in-depth study of the area before plunging headlong into action, trusting its experience with the urban poor to guide it in rural areas. Some of SEWA's projects worked, some did not. Why they did or did not was always a difficult question, one that SEWA had neither the ability nor the patience to answer. So when Marty turned her keen, scholarly mind and warm blue eyes to studying Maatisar, SEWA glowed with secret delight.

Here was the kind of research SEWA should have done. In analysing the village, its history, its resources, its people, with a deep understanding of local realities and never losing touch with the simple, practical problems that dominate daily life, she has come up with an invaluable document that is, in fact, a tool for social change.

Although it is not a study of SEWA's role in the village, her observations have led to a sea-change in SEWA's understanding. It has helped SEWA plan its development schemes and strategies.

Her data has helped SEWA understand how people behave during droughts, and the occupations and resources that are most affected. As a result, it has been possible to 'drought proof' by developing fodder farms, by water-harvesting and using latent resources even during good rainfall years. Such dedicated, thorough studies are invaluable tools for grassroots organisations. Hand in hand, they can bring about powerful social changes. It is my sincere wish that research and action marry more often.

Planning Commission   ELA R. BHATT
New Delhi
October 1990

Acknowledgments

Without the experience and support of the Self-Employed Women's Association (SEWA), this book simply would not have been written. SEWA staff introduced me to the study area and to the local problems of women and the poor; expressed interest in and sponsored my research; and provided the intellectual, logistical and moral support necessary to carry out my field work. I am particularly grateful to Ela Bhatt and Renana Jhabvala for their guidance and wisdom, to Usha Jumani for her thoughtful comments, and to Anila Dholakia for introducing me to Maatisar (our study village) and for answering our many questions. I am also grateful to SEWA's rural staff, who shared their insights during regular visits to Maatisar; SEWA's head office staff, who provided logistical and administrative support; and SEWA's drivers, who drove us to and from Maatisar on many occasions.

Also, without the patience and generosity of the people of Maatisar, this book would not have been written. They welcomed me and my research team into their homes, tolerated our endless questioning, and shared their recollections and knowledge. I am profoundly grateful to them for their kindness, hospitality and cooperation. And I remain deeply moved by their calm, strength and resilience during the 1985–87 drought.

To my research team—Darshana Vyas, Kalpana Pathak and Kausik Amin—I owe so much. They accompanied me on innumerable rounds of the village, earned the respect and affection of our informants, shared their own knowledge and insights with me, and took responsibility for significant portions of the fieldwork. I am particularly indebted to Darshana Vyas for her untiring efforts: without her the field work would certainly not have been completed. And I wish to thank Darshana's husband, Chauhan, for his support and encouragement.

The fieldwork was supported by a grant from the International. Development Research Council (IDRC). The analysis and writing phases were supported by grants from The Ford Foundation, the United States Agency for International Development (USAID), the International Labour Organisation (ILO), and the World Bank. I am grateful to these organisations for their interest and encouragement as well as their financial support. In particular, I wish to thank Vijay Pande and Susanne Mowat (IDRC), Franklin Thomas (The Ford Foundation), Owen Cylke (USAID), Andrea Singh (ILO), and Barbara Herz (The World Bank).

Several individuals assisted me in the analysis and writing of the book. I am very grateful to Raj Bhatia and to M.A. Gandhi for computerising and analysing our data, and to Mihir Bhatt for collecting some of the official data. For preparing the maps, I am grateful to Madhavi and Miki Desai. And for her editorial assistance, I am grateful to Liz McGrory.

The writing of this book was sponsored and supported by the Harvard Institute of International Development (HIID). I wish to thank HIID, especially Dwight Perkins, for providing a congenial atmosphere in which to write. For typing, proofing, and in other ways assisting me in preparing the manuscript, I also wish to thank Mary Lavallee, Elizabeth Dyer and Allegra Burnette.

There are other, countless people to whom I am grateful for their wisdom and encouragement. My informal advisors—those with whom I have had stimulating discussions about poverty, gender and rural livelihoods—are too numerous to name. However, I do wish to mention several individuals who went out of their way to advise and facilitate my research. I remember with respect Raj Krishna, who before his early death, encouraged me to undertake a study on household livelihood systems. I am very grateful to N.S. Jodha for his own work, which inspired mine, and for his advice; to Ranjith Senaratne who trained me in anthropology and who helped train my research team; to John and Pat Caldwell whose work on drought in India and Africa informed my own; to Bina Agarwal for her own work on women, families and social security; to Abe Weisblat who encouraged me to undertake this study; and to Robert Chambers who popularised so many of the issues I addressed in my research.

In Ahmedabad, I am especially indebted to Nirubhai Desai, Vimal Shah, Praveen Visaria and Sudarshan Iyengar, all associated with the Gujarat Institute of Area Planning, for their knowledge and advice. I also wish to thank M.D. Mistry of DISHA, whose courage and insights I admire; Anil Gupta of the Indian Institute of Management (Ahmedabad), whose work informed my own; and Indira Hirway of the Gandhi Labour Institute for her advice and help. Also, I wish to thank several people who offered me generous hospitality during my many trips to Ahmedabad: Ela and Ramesh Bhatt; Renana Jhabvala and Harish Khare; Kartikeya, Raju, and Mrinalini Sarabhai; Vimal and Sarla Shah; Usha Jumani; Mihir Bhatt; Anila Dholakia and her family; and M.D. Mistry and his family.

This book is a revised version of my doctoral dissertation, submitted to the Department of South Asia Regional Studies at the University of Pennsylvania. I am grateful to my dissertation committee—Alan Heston, Jere Behrman, Anil Deolalikar and Arjun Appadurai—who offered constructive advice on my research design, preliminary analysis and the dissertation itself.

I also wish to thank Amartya Sen and Jean Dreze, who became friends and advisors while I was writing the book. Their pioneering work, both individual and joint, on poverty, hunger and social security set a high standard for all of us writing on these topics. Both took time out of their busy schedules to advise and encourage me.

Finally, I want to thank three people without whose patience, understanding and encouragement this and other manuscripts would never have been completed: my husband Lincoln, who has been both a colleague and mentor throughout our mutual careers in international development; and our children, Gregory and Alexis, who were raised in and conditioned by the developing world.

Introduction

The Problem

Rural households, particularly in the arid and semi-arid areas of India, routinely plan for and manage uncertainty associated with regular seasonal fluctuations and periodic drought-induced crises. These uncertainties pose particular hardships for the poor who face chronic vulnerability in terms of their access to resources. In fact, the lives of the poor in India have been characterised by the almost total absence of security (Dreze and Sen 1988). This book describes and analyses the strategies adopted by different types of households to cope with seasonality and drought in a single village in a semi-arid region of Gujarat state in Western India.

The research was carried out during 1987, which turned out to be the third year of a severe drought in the region. High rainfall variability and drought are common phenomena in India. An estimated two thirds of the cultivated area is subject to drought (Rao et al. 1988). During the 1960s and 1970s in Gujarat, there were five widespread droughts (which affected more than 20 per cent of the villages), three severe droughts (which affected more than 50 per cent of the villages), and localised droughts in one or more arid areas every year.

In designing the study, I had not predicted that drought would recur during 1987. My original intention was to study how a cross-section of households generates livelihoods. I use the term 'household livelihood system' to refer to the mix of individual and joint strategies within a household, developed over a given period of time, that seeks to mobilize available resources and opportunities. Available resources are seen to include physical assets such as land; human assets such as time and skills; social assets such as family, kin, caste and patronage relationships; and collective assets such as common property resources or public sector services.

I identified several dimensions of household livelihood systems for particular focus: the significance of *gender* as a basic variable in understanding household behaviour; the importance of recognising not only the *multiple* activities but also the multiple sectors, markets and institutions in which households are engaged; the centrality of *non-market* activities, relationships and institutions to household livelihood systems; and the significance of *seasonality* in determining how households mix their resources and activities across a given year.

After the monsoon rains failed mid-way through the study year, I modified the study to incorporate a focus on the drought. Given the existing focus on seasonal coping strategies, it was not difficult to incorporate a focus on drought-induced strategies. Indeed, as I will discuss in Part III, household responses to drought often involve intensifying or modifying regular seasonal strategies.

Background

I first visited the study area in 1979. At that time, I was working for the Bangladesh Rural Advancement Committee (BRAC), a leading non-government organisation in Bangladesh, and had brought a team of BRAC staff on a study tour of rural development projects in India. The first project we visited was the Self-Employed Women's Association (SEWA), which had recently begun working in rural areas. As part of our SEWA visit, we were brought to Maatisar and neighbouring villages. Little did SEWA or I know that eight years later I would return to study Maatisar.[1]

From 1975 to 1987, first with BRAC and then with Oxfam America, I worked closely with over 50 non-government projects, in both India

[1] The real name of the village is not used in this book to protect its identity. Ela Bhatt of SEWA coined the pseudonym 'Maatisar'.

As she explained, 'sar' is a common suffix in local place names; 'maati' is a very ordinary Gujarati word meaning earth, dust or mud; and 'maatikam' (literally, 'earth work') is the local word for manual labour. The choice of Maatisar is particularly apt in that men and women from over half the households in the village dug, lifted and carried earth at relief works during the study year.

and Bangladesh, designed to help women from poor households improve their livelihoods and organise for change. Most of these projects were premised on two basic assumptions: that women's work is critical to the livelihoods of poor households and that standard definitions of work, worker and income do not capture how poor households generate livelihoods.

In order to test these assumptions, I decided to undertake a study of household livelihood systems in one of the project areas. After considering several alternatives, I chose the SEWA area and Maatisar village for two basic reasons. First, SEWA staff expressed interest in the utility of my proposed research for their ongoing work in the area. Second, Maatisar is located in a relatively remote, underdeveloped and arid area, and is fairly typical of the area in terms of size and composition (by landholding, caste and occupation).

The Argument

In carrying out the study, it became clear that rural households have developed a range of strategies to deal not only with seasonality but also with drought; further, that droughts are endemic in the study area and that drought-adjustment strategies are as intrinsic to local liveli-hood systems as seasonal-adjustment strategies. Therefore, I argue that both the possibility of drought and the predictability of seasonal fluctuations are constant factors in the livelihood calculus of most households and influence both their options and their strategies, even in normal years.

A growing body of literature on household coping strategies, both from Africa and Asia, focuses on the differences between seasonal and crisis coping strategies, the sequence and timing of these strategies, and the options or objectives which influence the choice of strategies.[2] I focus both on these and other issues. In brief, several coping strategies proved less viable under drought conditions than under normal seasonal conditions in Maatisar, notably: entering the local labour market (as the demand drops sharply under most drought conditions), drawing upon common property resources (as the competition over

[2] See Agarwal 1989; Behrman 1988a, b; Behrman and Deolalikar 1987, 1989, 1990; Caldwell et al. 1986; Chambers et al. 1981; Corbett 1988; Dasgupta 1987; Dreze 1988; Gupta 1981; Huss-Ashmore et al. 1988; Jiggins 1986; Jodha 1975, 1978, 1981; Longhurst 1986; Sen 1981.

scarce resources from common grazing lands or private fallows increases), and drawing upon social relationships (as patronage, caste and even kin-based relationships become less reliable). Further, many households reduced consumption earlier and more sharply and took smaller but more frequent loans during the drought than they did in normal slack seasons.

In comparing seasonal and crisis strategies, I consider four important variables: the *type* of strategy (i.e., whether it involves adjustments in work, consumption, assets or social relationships); the *level* at which the strategy is negotiated (i.e., whether within the household, between households, at the village level or with the government); the degree to which the strategy is *reversible* (i.e., whether the household can recover after the drought is over); and the *sequencing* or timing of household strategies (i.e., who adopts which strategies in what sequence, and why).

In addition to household responses, my analysis of the 1987 drought covers three related topics: the spatial and temporal dimensions of the drought; its impact on different occupational groups; and both local community and official government responses to it. In terms of the spatial and temporal dimensions of drought, I argue that it is important to distinguish between *localised* and *widespread droughts* and *single-year* and *prolonged droughts*. If the drought in Maatisar had not persisted for three years, the accumulated toll on farmers would not have been so great. As it was, the prolonged nature of the drought forced some surplus farm households not only to take loans after crop failures in order to invest in subsequent cultivation but also to deploy some household labour to relief works. Further, if the drought had been localised in and around Maatisar, the households that normally migrate each year would have been able to do so as usual. Because the drought was so widespread, the migrant labour markets collapsed to a significant degree, forcing many migrant households either to explore new migration routes or remain at home.

In analysing the impact of the drought on different occupational groups, it is important to distinguish between the impact of drought on *entitlements to food* and on *entitlements to produce food*: that is, to determine the impact not only on the day-to-day consumption needs of households, but also on the season-to-season and longer-term needs for fixed assets and working capital. Many households in Maatisar were forced into debt in order to replant in the 1987 monsoon season after their seed stock had been exhausted in the first planting, and to plant in the winter season after suffering monsoon crop losses. These households required not only fixed capital to improve or increase their irrigation resources but also working capital to invest in seeds and other inputs. However, the government did not extend any emergency loans during the 1987 drought period.

In comparing local community and official government response to the drought, I argue that the traditional social security system and the public social security system are effective under very different conditions. During peak seasons in normal years, caste, kin or family support mechanisms operate and the government provides a limited amount of public services. During slack seasons in normal years, caste neighbours often withdraw support leaving kin and family to cushion shortfalls. Few public goods or services are targeted to slack season conditions and requirements. The government is most responsive under drought or other crisis conditions, when kin-based support mechanisms are often strained beyond their capacity to respond. In sum, the traditional social security system operates best during peak seasons in normal years whereas the public social security system operates best under crisis conditions; neither is very effective during slack seasons in normal years.

Ever since the Famine Codes were promulgated by the British Administration towards the end of the nineteenth century, India's famine relief system, particularly the relief or public works schemes, have played an undeniable and crucial role in averting large-scale starvation. As a case in point, during the 1985–87 drought, relief works played an undeniable role in generating employment and helping, thereby, to avert widespread hunger in Maatisar. Men and women from more than half the households in the village participated in the relief works. Our data indicate that, during the drought year, adult labourers averaged 120 days of employment each, of which only 20 days were in the local labour market, 40 in the migrant labour market, and 60 at the local relief works.

Methods

This study is based on two different but complementary data sets: one quantitative (using survey instruments); the other qualitative (using ethnographic methods). My aim was to design survey instruments based on insights generated by preliminary ethnography and to use ethnographic methods to investigate topics which do not readily lend themselves to a survey format. We used ethnographic methods both before and after all surveys: to inform survey design, to verify survey findings, to probe sensitive subjects and to understand the dynamics of selected phenomena.

As designed, the study was deliberately inductive. One strength of inductive fieldwork was seen to be the opportunity to formulate new testable hypotheses rather than merely testing received theory. The study was also deliberately an empirical rather than an archival exercise. The recent history of the village, taking the early 1950s as the baseline, was reconstructed from fragmentary evidence gathered through life-histories, genealogies and other in-depth interviews.

In choosing research assistants, I looked for Gujarati men and women with some rural experience and without too many urban biases. I chose two women—one senior, who had carried out her own research on nomadic tribes in Gujarat, and one junior, who had spent time in a village during her college years; and one man, who had worked with several rural development projects. The research team spent most of 1987, at least half of each month, in Maatisar. I spent a total of three months in the village at four different times in the year. The senior woman on my team made periodic return visits to the village during the first half of 1988 to monitor household responses under continuing drought conditions until the monsoon rains arrived in June.

Our initial census of all households in the village provided both baseline socio–economic and demographic data and a sampling frame. We identified a stratified random sample of 59 households, every fifth household within each of five landholding groups. And we selected a sub-sample of 31 households by taking every second household from the sample, dropping a few which proved uncooperative, and adding a few purposefully chosen from the sample to represent female-headed households and selected occupations. As my research team used to say, the 31 sub-sample households became our 'brothers and sisters' because we spent so much time with them: they were subjected to all our methods, both quantitative and qualitative. The remaining households in the sample became our 'cousins' because we came to know them far better than the non-sample households.

To collect quantitative data, we field-tested and then used several survey instruments: an agro–economic survey; a time–allocation survey; a household consumption survey; and a fuel, fodder and water consumption survey. We conducted the agro-economic survey in the

59 sample households three times, once during each season in the study year. The form for this survey was modelled on household survey forms developed by both the National Council of Applied Economic Research (NCAER) and the International Crop Research Institute for the Semi-Arid Tropics (ICRISAT). To capture the full range of livelihood activities by all types of households, our survey form included long sections on self-employment, local and migrant wage labour, collection of free goods and interhousehold exchanges.

We conducted the time–allocation survey six times, twice during each season, on all persons aged five and above in each of the 31 sub-sample households. This survey involved a recall method which asks respondents to report the previous day's activities, giving the estimated amount of time spent on each, in the sequence in which they were performed. On the same day, surveys on household food, fuel, fodder and water consumption, also based on 24-hour recall, were conducted on each of the sub-sample households.

Our main qualitative methods included structured interviews, life-history interviews, genealogies and participant observation. In the early months of the study year, we conducted semi-structured interviews with selected informants on a wide range of village topics. Later, we conducted more structured interviews with selected informants to develop case studies of 15 key resources and institutions in the village, including land, common property resources, share-cropping, water, labour markets, moneylending, caste structure and dynamics, and the drought. We recorded these interviews, plus all relevant observations and conversations, on worksheets which were then coded by topic and by informant.

We probed the life-histories of three or four members from each of the 31 sub-sample households. The individuals were purposefully chosen to reflect age and gender hierarchies. The life-history interviews focused on the occupational and economic history of the individual at critical stages of his/her life (childhood, marriage, early and later married years, old age) and of the household at different stages of its life-cycle (joint, nuclear, extended). We focused on the options available when critical economic decisions were made (e.g., changing occupations and selling or buying assets) and the reasons for doing so. Through these individual life-histories, we were able to develop a composite history of each sub-sample household. The life-histories, case studies and genealogies served to elicit patterns of village dynamics and to introduce the dimension of time.

In addition, we carried out several small, focused surveys. The number and content of these surveys were determined by the findings of the other methods described above and the progress of the study more generally, including a mid-year adjustment to incorporate a focus on the drought. We carried out three surveys of migrants: two of labour migrants in early and late 1987; and one in late 1987 in south Gujarat of the shepherds from Maatisar who were forced to migrate with their cattle in search of fodder. We also carried out three surveys of participants in government relief works: during the summer and monsoon seasons in 1987 and in January 1988. We probed sensitive subjects through multiple small surveys to verify and amplify data collected in the agro–economic survey: on land sales and mortgages, share-cropping and moneylending. And we surveyed the retail prices of basic commodities every other month.

The basic aim of our study was to contribute to a broader under-standing of the dynamics of rural poverty in India by analysing house-hold livelihood strategies in a single village. Limited to a single village, the study does not attempt to draw broad generalisations about rural phenomena. Rather, it attempts to analyse why, how and under what circumstances households adopt different coping strategies.

Plan of the Book

The plan of the book is as follows. Part I describes Maatisar and discusses changes over time which have affected its resource base and occupational structure. Part II analyses the various seasonal strategies adopted by different households and the institutions, both economic and social, which regulate access to these strategies. Part III describes the 1985–87 drought in the region and analyses the various strategies adopted by different households in response to it. A concluding section summarises the main findings by comparing household, village and state responses to persistent vulnerability in Maatisar and discusses the policy implications of the study.

I

The Village

The Region

Maatisar village is located in Dholka *taluka* in Ahmedabad District of Gujarat state in Western India (see map of Gujarat state). The district headquarters and state capital is Ahmedabad city, often referred to as the 'Manchester of India' because of its textile mills and related industries. Ahmedabad District is cited as one of the most highly industrialised and urbanised districts of Gujarat. However, given that Ahmedabad city is a major metropolitan centre, the statistics for the district as a whole are somewhat misleading. Except for the urban area around Ahmedabad city, the district remains relatively underdeveloped. Industrialisation has begun in the northern portion of Dholka *taluka*, mainly near the towns of Dholka and Bavla, but the rest of the *taluka* is notable for its lack of industrial activity (Government of Gujarat 1984).

Ahmedabad District is divided into seven *talukas*, Dholka being one of the larger *talukas* of the district and the state as a whole. It comprises 116 villages and two urban centres and lies to the southwest of Ahmedabad city. The *taluka* administrative headquarters are in the historic town of Dholka, approximately 40 kilometres from Ahmedabad. The other urban centre is Bavla, a growing market and industrial town, some 30 kilometres from Ahmedabad and 25 kilometres from Maatisar.

The *taluka* is trisected by two highways, one a national highway which passes by Bavla and the other a state highway which passes by Dholka (see map of Ahmedabad District). The eastern boundary of

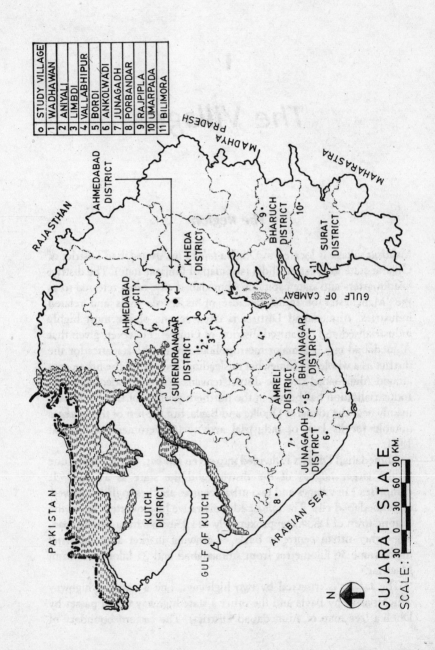

0	STUDY VILLAGE
1	WADHAWAN
2	ANIYALI
3	LIMBDI
4	VALLABHIPUR
5	BORDI
6	ANKOLWADI
7	JUNAGADH
8	PORBANDAR
9	RAJPIPLA
10	UMARPADA
11	BILIMORA

GUJARAT STATE

SCALE: 30 0 30 60 90 KM.

N

MADHYA PRADESH

MAHARASTRA

RAJASTHAN

PAKISTAN

AHMEDABAD DISTRICT

AHMEDABAD CITY

KHEDA DISTRICT

BHARUCH DISTRICT

SURAT DISTRICT

GULF OF CAMBAY

SURENDRANAGAR DISTRICT

AMRELI DISTRICT

BHAVNAGAR DISTRICT

JUNAGADH DISTRICT

KUTCH DISTRICT

GULF OF KUTCH

ARABIAN SEA

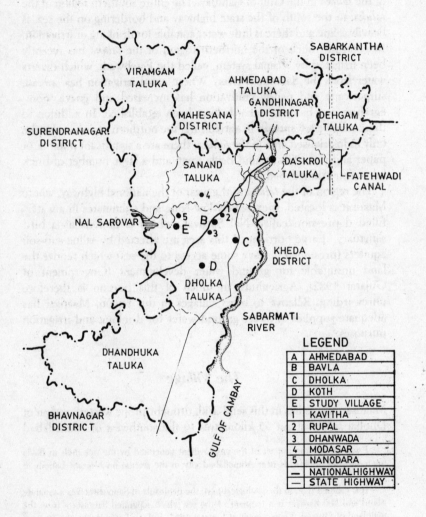

SABARKANTHA
DISTRICT

VIRAMGAM
TALUKA

AHMEDABAD
TALUKA
GANDHINAGAR
DISTRICT

DEHGAM
TALUKA

MAHESANA
DISTRICT

SURENDRANAGAR
DISTRICT

SANAND
TALUKA

A

DASKROI
TALUKA

FATEHWADI
CANAL

4

NAL SAROVAR

5   B
E   2
3
C

KHEDA
DISTRICT

D

DHOLKA
TALUKA

SABARMATI
RIVER

DHANDHUKA
TALUKA

LEGEND	
A	AHMEDABAD
B	BAVLA
C	DHOLKA
D	KOTH
E	STUDY VILLAGE
1	KAVITHA
2	RUPAL
3	DHANWADA
4	MODASAR
5	NANODARA
—	NATIONAL HIGHWAY
—	STATE HIGHWAY

BHAVNAGAR
DISTRICT

GULF OF CAMBAY

N

AHMEDABAD DISTRICT

SCALE: 9 0 9 18 27. KMS.

the *taluka* is skirted by the river Sabarmati, which ends at one corner of the *taluka* in the Gulf of Cambay. The entire southern region of the *taluka*, to the south of the state highway and bordering on the sea, is heavily saline and there is little water suitable for drinking or irrigation. In contrast, much of the northern region of the *taluka* has recently been irrigated by a canal system, called the Fatehwadi, which diverts water from the Sabarmati river. Where canal irrigation has spread, surgar-cane and paddy cultivation has increased and guava, pom-egranate and banana orchards have been established. In addition to these relative advantages in agriculture, the northern region is also the only industrialised area in the *taluka*: there are a significant number of paper and rice mills around Bavla town and a large number of brick kilns near Ahmedabad city.[1]

The region of the *taluka* to the west of the national highway, where Maatisar is located, is extremely low-lying and culminates in a water-filled depression called Nal Sarovar, which is famous as a bird sanctuary.[2] Large portions of this area are affected by saline sub-soil aquifers (presumed to have some access to the sea) which render the land unsuitable for ground water development (Government of Gujarat 1982). Agriculture in much of this portion is therefore unrewarding. Relative to other villages in this region, Maatisar has adequate supplies of sweet ground water for drinking and irrigation purposes.[3]

The Village

Maatisar village lies in this semi-arid, drought-prone western region of Dholka *taluka* about 55 kilometres to the southwest of Ahmedabad

---

[1] I will discuss the impact of the employment generated by the rice mills in Bavla town and the brickfields near Ahmedabad city in the section on Migrant Labour in Part II.

[2] It is claimed that, in the geological past, the peninsula of Saurashtra was a separate island and Nal Sarovar is a remnant of the sea which separated Saurashtra from the mainland of Gujarat (Government of Gujarat 1982: Vol. I). Large flocks of migratory birds stop annually at Nal Sarovar. During the 1985–87 drought, Nal Sarovar dried up completely, a very rare occurrence.

[3] Maatisar is situated on a physiographic border between mainland Gujarat and the Saurashtra peninsula. The maps in the Statistical Atlas (1982) of Gujarat show Maatisar as falling right on the border between areas to the north and east with relatively higher rainfall reliability, higher aquifers, better alluvial soils and semi-arid conditions, and areas to the south and west with relatively higher rainfall variability, saline soil and water sources, and more arid conditions.

city. It is a mixed-caste village, although the majority of households are from Scheduled or Backward Castes (Table 1).[4] Out of a total of 285 households in the village, only 12 are from higher castes: six are Brahmin and six Thakkar, a local Vaishya (trader) caste. As elsewhere in rural India, occupations are generally distributed along caste lines (Table 2). Most of the Brahmin households engage in cultivation and all of the Thakkar households engage in trade and moneylending.[5]

The Koli Patels are the traditional peasant caste of the village: two-thirds of the Koli Patel households claim cultivation as their major occupation and many others engage in cultivation as a secondary occupation. In addition, many Koli Patel households rear livestock and engage in wage labour. All of the Bharwad shepherd households rear livestock and 50 per cent of them also engage in cultivation. Most of the Prajapati potter households produce or sell pottery goods. A few also engage in cultivation and/or labour, and one has begun shopkeeping. Unlike elsewhere in the state, where Vaghris are generally vendors, the local Vaghris engage in either cultivation or wage labour or both. A few Vaghri households vend vegetables and other perishables in the village, and two have migrated once or twice to Delhi to sell utensils and barter used clothing.[6]

The weavers of Maatisar are Vankars, the largest caste group in Ahmedabad district (Government of Gujarat 1984). Whereas elsewhere the Vankars weave cotton, the local Vankars are the only weavers of wool in the *taluka*. In addition to weaving wool, they flay cattle and work as wage labourers, mainly in paddy planting and harvesting.

As would be expected, there are sub-hierarchies within this broad hierarchy of caste groups. The Brahmins carry the most social status as

[4] At the all-India level, the Hindu hierarchy of castes is traditionally divided into four groups or *varnas* (Brahmin, Kshatriya, Vaishya and Sudra). A fifth group of untouchable castes is regarded as being outside the system. The untouchable or outcaste communities are referred to as Scheduled Castes, because they were listed in a 1935 Schedule issued by the British Viceroy, or as Harijans (literally, 'the children of god'), the name given them by Mahatma Gandhi. Under another official classification, the Backward Castes refer to those castes which are the lowest in the four caste groups (i.e., Sudras or agriculturalists). It should be noted that there are no Kshatriya castes in Maatisar.

[5] One Thakkar household claimed salaried government work as its primary occupation, as the household head is a government schoolteacher. But that household also engages in trade and moneylending.

[6] Elsewhere in Gujarat, Vaghris grow and sell vegetables in urban centres within Gujarat state. Some migrate to Delhi and Bombay to barter stainless steel utensils for used clothing which they then recycle and sell.

Table 1
Population and Households by Caste

Caste group	Persons		Households	
	No.	%	No.	%
1. Higher castes				
Brahmin	47	3	6	2.0
Thakkar (traders)	40	2	6	2.0
2. Backward castes				
Bharwad (shepherd)	127	7	19	7.0
Koli Patel (peasant)	830	49	142	50.0
Prajapati (potter)	43	2	7	2.0
Rawal (camel carter)	13	1	4	1.0
Vaghri (vendor)	316	19	51	18.0
3. Scheduled castes				
Barot (genealogist)	14	1	5	2.0
Vankar (weaver)	163	10	28	10.0
Bhangi (scavenger)	29	2	6	2.0
4. Others	66	4		
Gosai (priest)	—		2	0.7
Nayyak	—		1	0.3
Muslim*	—		2	1.0
Others	—		6	2.0
Total:	**1,688**	**100**	**285**	**100.0**

* In this and other tables, for ease of presentation, the two Muslim households are listed as a 'caste'.

members of the highest caste, while the Thakkars command the greatest economic power and status. Among the Backward Castes, the Koli Patels have always been numerically strong but until recently, with the election of the current *sarpanch* (village headman), they never captured political power. The Bharwad shepherds are economically strong, especially since the expansion of the commercialised dairy sector, and have remained powerful political clients of the Thakkar ex-*sarpanch*. The Prajapatis (potters) are few in number and remain relatively weak, both socially and economically. Although officially classified as a Backward Caste, the Vaghris are only slightly above the Scheduled Castes in social status. As such, they attempt to gain social status through an elaborate set of taboos regarding their interactions with the Vankars, Bhangis and Barots.

Table 2
Primary Occupations by Caste

Caste groups	No. of HHs	Cult.	Livestock	Labour	Weaving	Trade	Others*
Brahmin	6	4	—	—	—	—	2
Thakkar	6	—	—	—	—	5	1
Bharwad	19	7	10	1	—	—	1
Koli Patel	142	93	1	35	—	1	11
Prajapati	7	1	—	2	—	—	4
Rawal	4	—	—	2	—	—	2
Vaghri	51	22	—	22	—	1	6
Barot	5	—	—	—	—	—	5
Vankar	28	—	—	1	22	—	5
Bhangi	6	3	—	2	—	—	1
Gosai	2	—	—	—	—	—	2
Nayyak	1	—	—	—	—	—	1
Muslim	2	—	—	—	—	1	1
Others	6	—	—	4	—	1	1
Total:	**285**	**130**	**11**	**68**	**22**	**9**	**44**

* 'Other' includes: caste services, artisan production, transport, salaried work and those that are non-active.

Among the Scheduled Castes, the Bhangis have the lowest status, although none of the Bhangi households engage in the traditional caste occupation, scavenging. The Vankars command some political status because their caste leader has linkages with the Scheduled Caste political lobby in the state, and some economic status because they are primarily and traditionally weavers rather than wage labourers. Although elsewhere Barots are generally classified as a Backward Caste (Shah and Desai 1988), the Barots of Maatisar are genealogists for the Vankar weavers and, as such, have acquired the lower status of the Vankars and live in the Vankar *vas* (neighbourhood).

In terms of political power, the two higher caste groups controlled the position of *sarpanch* (village headman) for 25 years: from 1960, when the *gram panchayat* (village council) system was introduced, until the elections in 1984. In fact, except for one four-year period when the *sarpanch* was a Brahmin, members of a single Thakkar household held the position of *sarpanch* for over two decades. The men of this family were the political heirs of the ex-feudal lord, Shermia. In the 1984 election, the Koli Patels, who have always been numerically strong in the village (nearly 50 per cent of all households), rallied together and elected a *sarpanch* from their own caste group, the son of a deceased but greatly revered caste leader.

The residential area of Maatisar is densely clustered and encircled by its agricultural land. Each caste or sub-caste group lives in a separate neighbourhood or *vas*: the Brahmins and Thakkars along the main street; the various Koli Patel sub-castes in the east, south and west of the village centre; the Bharwads in the north; the Vaghris and Scheduled Castes at opposite ends of the village (see map of Study Village).

To the north and west of its residential centre, the farm land of Maatisar abuts directly onto the agricultural land or the common grasslands of four other villages. To the south and east, the River Rodh separates the agricultural land of Maatisar from that of two other villages. The land mass of Maatisar totals nearly 3,000 acres, of which roughly 2,400 acres are agricultural land.[7] The agricultural land comprises approximately 300 acres of low-lying alluvial soil and some 2,050 acres of medium brown to sandy loam soil; roughly seven

---

[7] According to the 1981 official census and our study census, Maatisar village consists of a total land area of about 2,800 acres.

per cent of the low-lying and 26 per cent of the higher land are irrigated.[8]

Although the agricultural land encircles the village completely, this ring of fields is itself divided into six areas by four roads which pass by the village: the main paved road which runs from the main state highway to Sanand *taluka*, a branch of the main road which runs northeast from Maatisar, and dirt roads which run west and south from Maatisar. Within each area, there are one or more water tanks (nine in all) which are the common property of the village. Each of the land areas is named after the village tanks or, in one case, the river located in the area (see map of Study Village Lands).[9] In addition to private agricultural land, there are 18 plots of non-cultivable land, some 157 acres of permanent pasture land (called *gauchar*), and 59 acres of forest groves which are the common property of the village.[10]

There are two sources of surface water in the village: a river which flows to the south and the nine village tanks scattered through the private fields. The River Rodh, which flows through Sanand and

	1981 Census	1987 Study
Irrigated	49	558
Non-irrigated	2,333	1,789
Cultivable waste	264	216
Non-cultivable waste	183	183
	2,829	2,746

Informant data from the current study puts the figure for permanent pastures and forest groves at 216 acres, compared to the official figure of 264 acres for cultivable waste. The current study obtained no reliable figure for non-cultivable waste (areas numbered 1–18 on the map of Village Lands). Throughout the report, therefore, the 1981 census figure of 183 acres is assumed for 1987. According to the 1987 study census, assuming 183 acres of non-cultivable waste. the total land mass of the village is 2,746 acres. All figures have been rounded to the nearest whole number.

[8] The local names for the two types of soil are:

   kyari = low-lying alluvial soil

   goradu or *thaliya* = medium brown to sandy loam

[9] When villagers describe the location of their fields, they mention the names of these areas.

[10] The 18 plots of non-cultivable land, each of which has a name, are numbered 1–18 on the map of Village Lands. The forest groves include two plots of 10 acres each of permanent pastures which have been taken over by the Forest Department for tree-plantations (letter F on the map) and a 29-acre tract of wild *babul* near the River Rodh (called Rodhna Kanthe, number 7 on the map). The permanent pasture land is lettered P on the map.

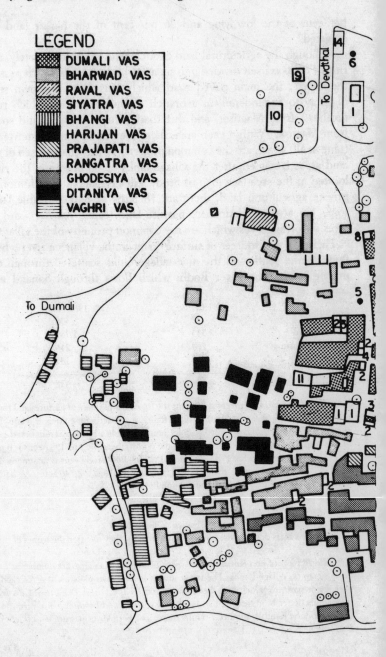

LEGEND

▨	DUMALI VAS
▤	BHARWAD VAS
▨	RAVAL VAS
▨	SIYATRA VAS
▥	BHANGI VAS
▨	HARIJAN VAS
▨	PRAJAPATI VAS
▨	RANGATRA VAS
▨	GHODESIYA VAS
■	DITANIYA VAS
▤	VAGHRI VAS

To Devdhal

To Dumali

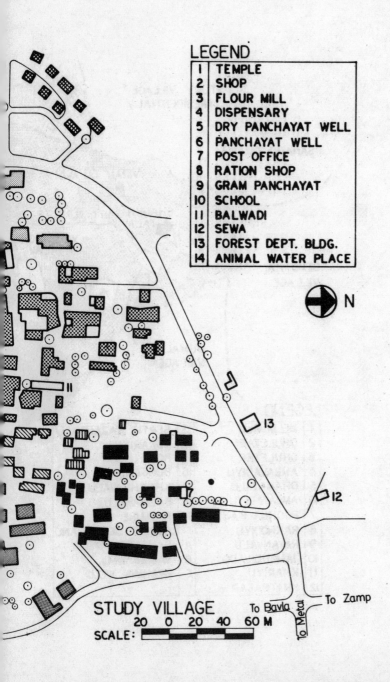

LEGEND

1	TEMPLE
2	SHOP
3	FLOUR MILL
4	DISPENSARY
5	DRY PANCHAYAT WELL
6	PANCHAYAT WELL
7	POST OFFICE
8	RATION SHOP
9	GRAM PANCHAYAT
10	SCHOOL
11	BALWADI
12	SEWA
13	FOREST DEPT. BLDG.
14	ANIMAL WATER PLACE

N

STUDY VILLAGE

To Bavla   To Zamp

To Metal

SCALE: 20 0 20 40 60 M

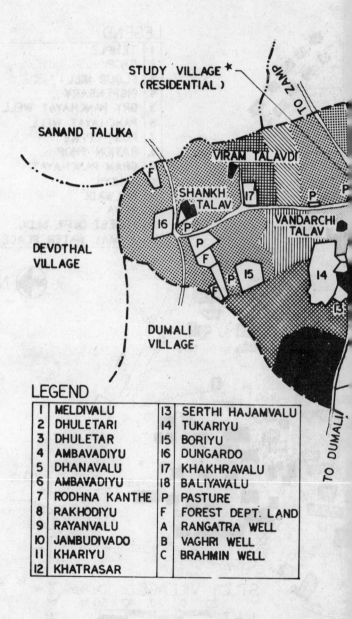

STUDY VILLAGE ★
(RESIDENTIAL)

TO ZAMP

SANAND TALUKA

VIRAM TALAVDI

F

SHANKH
TALAV

17

P

P

16

P

VANDARCHI
TALAV

P

DEVDTHAL
VILLAGE

F

P

15

14

F

13

DUMALI
VILLAGE

TO DUMALI

LEGEND

1	MELDIVALU	13	SERTHI HAJAMVALU
2	DHULETARI	14	TUKARIYU
3	DHULETAR	15	BORIYU
4	AMBAVADIYU	16	DUNGARDO
5	DHANAVALU	17	KHAKHRAVALU
6	AMBAVADIYU	18	BALIYAVALU
7	RODHNA KANTHE	P	PASTURE
8	RAKHODIYU	F	FOREST DEPT. LAND
9	RAYANVALU	A	RANGATRA WELL
10	JAMBUDIVADO	B	VAGHRI WELL
11	KHARIYU	C	BRAHMIN WELL
12	KHATRASAR		

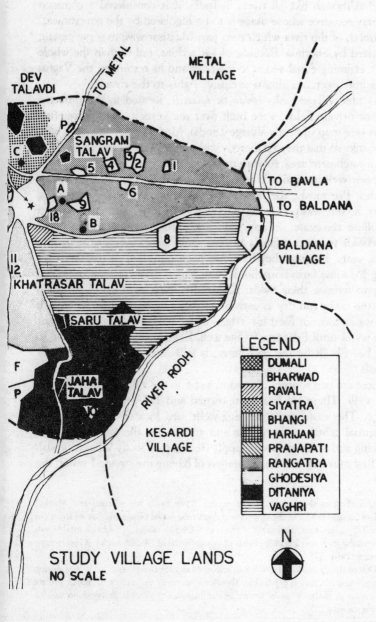

DEV
TALAVDI

TO METAL

METAL
VILLAGE

SANGRAM
TALAV

TO BAVLA

TO BALDANA

BALDANA
VILLAGE

KHATRASAR TALAV

SARU TALAV

RIVER RODH

JAHA
TALAV

KESARDI
VILLAGE

LEGEND

▨	DUMALI
	BHARWAD
▨	RAVAL
▦	SIYATRA
▤	BHANGI
▦	HARIJAN
	PRAJAPATI
	RANGATRA
	GHODESIYA
■	DITANIYA
▤	VAGHRI

N

STUDY VILLAGE LANDS
NO SCALE

Dholka *talukas*, is an annual river and dries up soon after the monsoon.[11] Although like all rivers in India, it is considered a common property resource whose usage is to be regulated by the government, the stretch of the river which runs past Maatisar was, to some extent, privatised by Shermia. Because of his actions, rather than the whole village claiming equal access to the river and its resources, the Vaghri community exercises almost exclusive rights to the river.

The nine village tanks (*talav* or *talavdi*), located in the different areas of private fields, were built over the years as animal watering points (see map of Study Village Lands). Most of them are built with high banks so that they fill directly with the monsoon rains rather than from a catchment area. As with the *gauchar* land, the village tanks have not been well-maintained, regularly desilted or regulated in recent decades. Previously, the tanks were maintained strictly as watering points; no one was permitted to draw water for irrigation purposes or to pollute the water in any way. While the common rights of all households to water animals at these tanks have been maintained, in recent years, because they have not been punished or penalised for doing so, some farm households have begun drawing water from the tanks to irrigate their fields. Alledgedly, even after good monsoon rains the tanks run dry as early as October or November, whereas if tank water was not used for irrigation the tanks would retain at least some water until February.[12] One well, Devtalau, which is believed to have been built by the god Shiva, is still used exclusively to water animals.

There are two sources of ground water in the village: dug-wells and tube-wells. There are four caste-owned and 177 private wells in the village. The caste wells, all dug-wells, are located in or near the residential centre of the village and are used as the main sources of drinking and domestic water supply (see map of Study Village Lands). The Brahmin well has the reputation of having the sweetest water; the

---

[11] According to the *District Gazetteer*, the 'River Rodh issues from near Mankol village of Sanand taluka of the district and flows near Juwal village and has a catchment area of 278 square kms. Thereafter it enters into Dholka taluka. . . . After a total length of 33 kms the river spreads in the fields of village Shiyal of Dholka taluka' (Government of Gujarat 1984: 11).

[12] Due to the drought, the tanks had remained dry for two years prior to and during our study year. It was not possible, therefore, to verify the extent to which private exploitation of the tank water for irrigation purposes pre-empts its common use for watering animals.

Vaghri well is equipped with a pump and is, therefore, also tapped for irrigation. The Koli Patel well is used most commonly for domestic water needs rather than as a source of drinking water. These three wells are commonly used by all caste groups, except the Vankars, Barots and Bhangis who use the Vankar well. Private tube-wells and dug-wells are located in private fields and are used primarily for irrigation, though they are also used for watering animals, washing clothes and other purposes.

The *gram panchayat* (village council) of Maatisar owns one tube-well which it is supposed to operate for use by the whole village. The tube-well, with an attached animal trough, is located in the northern corner of the village. This tube-well was not operated during the first two years of the 1985–87 drought and was activated only for intermittent periods of time during our study year. The local political story behind this is an interesting one. When the current *sarpanch* was first elected, his council decided (under the advice, allegedly, of the Gujarat Water Supply and Sewerage Board) to replace the *panchayat*'s diesel pump with a submersible electric pump. However, they were not told that the submersible motor would be more difficult to maintain and repair and that electrical supply would be sporadic, especially during seasons when water is in greatest demand.

In order to pay for the cost of running a well, the village *panchayat* is authorised to raise revenue by charging an annual animal tax of Rs 3 per large animal and Rs 1 per small animal. Given political pressures, the *sarpanch* had been unable and unwilling to raise the necessary revenue. His opposition lobbied villagers to resist paying the animal tax and the *sarpanch* was hesitant to anger his constituency. The *taluka panchayat* (*taluka* council) agreed to pay two electrical bills but a third bill for Rs 1,800 went unpaid for two years. In early 1987, due to the continuing drought conditions, the *taluka panchayat* agreed to pay the outstanding electricity bill and all electricity expenses until the monsoon rains. The Gujarat Electricity Board activated the pump in early April, with the condition that residents from two neighbouring villages also have access to the well. When the rains failed in July 1987, the *taluka panchayat* ordered that electrical supply to the pump be continued indefinitely, subject to sporadic power failures.

The other common property resources (CPRs) which belong to and are supposed to be managed by the *gram panchayat* include the community threshing grounds, *panchayat*-owned trees and the boundaries along public roads. For fuel and fodder collection, there is open and free access to boundary plantations along public roads and to leaves, twigs and branches from *panchayat* trees. Under the previous *sarpanch*, the community threshing grounds were allotted for a public housing scheme.[13] By the time this decision was reached, the technology of threshing had undergone a major change. Since the introduction of mechanical threshers, very little, if any, wheat or barley has been threshed by bullocks in the traditional way. Further, the villagers found it was more efficient to locate the mechanical threshers near the fields rather than at the traditional threshing grounds on the outskirts of the village. Privately-owned, open areas near cultivated fields are now used, with the owners' permission, for threshing.

Political and Economic Changes over Time

In collecting data on trends over time, we used the early 1950s as a benchmark for village history which, to use the village phrase, were 'in Shermia's time'. At that time, there was roughly half the population that there is today (see Table 3).[14] Based on information collected while conducting life-histories and compiling genealogies, we were able to trace several broad patterns of change in Maatisar since the early 1950s.

The recent political history of Maatisar can be seen to have passed through three phases since Independence in 1947: an initial feudal phase dominated by the local feudal lord; a long semi-democratic phase after the introduction of the *gram panchayat* system; and the current democratic phase dominated by caste politics. For 10 years after Independence, Maatisar remained under the control of Shermia, a local feudal lord whose ancestors had been granted rights to collect taxes and control much of the land in Maatisar and 11 other villages. With the land reforms in the mid-1950s, this feudal lord and the system he represented were abolished. After the formation of the state

[13] This scheme came under the Government of India's Twenty-Point Programme, designed to address the problems of the poor.

[14] The official census of 1951, at which time Gujarat came under the Bombay Presidency, does not provide data on Maatisar village, only on Dholka *taluka*. Table 3 presents comparative demographic data from the 1961 and 1981 official censuses and our 1987 study census. Assuming the same rate of population growth for the decade from 1951 to 1961 as over the two decades from 1961 to 1981, the population in 1951 would have been 875.

Table 3
Village Characteristics: 1961, 1981 and 1987

Characteristics	Official census		Study census 1987
	1961	*1981*	
No. of households	205	234	285
Population			
Total	1,006	1,274	1,688
Male	524	664	890
Female	482	610	798
Literacy rate			
Total	12%	16%	20%
Male	16%	25%	30%
Female	6%	6%	9%

* In the study census, those who have attended one or two years of primary school and claim they can read and write are called 'literate'.

of Gujarat (formerly part of Bombay Presidency) and the introduction of the *gram panchayat* system of local government in 1963, Maatisar entered a semi-democratic phase.

Under the *panchayat* system, each village through a one-person–one-vote system elects a village council and headman to four-year terms. Between 1963 and 1984, only three men served as *sarpanch*. One of these, a Brahmin, served for only one term. The other two, a Thakkar and his nephew who had close social and economic ties with Shermia, enjoyed a combined tenure of more than 20 years. These de facto heirs to feudal rule were not defeated until the 1984 election, when the Koli Patels, who are numerically strong in the village, elected their own candidate. This shift in power from the socially-higher castes to a numerically-dominant caste is not an isolated phenomenon but reflects the growing power of minority caste political factions in the state—notably, of the Scheduled and Backward Caste lobbies.[15]

However, the current *sarpanch* has yet to develop significant ties with *taluka*-level officials and has not, therefore, completely displaced the authority of the ex-*sarpanch*. During the 1985–87 drought, for example, the ex-*sarpanch*, rather than the current *sarpanch*, was asked to serve on the *taluka*-level relief committee. Over the past 15 years,

[15] Apparently, Koli Patels have gained control over a large number of *gram panchayats* in Dholka *taluka* in recent years (personal communication, R. Bhat).

the Vankar leader in Maatisar has acquired significant local power and wider political linkages without running for office. His patron, a schoolteacher, is the political client of several regional Scheduled Caste politicians, including a Congress-I Member of the Gujarat State Legislative Assembly. In 1975, the local Vankar leader was appointed postmaster of Maatisar, a postion which he still holds. Through this position and his political connections, he has emerged not only as the Vankar leader but also as the acknowledged local broker of government loans.

During the 1960s, given the national preoccupation with the Green Revolution in irrigated areas, very few development or extension services reached Maatisar. During the 1970s, however, the situation began to change. Government planners began to pay increasing attention to small-holder farms and dryland farming; several nation-wide anti-poverty programs were introduced; banks, which had been nationalised in 1969, were given targets to reach the rural poor; and, after a highly successful pilot programme in another region of Gujarat, the commercialised dairy sector began to expand its area of operation. By the late 1970s, all of these programs had, albeit with varying coverage and impact, reached Maatisar.

Moreover, in the late 1970s, a leading non-government organisation, the Self-Employed Women's Association (SEWA) of Ahmedabad, decided to work in Dholka *taluka* using Maatisar as its rural headquarters. Under SEWA's leadership, two local cooperatives for women (dairy and weaving) were established, a local creche was opened, IRDP loans for milch animals were channelled to women, and schemes in cotton spinning, roof tile manufacturing and bamboo crafts were introduced. As a result of these combined government and non-government efforts, the village has a functioning school, an electricity connection, a ration shop, a public tube-well, two child care centres, two functioning cooperatives, and frequent visits from various government and non-government workers.[16]

Meanwhile, during the 1960s and 1970s, local infrastructure was gradually expanded and improved. The main local roads were paved and the bus service expanded to include trips between Maatisar village and the nearest market town, Bavla, several times a day. Combined with other forces, improved transportation had a number of implications

[16] Compared to other states, Gujarat is known for its relatively competent administration and relatively extensive provision of social services (Dreze 1988).

for trade and economic activity in the village. Milk trade between Maatisar (plus other villages) and a private dairy in Bavla was started; Maatisar residents began migrating for seasonal employment opportunities; and Maatisar farmers began purchasing inputs from and selling produce at Bavla town.[17] After the first diesel pumps were purchased in the mid-1950s, households began to grow winter wheat and other winter crops more extensively. The extension of the Fatehwadi Canal Command Area in the 1970s to villages within Dholka *taluka* led to the introduction of high-yielding varieties of several crops in the region.

The history of land in Maatisar, as with the history of other resources and institutions in the village, is directly related to the history of Shermia, the ex-*talukdar* of the region.[18] According to village lore, Shermia's ancestors were given the *talukdari* or revenue-collecting authority by the British for this region in the mid-1800s. As *talukdar*, Shermia was granted use rights to a fixed amount of government land and was authorised to manage all the land, both private and public, in each village under his jurisdiction in exchange for collecting revenue for the state. In Maatisar, Shermia allotted some of his 'private' land to sub-tenants in exchange for a fixed amount of tax, called *mehsal* or *vighoti*, and some to his favoured clients in exchange for mandatory caste-based services, called *veth*.

During the British period in India, under the Survey and Settlement System, the government allotted to each village or cluster of villages a certain amount of government land as permanent pasture land according to the number of head of cattle each village owned.[19] Under the pre-Independence arrangement in Maatisar, the control and management of all village land, including the permanent pastures, was assigned to Shermia. Villagers paid Shermia a tax in kind for the land they cultivated, as well as fees for access to the common pastures.[20]

[17] Before local transportation was improved, Maatisar farmers relied more heavily on local traders for inputs and sales.

[18] *Talukdars* were feudal landlords vested with the authority to collect revenue.

[19] The Survey and Settlement System was introduced initially in British-ruled Gujarat (including Dholka *taluka*) and was extended to the whole of Gujarat after Independence (Iyengar 1988).

[20] It was reported that Shermia collected an annual animal tax of Rs 1 per animal. Archival data on the details of these charges and arrangements in the pre-Independence period was not collected. However, Jodha (1985a) presents a description of the management of common property resources in feudal times in Rajasthan. As Jodha notes, the pattern varied only in minor details from place to place with the exception of those areas

Shortly after Independence in 1947, when legislation was introduced to abolish tenancy,[21] Shermia is said to have negotiated with the state government to continue his revenue-collecting jurisdiction for an additional 10 years, allegedly to the full term of 100 years offered to his ancestors. In Gujarat generally (then part of the Bombay Presidency), the tenancy reform legislation of early Independence granted permanency, not ownership, to tenants. It was not until 1955–57 that tenancy was actually abolished and tenants were granted ownership of land.

According to village lore, once it became clear that the government was going to enforce strong tenancy reforms, Shermia orchestrated transfers of land to his preferred tenants and clients. First, he paid the revenue tax required to register in his own name about 150 acres of government land for which he had previously been granted use rights. He then renegotiated and registered the titles to this land in the names of his heirs, his favoured clients and his tenants. Interestingly, the majority of Shermia's clients (chosen presumably in recognition of their services or loyalty to him) came from castes that traditionally did not own land: ten Vaghri, one Bhangi and three Barot households. These households were allotted land by Shermia as payment, *pasayita*, for providing *veth* services over the years. In addition, nine Koli Patel households were granted land by Shermia; among these were four brothers who had worked as attached labour and two others who had worked as peons for Shermia. These tenants acquired land in exchange for paying a stipulated amount of revenue, *vighoti*. Three Bharwad client–friends of Shermia's simply occupied some of his land as they were not entitled to it under either the *vighoti* or *pasayita* systems.

In addition to some 150 acres of public cultivable land which he transferred in this way, Shermia allotted some 46 acres of public forest land covered by *babul* trees and the rights to the riverbed of the River Rodh. He gave the 46 acres of *babul*-covered land to a single Vaghri household, reportedly saying, 'If you can clear this land, you can

---

directly under the administration of rulers of princely states. In brief, Jodha describes how feudal landlords built up private revenues from CPRs by fixing a grazing tax per head of animal, auctioning produce from CPRs, fixing different levies on the users of the land, and demanding penalty payments for violation of regulations. Despite the exploitative aspects of the system, the villages benefited from 'a management system that protected, maintained and regulated use of common property resources' (Jodha 1985: 254).

[21] This legislation included the Bombay Tenancy and Agricultural Lands Act, 1948 and the Bombay Talukdari Tenure Abolition Act, 1949.

cultivate it.' In fact, only 17 of the 46 acres were actually cleared and privatised. The uncleared balance still operates as a common property resource, from which anyone from the village is free to collect *babul* as firewood. Because of this 29-acre tract of *babul*, fuelwood remains in relatively good supply in Maatisar.

In addition to the forest tract of *babul* trees along the River Rodh, Shermia governed the use of the river itself: its water, fish, bed and banks (some 57 acres of land cultivable from September to May after the river runs dry). All of these resources would normally be considered common to the villages the Rodh passes through, as rivers in India are regulated by state governments. In the case of the stretch of the River Rodh which runs to the east of Maatisar and west of Kesardi village, Shermia partially privatised these resources by registering the land in his son's name and then, by a verbal agreement, granting the right to cultivate the riverbed to the whole community of Vaghris in Maatisar (in return for their caste-based services to him over the years). Eventually, Shermia's sons were forced to forfeit their claims to this land. In theory, whoever then wished to cultivate the riverbed could apply for permission each year from the village *panchayat*. In practice, the Vaghris of Maatisar regularly cultivated over 75 per cent of the riverbed land, while a few Koli Patels from Kesardi cultivated the remaining 25 per cent on the Kesardi side of the river.

Recently, however, the assumed rights of the Vaghris of Maatisar have been challenged by the Kesardi Koli Patels. About 10 years ago, some Koli Patels from Kesardi tried to 'occupy' the full area of riverbed land by sowing sorghum seeds. At the same time, the Vaghris from Maatisar were trying to plant melon seeds on the stretch of riverbed which they normally occupied. The confrontation led to a major conflict which was taken to court for jurisdiction. At that time, Shermia advised, on the basis of old survey maps that showed all of the River Rodh as lying within the boundaries of Maatisar, that the settlement should be in favour of the Maatisar Vaghris and that the Koli Patels of Kesardi should 'occupy' only that land which the Maatisar Vaghris granted them.

For the next several years, the river remained full so that no cultivation was possible and no conflicts arose. Meanwhile, however, Shermia died and one of his sons became friendly with the residents of Kesardi. Moreover, the local *talati* (the village accountant who previously lived in Maatisar) shifted his residence to Kesardi and commissioned a new set of maps, which showed that over 75 per cent of the local stretch of the River Rodh fell within the boundary of Kesardi.

In the winter season of 1986–87, when the River Rodh was dry, the Koli Patels of Kesardi again occupied most of the riverbed land. The *sarpanch* of Maatisar sent a Koli Patel caste leader (*panch patel*) from Maatisar to negotiate with the Koli Patels from Kesardi. However, this time the arbitration was in favour of the Kesardi Koli Patels, allotting most of the land to them and only a small portion to the Vaghris of Maatisar.

In October 1987, in preparation for the 1987–88 winter season, four or five Vaghri households from Maatisar planted some mustard, melon and vegetable seeds to reclaim their rights to the riverbed land. However, the Koli Patels from Kesardi started planting on the same land. The Vaghris again requested Maatisar's *sarpanch* to take action on their behalf, but this time, the *sarpanch* refrained. It is rumoured that the *sarpanch* was unwilling to intervene because he was afraid to challenge the Koli Patels of Kesardi, who had recently murdered a Bharwad of that village.[22] One of Shermia's sons persuaded the Maatisar Vaghris to let some very poor Koli Patels from Kesardi cultivate winter wheat. The Vaghris agreed but planned to 're-occupy' the land to grow melons in the summer of 1988.

After the land and tenancy reforms of the 1950s and 1960s and the institutionalisation of the *gram panchayat* system in 1963, the management of common property resources in countless villages, including Maatisar, was handed over to the *gram panchayats*. They were expected to manage the CPRs for the optimal benefit and use of the village community and were entitled to levy fees and to auction certain CPRs as a means of raising revenue. However, although the provision of common access continued as in the past, in most villages the old system of management disappeared. As noted by one of the ex-*sarpanchs* with regard to the management of CPRs in Maatisar, the *gram panchayat* has 'neither raised revenue nor provided maintenance'.[23]

Some five years ago, under a joint programme of the District Rural Development Authority and the Forest Department, 20 acres of

---

[22] The *sarpanch*'s wife is reported to have said: 'I don't want my husband killed by Kesardi folk.' As will be described later, a group of Bharwads from Maatisar once beat and threatened to kill the current *sarpanch*. There is a long and continuing history of animosity between the farmers (mostly Koli Patels) and the shepherds (all Bharwads) in the region.

[23] Data on the physical status of the CPRs from the 1950s to the present was not collected. However, it was reported that the number of trees has been reduced significantly and that certain shrubs/grasses are no longer readily available.

permanent pasture land (in two separate plots of 10 acres each) were brought under a reforestation project. Although a few Maatisar residents have been employed in the planting and maintaining of these plots, to date there has been no significant production or revenue generated by this scheme. Moreover, it is unclear whether the reforested plots will continue to be managed by the Forest Department or will be handed over to the *gram panchayat*. Although villagers are allowed to collect headloads of grass from these plots, they view this forestry scheme as further privatisation of common property land.[24] Due to the privatisation of government agricultural land engineered by Shermia and the loss of 20 acres to the government reforestation scheme, common property land declined by about 33 per cent from roughly 555 acres in 1951 to just under 370 acres in 1987.[25]

Soon after tenancy was abolished in the mid-1950s, additional land reform legislation served to further redistribute landholdings in Maatisar. In 1961, the newly-formed Gujarat state passed and enforced the Gujarat Agricultural Lands Ceilings Act setting a ceiling on private ownership at 19 acres for irrigated land and 132 acres for dryland (Government of Gujarat 1979).[26] This Act was amended in 1974, when the ceiling was further lowered to 13–19 acres for irrigated land and 26–39 acres for dryland (Breman 1985: 50). Under the provisions of this Act and its amendment, 10 Vankar households were able to negotiate plots of two acres each from the surplus holdings of a few Koli Patels.

The combined effect of these land reform measures was a limited redistribution of land both between those with different sizes of holdings as well as to caste groups which had traditionally not owned

---

[24] The transfer of revenue and other CPR land to the Forest Department is not uncommon in Gujarat, whereby the availability of freely accessible CPR land is reduced (Iyengar 1988).

[25] Under current state norms, there should be 16 hectares of *gauchar* land for every 100 adult cattle (Aga Khan Rural Support Programme 1989). In Maatisar, there are almost 18 hectares of *gauchar* land for every 100 adult cattle unit (ACU). One ACU equals 300 kgs of body weight. The conversion rates for adult (0.85) and young (0.5) cattle, adult (1.0) and young (0.6) buffalo and goats (0.19) were taken from Iyengar 1988: 119.

[26] 'The first ceiling measure was introduced in 1961. The basis was an income of Rs 1,200 from farming which was translated into a certain quantum of land made up of different categories where it differed in productivity and infrastructure base. Such an area of land was to be called a family holding and it was to serve as a basis for ceilings limit' (Government of Gujarat 1979: 100).

land: the Vaghris, Bharwads, Vankars, Bhangis and Barots. Through these processes, roughly 170 acres, or six per cent, of the total cultivable land in Maatisar was redistributed.

Only the Vaghris, the Bharwads and the single Bhangi who received land under these land reform measures actually cultivated it. The three Barots who received land from Shermia soon sold it since, as genealogists, they were not interested in cultivation. Four out of the 10 Vankar households allotted land under the Land Ceilings Act also sold off this land. By contrast, the Vaghris retained and cultivated the land they received. At present, just under half of the Vaghri households, mostly descendants of Shermia's clients, currently own land; and over half of the Vaghri households report cultivation as their major source of income.[27] The single Bhangi household which acquired land from Shermia has prospered relative to other Bhangis by engaging in agriculture. The Bharwads who occupied some of Shermia's land engaged in cultivation and began to expand their holdings.

Inspired in part by these pioneer Bharwad farmers, a significant number of Bharwad households have acquired land and engage in cultivation to the point where less than half of the Bharwads are now landless and two Bharwad households own more than 35 acres of land. Interestingly, only a few households from two caste groups own more than 35 acres of land each: eight Koli Patel households from the traditional peasant caste, the largest in the village, and the two Bharwad households from the traditional shepherd caste, a relatively small group. Table 4 depicts the distribution of land by landholding, occupation and caste.[28]

As a group, the Bharwads have acquired the most land over the past 15 to 20 years—roughly 75 acres by mortgaging in land and 82 acres

[27] In Gujarat generally, Vaghris are known as itinerant vendors, selling what they produce or catch: birds, fish and vegetables (which they grow on river banks). Individual Vaghris specialise as *buas* (charmers or exorcists of the mother goddess) and as fortune-tellers.

[28] In this study, households are grouped into five landholding classes:

	Bighas	Acres
Landless	0	0
Small	1–7	.5–4
Medium	8–20	4.5–11.5
Large	21–60	12–34.5
Surplus	>60	>34.5

In this area, an acre equals 1.75 *bighas*.

Table 4
Distribution of Land (Total, Paddy, Normal in Acres) by Landholding, Occupation and Caste

Household groups	Households		Total land		Paddy land		Normal land	
	Total	%	Total	Per HH	Total	Per HH	Total	Per HH
1. Landholding								
Landless	118	41	0	0.0	0	0.0	0	0.0
Small	34	12	79	2.3	10	0.3	66	1.9
Medium	62	22	526	8.5	86	1.4	440	7.1
Large	61	21	1,317	21.6	147	2.4	1,148	18.8
Surplus	10	4	495	49.5	53	5.3	395	39.5
2. Occupation								
Cultivation	130	46	2,068	15.9	256	2.0	1,745	13.4
Livestock	11	4	93	8.4	7	0.6	86	7.8
Labour	68	24	120	1.8	20	0.3	100	1.5
Weaving	22	8	8	0.4	0	0.0	8	0.4
Trade	10	3	36	3.6	3	0.3	33	3.3
Others	44	15	93	2.1	11	0.2	78	1.8
3. Caste								
Koli Patel	142	50	1,721	12.1	222	1.6	1,431	10.1
Vaghri	51	18	234	4.6	24	0.5	210	4.1
Vankar	28	10	11	0.4	1	0.0	10	0.4
Bharwad	19	7	200	10.5	26	1.4	174	9.2
Prajapati	7	2	25	3.5	2	0.3	22	3.2
Brahmin	6	2	114	19.0	13	2.1	98	16.3
Thakkar	6	2	46	7.7	3	0.6	43	7.1
Bhangi	6	2	39	6.5	5	0.8	34	5.7
Barot	5	2	0	0.0	0	0.0	0	0.0
Rawal	4	1	5	1.1	0	0.0	5	1.1
Others	11	4	23	2.1	1	0.1	22	2.0
All households:	**285**	**100**	**2,418**	**8.5**	**297**	**1.0**	**2,049**	**7.2**

through purchasing land.[29] Under recent land legislation in Gujarat, those who are not traditional farmers are not allowed to purchase agricultural land. The Bharwads circumvented this regulation by acquiring the land in stages. First, they had the land mortgaged or 'gifted' to them. Then they cultivated the land, earning the title 'farmer'. Once they were classified as farmers, the Bharwads were able to purchase land. At present, seven out of 19 Bharwad households claim cultivation as their primary occupation.

Although widows are legally entitled to their husband's share of land, households headed by widows have, as a group, lost the most land over the past 15 to 20 years. Out of 16 households headed by women, two have sold land (a total of seven acres) and five have mortgaged it (a total of almost nine acres). Young widows, especially those without grown-up sons, are particularly vulnerable to land alienation for one or more of the following reasons: they are often unable to cultivate or manage the land single-handedly and are frequently forced by their in-laws to forfeit their use rights to their husband's share of land;[30] or they are forced to sell or mortgage land to raise capital to meet the subsistence needs of their families. Further, when it comes to those productive assets which cannot be divided and are often held jointly by the husband's family (i.e., pump sets, bullock-carts, bullocks), the young widow has no legal claim; her use rights to these assets are at the discretion of her in-laws. For instance, if a young widow wants to share-crop out her share of land, she cannot always claim rights to her in-laws' pump set or bullocks when she negotiates the share-cropping contract.

Changes in Occupations

In Maatisar, as in many villages in India, the traditional economy was organised largely along caste lines: each caste group in the village

[29] As a rule, Bharwads do not own land or engage in cultivation. In Saurashtra, where the vast majority of Bharwads live, over 75 per cent of them are 'semi-nomadic', moving with their herds for grazing at different seasons in the year. Of those that are settled, very few own land or practise cultivation.

[30] In most cases, widows of men in joint families are not formally deeded their legal share of their husband's land. In some cases, they are forced to forfeit the use rights to their legal share to their in-laws in return for an equivalent share of the produce. In other cases, they are forced to forfeit the use rights to their legal share to their in-laws in return for little, if any, share in the produce.

carried out its hereditary occupation which served to generate the range of goods and services necessary for collective and individual subsistence. In addition, as in other villages which came under the *talukdari* system of tenancy, each caste group in Maatisar provided compulsory *veth* services to the feudal landlord.[31] Even in the early 1950s, shortly after Independence and before land reforms were implemented in the area, this pattern held. Occupations were more strictly distributed along caste lines and the pattern of relationships and obligations more feudal than at present.[32]

In the early 1950s, the primary occupation of nearly all households was the hereditary occupation of the caste to which they belonged.[33] The Brahmins cultivated land. The Thakkar traders were engaged in shopkeeping and moneylending. The Koli Patels, nearly all of whom owned land, were the major cultivators of the village, although some were labourers. The Bharwad shepherds were engaged exclusively in animal husbandry, including cattle breeding and veterinary care services for the village at large. The Vaghris supplemented seasonal hunting, fishing and local vending with wage labour. The Vankars supplemented weaving with seasonal wage labour. The potters produced and sold pottery and engaged in cultivation. And the various service castes (carpenter, priest, barber, genealogist) were engaged in their respective caste services.

In addition to their primary occupation, each caste group carried out certain compulsory *veth* services for the feudal lord, Shermia.[34] Under the *veth* system, Shermia received a wide range of services: cooking by the Brahmins; food supplies and accounting services from the Thakkars; milk and ghee from the Bharwads; transport and storage

---

[31] 'The *taluqdars* resembled independent princely states' (Government of Gujarat 1979: 40).

[32] No baseline data on Maatisar in the 1950s are available. We have tried to reconstruct a rough picture of the village at that time from life-histories, genealogies and informant interviews.

[33] At that time, the population and number of households were roughly half what they are today. Increasing population density and division of inherited property (both land and other assets) have contributed to an overcrowding both of traditional occupations and land.

[34] *Veth* services are compulsory services demanded by and carried out for a feudal lord, without compensation or payment. At the discretion of the feudal lord, certain favours or payments called *pasayita*, such as the allotment of land, were occasionally offered. Refer to the preceding section for a discussion of clients who received land as *pasayita* from Shermia.

services by the Koli Patels; supply of fish, hare, partridge and *dattan* (reeds for brushing teeth) from the Vaghris; water and water pots from the Prajapatis; firewood and messenger services from the Vankars; sweeping, cleaning and bathing services from the Bhangis; utensil-cleaning, *hookah*-preparing[35] and hair-cutting services from the single village barber; drumming by the Rawals; singing and storytelling by the Barots.

With the land reforms of the mid-1950s, these *veth* services were abolished. The other significant change in occupations since that time has been the increased diversity and intensity of secondary activities, particularly among the Backward and Scheduled caste groups (Table 5). Although relatively few households have actually left their hereditary caste occupation, many now combine these occupations with multiple secondary occupations or another primary occupation. At present, for example, one-third of the Bharwads supplement the rearing of live-stock with cultivation, and another third declare cultivation as their primary occupation. Similarly, one half of the Koli Patels supplement their earnings from cultivation with wage labour, and another one-third declare labour as their primary occupation. As the scope for hunting and fishing has been greatly reduced, one half of the Vaghri households declare cultivation as their primary occupation, and the other half claim wage labour. The Vankar weavers also spend more time supplementing their earnings from weaving with wage labour. Two out of three carpentry households and the younger generation of genealogists have migrated to Ahmedabad as carpenters, masons or construction workers. Moreover, at present, some 50 households migrate for wage employment each winter; many households, other than Thakkars, engage in moneylending; and many rear animals.

The current occupational structure in Maatisar is presented in Table 6. We have identified seven occupations in which significant numbers of households are engaged: cultivation, livestock, wage labour (both local and migrant), trade and moneylending, caste occupations, other self-employment and salaried work. In the following sections, each of these occupational groups are described with particular reference to changes which have occurred over time, and the current distribution of these occupations across caste and landholding groups. Part II describes the current dynamics and seasonal rhythms of these occupations.

---

[35] The *hookah* is a water bowl tobacco pipe.

Table 5
Primary and Secondary Occupations by Caste

Caste groups	Early 1950s		1987	
	Primary	Veth	Primary	Secondary
1. Brahmin	Cultivation	Cooking	Cultivation	Moneylending Salaried work
2. Thakkar	Trade Moneylending	Food supply Accounting	Trade	Moneylending Salaried work
3. Bharwad	Livestock rearing	Milk supply	Livestock rearing Cultivation	Moneylending
4. Koli Patel	Cultivation Labour	Transport Storage	Cultivation Labour	Moneylending Livestock Labour
5. Prajapati	Pottery Cultivation	Water supply Water pots	Pottery Cultivation	Labour Salaried work
6. Vaghri	Hunting Fishing Vending Labour	Fish and game supply	Labour Cultivation	Vending
7. Barot	Genealogy	Storytelling Singing	Genealogy Permanent migration	Singing Drumming
8. Vankar	Weaving Labour	Firewood supply Messenger	Weaving Labour	Salaried work Labour
9. Bhangi	Scavenging	Scavenging Bathing	Cultivation Labour	Artisan production
10. Muslim	Barber	Hair-cutting Utensil-cleaning *Hookah*-preparing	Barber Carpenter	Midwife
11. Rawal	Transport	Transport	Transport	Drumming

Cultivation

There are two major agricultural seasons in Maatisar. The *kharif* (monsoon) crops—consisting mainly of coarse grains, pulses and some paddy—are sown in June–July and harvested in October–November. The *rabi* (winter) crops—consisting mainly of barley, wheat, lucerne and some mustard—are sown in November–December and harvested in March–April. Longer crops (cotton, castor and green gram), which are planted during the monsoon and harvested in winter, bridge the

Table 6
Occupational Structure

Occupation groups	No. of HHs Engaged as	
	Primary	Secondary
1. Cultivation	130	64*
2. Livestock		
Livestock rearing	11	74*
Dairying		
3. Wage employment		
Casual	53	63*
Attached	15	–
Migrant	36	14
4. Trade and moneylending		
Shopkeeping + Moneylending	5	–
Shopkeeping	3	–
Vending	1	9
Moneylending	0	48
5. Traditional caste occupations		
Artisan: Weaver	22	6
Potter	3	4
Service castes: Barber	2	–
Carpenter	1	–
Genealogist	5	–
Priest	2	–
Midwife	–	5
Mattress-stitching	–	5
6. Self-employment		
Skilled: 'Doctor'	1	–
Tailor	4	–
Mechanic	1	–
Driver	1	–
Transport		
Spinning	–	28*
Bua [spirit possessor]	–	18*
Unskilled: Rope-making	–	28*
Water fetching	–	18*
7. Salaried work		
Government: Full-time	10	–
Part-time	–	13
SEWA: Full-time	8	–
Part-time	–	7

* Extrapolated from secondary activities of sub-sample.

two seasons. Sorghum, melons and a few vegetables are grown in summer.

Relative to irrigated regions of south Gujarat, the agriculture practised in Maatisar has remained traditional in terms of its emphasis on food rather than non-food crops, and mechanisation. Except for the threshing of wheat and barley, which has been rapidly and almost totally mechanised in the past few years, and irrigation, which has been mechanised more slowly, Maatisar farm households follow traditional cultivation practices and use traditional implements. However, many new crops have been introduced and chemical fertilisers are increasingly used.

Over the past two decades, several crops new to the area have been introduced: paddy in the monsoon season (in place of *bunti*, a coarse grain) and wheat and lucerne on irrigated land in winter. The cultivation of *bunti* has stopped altogether and castor and cotton cultivation has been reduced. The factors behind these changes include technological changes such as new crop varieties, improved irrigation technologies such as pumps, and market forces, including price incentives and increased access to markets due to improved transportation. With the extension of the Fatehwadi Canal system to the northern part of Dholka *taluka*, new crops and varieties were tested under irrigated conditions. Information about them spread to villages on the perimeters of the canal-irrigated area. *Bunti* was soon displaced by local varieties of paddy, even in non-irrigated villages, given the yield and price advantages of the latter.[36]

The introduction of high-yielding varieties of wheat as a substitute winter crop for barley was the result of several factors. The first was a technological breakthrough: the traditional or *desi* varieties of wheat could not sprout in the local *kyari* soil, but three high-yielding varieties could. Second, once it was proven that wheat could be grown locally, the higher yields and the higher price per maund of wheat, relative to barley, provided incentives to grow wheat.[37] Finally, the gradual

[36] Paddy yields average 40 to 50 *maunds* per *bigha* (at Rs 50 per maund) as opposed to *bunti* yields of five *maunds* per *bigha* (at Rs 15 per *maund*) and can be grown under rain-fed conditions during a good monsoon season. A *maund* equals 20 kilograms.

[37] The data from a small survey during the winter season of 1986–87 indicate that the per *bigha* average yield of wheat was over 16 *maunds* (ranging from a low of just over 5 to a high of 40 *maunds*) which sold for an average price of Rs 57.90 per *maund*. The per *bigha* average yield of barley was nearly 11 *maunds* (ranging from a low of 5.5 to a high of 18.75) which sold for an average of Rs 33.75 per *maund*.

improvement and eventual paving of the main road which links Maatisar to the nearest market town, Bavla, meant that crops could be grown for sale in Bavla. Whereas barley had been grown exclusively for consumption, wheat began to be grown for both consumption and sale.

Shepherds had traditionally raised their herds completely on common lands. However, over the years several forces have led them and others to begin cultivating fodder crops, largely for their own herds but also for sale. The first is that the commercialisation of milk and resultant changes in the size and composition of the local herd increased the local demand for fodder. In addition, growth in the animal population increased pressures on common land, one-third of which has been privatised as described previously. Thirdly, annual grasses grow on the permanent pastures only when there is adequate rainfall. Finally, pump irrigation has facilitated the cultivation of fodder crops, both lucerne in winter and sorghum in summer.

Out of a total of 285 households, 130 (or roughly 46 per cent) declared cultivation as their primary occupation during our initial census of the village. Among the various caste groups, the highest percentage of those who declared cultivation as their primary occupation were among the traditional cultivators: Brahmins (67 per cent) followed closely by Koli Patels (66 per cent). However, as noted in Table 2, significant percentages of Bharwads, Vaghris and Bhangis also claimed cultivation as their primary occupation.

Agricultural land in Maatisar is unevenly distributed between households (see Table 4). At one end, slightly more than 40 per cent of households are landless. At the other end, less than four per cent of households (referred to hereafter as surplus farmers) own more than 20 per cent of the land, averaging 50 acres per household. This skewing is corrected in part when examining ownership per capita. Interestingly, operational patterns appear to have only a limited effect on land distribution.[38]

Landless cultivators by definition operate more land than they own. As a group, during the winter of 1986–87, they operated nearly four per cent of the land cultivated, an average of just over half an acre per

[38] Because the study was carried out in a drought year, when the rate of tenancy was reported to be lower than in normal years, the actual impact of tenancy on land distribution cannot be determined.

household.[39] Interestingly, all other landholding groups operated less land than they own. Surplus households operated almost six acres less, on the average, than they own. The small, medium and large farmers all operated, on the average, slightly less than they own. Table 7 compares land owned and operated per household and per capita for each landholding, occupation and caste group.

It is important to note that not all landless households are either landless labourers or poor. In Maatisar, which has sizeable pastoral, artisan and trading communities, landholding as a proxy for 'class' is particularly misleading. Only half of the landless households can be considered 'poor': the 50 which claim labour and the seven which claim cultivation as their primary occupation. Most of the other land-less households are engaged in significant non-farming occupations—rearing of livestock, weaving, trade, salaried work, artisan production, caste services or transport services. For the purposes of analysis, despite this variation, all landless households are grouped together wherever landholding groups are discussed.

Table 8 summarises the distribution of land, wells, pumps and animals by landholding, occupation and caste. Certain predictable patterns emerge. The first is that cultivation as a primary occupation is strongly correlated with landholding. Second, cultivators own the highest percentage of all animals (except cows) and average the highest number of bullocks per household. Also, as might be expected, the shepherds own the largest percentage of cows and average the largest number of all animals (except bullocks) per household.

Since the mid-1950s, villagers have steadily purchased pump sets. By 1987, there were some 122 pumps in the village owned by 92 households.[40] Pump irrigation is used predominantly in the winter season to grow wheat, barley, lucerne and mustard; occasionally in summer to grow sorghum, melons and vegetables; and infrequently in the monsoon to grow sorghum when rain-fed paddy fails. Before

[39] Our data on share-cropping is from the winter of 1986–87, when share-cropping was reported to be below normal given the accumulated effects of two years of drought. During this period, 13 out of 118 landless households share-cropped land averaging 6.5 acres each. Interestingly, most were from caste groups whose hereditary occupation is not cultivation: nine out of the 13 households were Vaghri, two Bharwad, only one Koli Patel and one other.

[40] Between them, 111 households in the village own 177 wells, both dug- and tube-wells. Some of the dug-wells have gone dry.

Table 7

Land Owned and Operated (Total, Per Household, and Per Capita in Acres) by Landholding, Occupation and Caste*

Household groups	Total		Land owned			Land operated**		
	HHs	People	Total	Per HH	Per Capita	Total	Per HH	Per Capita
1. Landholding								
Landless	118	592	0	0.0	0.0	86	0.7	0.1
Small	34	201	79	2.3	0.4	68	2.0	0.3
Medium	62	361	526	8.5	1.5	483	7.8	1.3
Large	61	432	1,317	21.6	3.0	1,249	20.5	2.9
Surplus	10	102	495	49.5	4.9	439	43.9	4.3
2. Occupation								
Cultivation	130	819	2,068	15.9	2.5	2,061	15.9	2.5
Livestock	11	89	93	8.4	1.0	83	7.5	0.9
Labour	68	380	120	1.8	0.3	127	1.9	0.3
Weaving	22	136	8	0.4	0.1	2	0.1	0.0
Trade	10	56	36	3.6	0.6	0	0.0	0.0
Others	44	208	93	2.1	0.4	53	1.2	0.3
3. Caste								
Koli Patel	142	830	1,721	12.1	2.1	1,671	11.8	2.0
Vaghri	51	316	234	4.6	0.7	286	5.6	0.9
Vankar	28	163	11	0.4	0.1	5	0.2	0.0
Bharwad	19	127	200	10.5	1.6	185	9.7	1.5
Prajapati	7	43	25	3.5	0.6	11	1.6	0.3
Brahmin	6	47	114	19.0	2.4	110	18.4	2.3
Thakkar	6	40	46	7.7	1.2	0	0.0	0.0
Bhangi	6	29	39	6.5	1.3	53	8.8	1.8
Barot	5	14	0	0.0	0.0	0	0.0	0.0
Rawal	4	13	5	3.5	0.6	0	1.6	0.3
Others	11	66	23	2.1	0.3	3	0.3	0.1
All households:	285	1,688	2,418	8.5	1.4	2,324	8.1	1.4

* **Source**: Census
** **Season**: Winter 1986–87

Table 8

Distribution of Assets (Land, Wells, Pumps, and Animals) by Landholding, Occupation, and Caste

Household groups	Total No.	Land (acres)	Wells	Pumps	Bullocks	Cows	Buffaloes
1. Landholding							
Landless	118	0	0	0	6	91	45
Small	34	79	11	7	6	19	18
Medium	62	526	60	49	61	73	87
Large	61	1,317	88	55	101	271	112
Surplus	10	495	18	11	23	50	35
2. Occupation							
Cultivation	130	2,068	162	111	175	261	158
Livestock	11	93	3	3	12	196	91
Labour	68	120	4	2	3	18	24
Weaving	22	8	0	0	0	5	8
Trade	10	36	2	2	0	3	4
Others	44	93	6	4	5	22	12
3. Caste							
Koli Patel	142	1,721	132	85	135	124	116
Vaghri	51	234	19	16	25	9	37
Vankar	28	11	0	0	0	5	9
Bharwad	19	200	9	7	21	321	107
Prajapati	7	25	2	2	3	8	11
Brahmin	6	114	9	7	8	17	5
Thakkar	6	46	3	3	0	4	4
Bhangi	6	39	1	1	2	0	4
Barot	5	0	0	0	0	2	0
Rawal	4	5	1	1	0	6	3
Others	11	23	1	0	1	8	1
All households:	285	2,418	177	122	195	505	297

pump sets were introduced, only barley and mustard were grown in winter and only limited quantities of sorghum, melons and vegetables could be grown in summer. As might be expected, pump sets are owned primarily by medium, large and surplus farm households.

Rearing of Livestock

The one significant change in livestock ownership over the past 20 to 30 years has been the marked shift in favour of buffaloes, due to at least four factors. First, once dairying became commercialised, buffaloes were increasingly valued for the rich fat content of their milk. Second, because common pastures have been degraded and the extent of fallows (both in time and space) has decreased due to increased irrigation, buffaloes have been favoured because they do well under stall-fed conditions. Third, diesel pump sets and mechanical threshers have displaced bullocks from irrigation and threshing operations, thereby reducing the demand for them. And fourth, over the past decade SEWA has helped asset-poor households negotiate bank loans to purchase buffaloes.

The Bharwads, in particular, have made several shifts with regard to livestock and dairying. Whereas traditionally they reared mainly sheep, goats and cows, the Bharwads now rear mainly buffaloes, bullocks and cows. When a local Bharwad first started trading in milk, buying in the village and selling to the private dairy in Bavla town, the Bharwads began to sell off their sheep and goats in order to buy buffaloes. As their profits from selling milk increased, the Bharwads began to invest in land. Some of the Bharwads are now the largest landowners and moneylenders in the village and earn as much or more from these non-livestock resources as from their livestock. As farmers, they have also invested in a few bullocks.

Over the past three decades, both the size and the composition of the total village herd, not just the Bharwad herd, have changed. At present, the shepherds maintain a few bulls for breeding, varying-size herds of cows and buffaloes for milk production, some bullocks for farming, and a few small herds of goats. A significant number of farm households have small mixed herds of bullocks for draft power and cows and buffaloes for milk production. The Vaghris and Vankars keep mainly goats. Recently, with loans brokered by SEWA from the nationalised banks, some labour and weaving households have also acquired milch animals, mostly buffaloes.

In the 1950s, raw milk and milk products were consumed, sold and distributed within the village. By the early 1970s, some raw milk was sold outside the village to a private dairy through some of the local Bharwads. At present, raw milk is sold largely to a government dairy through a local dairy cooperative. Due to the efforts of SEWA, the first women's dairy cooperative in Ahmedabad District was registered in Maatisar in 1979. Since then, the government's dairy system has largely displaced the private milk trade controlled by the Bharwads. For many households, commercialised dairying has meant that the share of milk sales in household incomes has increased. However, given their increasing participation in cultivation and their loss of control over the milk trade, the relative share of milk and milk products in the total income of shepherd households has decreased.

The benefits from rearing livestock include not only animal products and draft power but also transport services and renewable sources of fuel and manure. For cultivators, perhaps the most important benefit from livestock is draft power. At present, bullocks are primarily used to pull ploughs and carts. Until recently, they were also used to thresh wheat and to lift water (the traditional *kos* system of irrigation relied on bullock power). The importance of the draft power of bullocks to cultivators is reflected in the fact that agricultural households own 90 per cent of the bullocks in the village.

Although residents in neighbouring villages own tractors and a few vans which can be hired for transport services, no one in Maatisar owns a mechanised vehicle. The only local means of transport, other than individual bicycles, are five camel-carts, 57 bullock-carts and one horse. Bullock-carts are most commonly used by their owners to haul loads to and from the fields and, occasionally, to markets outside the village. Two of the camel-carts (plus camels) are owned by a Rawal household, the traditional camel-carters; the other three are owned by Koli Patels. These camel-carts are regularly used to transport goods to and from Bavla. The transport charges vary according to the volume of the load.[41] The single horse in the village is owned by one of the

---

[41] The transport charges between Maatisar and Bavla town, whether by bullock-cart or camel-cart, are as follows:

  One Way:
    Rs 2.50 per sack (e.g., fertiliser)
    Rs 40 per cart load (e.g., of cotton)
    Rs 1 per *maund* (20 kgs.)
  Round Trip: Rs 50–55 per cart

wealthy Bharwads. Under a contract for Rs 700 per month from the government dairy, he uses the horse to transport milk every day from a neighbouring village, which is off the commercial dairy route, to the milk depot in Maatisar.

Raw buffalo and cow milk is both consumed and sold, either locally or through the government dairy system. There are two milk products processed in the village: *chaas* (buttermilk) and *ghee* (clarified butter). Villagers report that there has been a decline in the processing of milk products over the past two to three decades, due in part to the increased sales of raw milk. In the past, *chaas* was distributed free by employers to their labourers and within neighbourhoods. Some *chaas* is still distributed free within extended kinship or sub-caste groups while some is sold outside caste neighbourhoods. At present, a few households, mostly Thakkar traders, process surplus milk into *ghee*, which is consumed or sold locally (at Rs 60 per kg).

There are several other animal products which have subsistence or commercial value to Maatisar households, primarily cow-dung for fuel or manure and animal bones and skins. Most cow-dung is collected freely and used for subsistence purposes, though some is collected and processed for sale as manure or dung-cakes. Two caste groups, the Vankars and Bhangis, flay dead animals and sell the bones and skins to the Chamars (tanners) in a neighbouring village.[42]

Although men and boys graze the animals in all Bharwad and most other households, women in all households handle most of the routine maintenance and care of animals, including watering, feeding and milking, cleaning the cattle sheds, and collecting fodder.[43] Minor veterinary ailments are treated first by members of the family or kin group. One of the Bharwads is the local veterinarian for the whole village, treating minor fractures and handling deliveries (reportedly without charging a fee for his services). For more complicated or severe conditions, veterinary doctors, both government and private, are called from Bavla town or Kerala village where the government

[42] There are no Chamars in Maatisar. Flaying animals, one of the traditional caste occupations of the Chamars, has been assumed by these two other Scheduled Castes. Chamars from a neighbouring village visit Maatisar on a regular schedule to repair shoes, sandals and other leather goods. Residents from Maatisar purchase shoes and sandals from Chamars in other villages and from an itinerant vendor.

[43] SEWA decided to organise and register all-women's dairy cooperatives in Maatisar and other villages in recognition of women's major contribution to dairying. Because the cooperatives are registered in women's names, the women receive the milk payments and other benefits directly.

runs a first-aid veterinary centre. The average cost per visit by the outside veterinary doctors is Rs 100–150. There is one stud bull for breeding in the village, which belongs to one of the richer Bharwads. The fee for stud services is Rs 30, payable if and when the cow becomes pregnant.

In normal years during the monsoon season, the government makes provisions for a system of patrolling private fields, called *bhelan*. Applications for patrolling must be submitted (either by individual farmers, groups of farmers or village leaders) to the Deputy Superintendent of Police (DSP). The DSP then decides whether or not to authorise the Gram Raksha Dal (Village Protection Force) to activate patrolling. The Gram Raksha Dal (GRD) recruits, briefly trains, and retains as a reserve units of men in each village.[44] In Maatisar, there are 22 men in the GRD under the leadership of a Koli Patel. *Bhelan* patrolling is usually activated for four months in the year, from just before the monsoon season ploughing until after the monsoon harvest. The men in the patrol are paid at the rate of Rs 17 per day. During the current drought, the GRD unit in Maatisar was on active patrol during the 1985 and 1986 monsoon seasons but not in 1987, as few crops were planted and still fewer survived.

Despite this system of patrolling, conflicts between farmers (mostly Koli Patels) and shepherds (all Bharwads) are not uncommon in the region. Although none were reported in Maatisar itself, two or three murders were reported from neighbouring villages, either of shepherds by farmers or vice versa: all resulted from conflicts over grazing. This underlying tension between the two communities is reflected in the politics of the *gram panchayat* in Maatisar. The main political clients of the Thakkar ex-*sarpanch* are the Bharwads. Soon after the Koli Patel *sarpanch* was elected in 1984, a group of Bharwads cornered and began to beat him in the *panchayat* office. According to the *sarpanch's* wife, she grew suspicious because her husband was late returning home, went to the *panchayat* office to find him, thereby scaring off the Bharwads who otherwise, she claims, would have killed him. At present, there is a truce or stand-off between the two communities. However, as both communities are represented by regional caste lobbies, the underlying tension might well escalate or be used for political ends at any time.

[44] The Gram Raksha Dal (GRD) is under the Civil Defence Department of the state government, which in turn is under the Home Ministry.

There appear to be two major places where animals are purchased: a cattle fair in Kutch District and Maatisar itself. Twice each year, Muslim cattle breeders from Kutch pass through Maatisar to sell bullocks. The bullocks can be paid for in three equal, annual instalments, collected after either the wheat or the paddy harvest. The Kutchi breeders are also willing, for a price, to replace poorer-quality animals with better-quality ones. But if at all possible, Maatisar residents avoid selling animals, and only a few instances of sale were reported. In one case, an elderly couple who now share-crop out their land sold their bullocks to pay for a 'baby shower' ceremony for their daughter. Their old, dismantled bullock-cart stands leaning against the side of their hut.

The distribution of animals is skewed in favour of those who own the most land. Together, the large and surplus farm households (who represent only 25 per cent of total households) own about 60 per cent of the bullocks, cows and buffaloes in the village. The medium households (22 per cent of total households) own about 30 per cent of the bullocks and buffaloes, but only 15 per cent of the cows, while the small farm and landless households own far less than their share of all animals. But interestingly, landless households own three per cent of the bullocks and a significant number of cows, buffaloes and goats (see Table 8).

The distribution of animals by occupation is skewed, logically if not equitably, in favour of those households which declare cultivation or the rearing of livestock as their primary occupation. Together, these households own over 90 per cent of the bullocks and cows and almost 70 per cent of the buffaloes. Only these two groups of households average more than one bullock and one cow per household, and only the livestock group averages more than one of each type of animal per household. Although the distribution of animals is skewed in favour of cultivators, it is important to note that many farm households do not own one or another type of animal; most critically, nearly 40 per cent do not own bullocks.[45] In addition, large farmers or livestock rearers frequently share-crop out their dry or unproductive animals to poorer households to maintain. When the share-cropped animals deliver or start lactating again, they are returned to their owners. The net addition to the value of such animals (e.g., calves or additional height/weight) is divided equally between the two parties.

[45] I will address this point in the section on share-cropping in Part II.

Labour

About 70 households, nearly one-fourth of the village, claim wage labour as their primary occupation. In addition, some 60 households engage in wage labour as a secondary occupation. Of the total households engaged in wage labour (130), about 50 migrate for some part of the year in search of employment opportunities.[46] Table 9 shows the distribution of all households engaged in labour either as a primary or secondary occupation, and as local, migrant or attached labour. Of the 70 households which claim wage labour as their major source of income, over two-thirds (48 households) are landless. And nearly one-third (22 households) are Vaghris who are hired locally for paddy planting and harvesting and migrate during winter to nearby Saurashtra for groundnut and sugar-cane harvesting and processing.[47]

Table 9

Households Which Engage in Wage Labour: As Primary or Secondary Occupation and as Casual, Attached or Migrant Labour

Occupation group	Primary	Secondary	Local		Migrant
			Casual	Attached	
Cultivation	0	38	38	0	5
Livestock	0	1	1	0	0
Labour	68	0	53	15	36
Weaving	0	9	9	0	9
Trade	0	0	0	0	0
Others	0	9	9	0	0
Total:	**68**	**57**	**110**	**15**	**50**

Demand for hired farm labour in and around the study village is limited by several factors. The first is that mechanical threshing has virtually replaced manual threshing of wheat and barley, thereby displacing labour from those operations. Secondly, the majority of farmers are from Backward Castes whose use of family labour, both

---

[46] During the 1986–87 winter season, 42 households migrated. This number was said to be lower than for normal years because of the drought. Part II discusses seasonal migration in some detail.

[47] Saurashtra is a physiographic, not administrative, unit of Gujarat. Also known as Kathiawar, it is the most conspicuous peninsula of Western India and includes the districts of Surendranagar, Jamnagar, Rajkot, Bhavnagar, Amreli and Junagadh (see map of Gujarat State).

male and female, in agriculture is not constrained by caste-based considerations. That is, in these castes, manual work is not perceived to degrade the caste status of the family, there are no caste norms against women or men performing certain agricultural operations.[48] Moreover, rather than hiring labour, Koli Patels (the main peasant caste) often exchange labour with other Koli Patels who are their residential or farm neighbours.[49]

Rough estimates indicate that, in years of good rainfall, a male casual labourer could find local farm employment for a maximum of 220 days in the year and a female casual labourer for a maximum of 180 days. It is likely, however, that most labourers average fewer days of local farm labour each year: 175 days for male and 135 days for female.[50] These estimates are based on the assumptions that the demand for female and male labour is equal in all operations except ploughing (which is carried out exclusively by male labour), that the demand for hired labour in interculture activities (weeding, irrigation and pest control) is extremely low, and that the demand for hired labour in other operations is roughly as presented below:

Crops	Ploughing	Planting	Harvesting	Post-harvest
Paddy[51]	(10)	20–35	20–45	5
Monsoon	(10)	(10)	15–20	0
Winter	(20)	(10)	35	5
Summer	0	0	15	0

[48] The only two caste groups engaged in agriculture who would hire labour, rather than use family labour, in response to caste norms regarding either manual work or women's work, are Brahmins and Bharwads. However, of the total households which declare agriculture as their primary occupation, only three per cent are Brahmins and just over five per cent are Bharwads.

[49] The arrangements for exchange labour are quite straightforward: each party provides the other an equal number of labour days in the same operation. During the major harvest of the study year (barley and wheat harvest in March–April 1987), the volume of exchange labour was quite high.

[50] Because of the drought during our study year, we could not measure normal crop-wise levels of labour input. We arrived at the estimates I have used here by asking labourers how many days they could expect to get employment in the different operations for each crop in normal years. Breman (1985: 281) reports that from 'various agro–economic studies it appears that, while farm servants are kept busy the whole year round, casual labourers find work on only 200 days'. On the basis of a survey of 2,694 households of agricultural labourers from 27 villages in Gujarat, G. Shah (1978) calculated that casual labourers worked for 186 days per year and attached labourers for 351 days per year. For Gujarat as a whole, the Rural Labour Enquiry (RLE) of 1974–75 recorded 206 full days of employment for men and 160 for women.

[51] The brackets indicate operations for which a limited number of labourers are hired.

Further, opportunities for employment as permanent farm labour or as non-farm labour are very limited and long-term employment contracts are not common.[52] During our study year, only 15 regular farm servants, including four young boys, were working under (mostly) annual contracts for 11 households in the village.[53] Moreover, the demand for non-farm labour is extremely low,[54] and the village labour market is largely closed. During periods of peak labour demand, some local labour is recruited to one or two neighbouring villages.[55] Very few labourers are recruited into Maatisar, with the exception of a few relatives from neighbouring villages. Because of limited demand in the local labour market, a significant number of labourers migrate each year during certain seasons.

Trade

There are eight shops in the village, all of which are small, street-front rooms or partitioned spaces connected to residential units at the back. Six of these are owned and managed by Thakkars (the trader caste); one is owned and managed by a Marwari immigrant from Rajasthan; and the eighth is owned and managed by a Prajapati (potter). All sell essentially the same range of goods: the main staples of the village (cereals and pulses); potatoes and onions; seasonal green vegetables; tea; kerosene and cooking oil; a few snack items; soap and tooth-powder; ribbons and bangles; matches; mosquito coils; batteries;

[52] Breman (1985: 263) argues that it is the character of highly irrigated farming that requires farmers to contract full-time farm servants. 'The need for one or more permanent labourers begins at the level of the middle farmers, i.e., those with holdings of 5 acres and above—a need dictated in the first place by the character of irrigation farming.' Conversely, as data from Maatisar confirm, the character of semi-arid agriculture reduces the need for farmers to contract full-time farm servants. Moreover, most farmers in Maatisar are from Backward Caste groups which deploy a high degree of family labour, further reducing the need for farm servants.

[53] The majority of farm servants were Koli Patels and the majority of employers were Bharwads. The adult servants, all male, were hired almost exclusively for farm work. Even in the Bharwad households, the servants were hired mostly for farm work, leaving animal care largely to family labour. The young boys were hired for light farm work and animal care.

[54] A few labourers are hired locally for the following activities: women for fetching water, cleaning utensils, washing clothes and stitching mattresses; young boys to graze animals and run errands; and men for constructing houses and to graze and care for animals.

[55] Villages in which there are significant numbers of Rajput households (locally, the Darbar caste). Rajputs regularly hire labour because Rajput traditions discourage the use of women in family farm labour.

rope; and a few spare parts for lanterns, kerosene stoves and pump sets. In addition, there is a large ration shop licensed and operated by the current *sarpanch*, a Koli Patel.

Next to two of the shops on the main streets of the village are flour mills: one run by the Thakkar ex-*sarpanch*, the other by another Thakkar.[56] The latter mill-owner also runs a repair shop for repairing the rubber tyres on bullock and camel-carts. Under the large, shady tree by the bus-stop on the main road, a Koli Patel household operates a push-cart stall selling *bidis* (hand-rolled cigarettes), *paan* (a mixture of betel nut with lime wrapped in a betel leaf for chewing) and snack items.[57]

Each of the eight main shops caters to the public at large but also to a specific clientele. The distribution of customers by shop appears to have been determined both by proximity of residential neighbourhoods to different shops and the discretion of the shopkeepers who may prefer to deal only with certain caste groups. About half of daily sales are made on credit, so that customers become 'tied' for their line of credit and by their outstanding loans to specific shopkeepers.

The majority of customers make multiple small purchases, as many as four or five in a single day. During our rounds in the village, we regularly saw young boys or girls being given a few coins or a small amount of grain by their mother and running off to one of the shops to purchase a small bowl of grain, a small container of oil, or a few biscuits for themselves. Some customers shop weekly, and a few shop every two weeks.[58] A significant volume of the shops' sales is done on barter or credit. It is acknowledged by both shopkeepers and customers that higher prices are charged when purchases are made in small instalments and on barter or credit rather than in cash.

The ration shop licensed and run by the current *sarpanch* is a larger, less congested space than the other shops and serves as a regular

[56] During the study year, in the middle of the peak drought period, a third flour mill was opened by one of the Brahmins.

[57] Later, I describe the history of this family and how it came to own the push-cart stall as an example of upward mobility.

[58] In the shop with the largest volume of trade, that owned by the Thakkar ex-*sarpanch*, over 17 of his 27 regular customers shop four or five times a day; five shop daily; one weekly (a Brahmin); and four twice a month (all the richest Bharwads, perhaps the richest households in the village). In the shop with the second-largest volume of trade, all nine of the regular customers (mostly Koli Patels and Vagris) shop two or three times a day. And in the shop with the third-largest volume of trade, nine of the regular customers shop several times a day, two shop once a day and three shop several times a week.

meeting-place for his friends and supporters. It is stocked only with bags of grain or sugar and tins of oil. Those with ration cards can purchase rice, wheat, sugar and cooking oil at a subsidised price. During the drought period, this shop also served as the depot from which wheat payments for relief works were distributed. During this time, the *sarpanch*–proprietor expanded and upgraded the ration shop premises, allegedly on illegal profits from his role in implementing relief works (more on this in Part III).

In addition to what is sold from the shops or storefronts listed above, certain commodities are sold by itinerant vendors who roam the village or 'set up shop' in front of public places such as the temple or the post office on a regular basis. We interviewed 16 itinerant vendors who visited Maatisar during our study year: four came on a weekly basis, three every other week, one monthly, four seasonally, and four occasionally. The majority sold perishables: vegetables, melons, chillies, fish, popsicles. Two sold sandals (*chappals*); two sold *saris* or other cloth items; two sold metal utensils; and one sold kerosene. In addition, a team of Muslim metal-workers from Ahmedabad visits the village once a year to repair utensils.

Twice a year, two separate groups of nomads come to Maatisar to trade. One group from Rajasthan, led by a woman, comes twice a year to sell salt; on their first trip through the village they sell the salt, which is transported on donkey-back, and on the return trip they collect payment, largely in kind. The second group, Muslim cattle breeders from Kutch whom I have mentioned earlier, come twice a year to sell bullocks. In addition, groups of nomads regularly pass through the village with their herds of cattle or camels, as Maatisar is on an annual migratory route from Kutch District to Kheda District.

During the study year, 10 local vendors sold perishable items on a seasonal basis within Maatisar and some of its surrounding villages. Other than popsicles sold by one local vendor, all the products sold were locally-grown fruits and vegetables: melons, berries, mangoes, various types of beans, green onions and ladyfingers (okra). All of the local vendors were Vaghris or Koli Patels, the majority were women, and most had grown what they were vending. In addition to these vendors, three households brew and sell local liquor and one household sells kerosene.

Moneylending

Moneylenders in rural India are generally thought to be fewer in number and of a different class or caste than households which take loans. However, in Maatisar, a significant number of households engage in one or more types of moneylending; many households are at once lenders and borrowers; and households borrow and lend both within and across caste or class boundaries. Both lenders and borrowers, but particularly lenders, were reluctant to report or discuss moneylending. To probe this topic we had to broach the subject indirectly, collect data from multiple sources, and check and recheck our data regularly.

Including loans given against mortgaged land, some 53 households (over 18 per cent of total households) were reported to engage in moneylending. Excluding those households which only gave loans against mortgaged land (19) or which only advanced credit to attached labour (2), some 32 households (11 per cent of total households) were reported to be engaged in moneylending. However, only the Thakkars, whose hereditary occupation includes both moneylending and trade, could be considered professional moneylenders. It should be noted that these totals do not include short-term, interest-free loans (in cash or kind) reported to be common in the village. Table 10 presents the distribution of moneylending households by caste and by type of moneylending.

Of the eight shopkeepers, seven sell consumer goods to customers on credit and five extend credit against pawned consumer durables at high rates of interest. One of the shopkeepers, the Thakkar ex-*sarpanch*, is one of the largest moneylenders in the village. Allegedly, he is currently owed between two to three *lakh* (hundred thousand) rupees in outstanding loans.[59] Another Thakkar trader reported that he inherited (from his father) clients with two to three *lakh* rupees in outstanding loans. In 1987, he claimed to have recently stopped moneylending and credit sales in order to recoup his finances with a thought to migrating to Ahmedabad city in the near future.[60]

[59] One loan for Rs 90,000 was made to the largest Koli Patel landowner for seeds and fertiliser some 10 years ago. It is rumoured that the Koli Patel landowner still owes the ex-*sarpanch* Rs 20,000, which he refused to repay even in a year of high yields (1983), and that the ex-*sarpanch* has therefore closed his account in his shop. Interestingly, during the drought of 1987, that same Koli Patel landowner purchased the first mechanical thresher in the village. He did so despite the losses he suffered in the drought and despite his outstanding loan to the largest trader in the village.

[60] According to this Thakkar, he has invested the following amounts in buildings in Ahmedabad city: Rs 71,000 (of which Rs 20,000 was taken on loan) on purchasing a building in an existing housing society and Rs 81,000 (of which Rs 20,000 was a loan) on

Table 10
Moneylenders by Caste and Type of Moneylending

Caste	Total HHs	Moneylending HHs	Type of moneylending					
			Land mortgage	Credit sales	Pawn	Labour advance	Credit advance	Others
Thakkar*	6	6	2	7	5	1	2	5
Bharwad	19	10	9	0	2	5	0	5
Koli Patel	142	23	16	0	4	4	0	6
Vaghri	51	7	4	0	1	0	0	2
Brahmin	6	2	0	0	2	1	0	1
Prajapati	7	2	1	1	1	0	0	1
Vankar	28	1	0	0	1	0	0	1
Priest	2	1	0	0	1	0	0	1
Schoolteacher	2	1	0	0	1	0	0	1
Others	22	0	0	0	0	0	0	0
Total:	285	53	32	8	18	12	2	23

* The Thakkars are the traditional or professional moneylenders of the village.

The Thakkars began disinvesting in moneylending about 10 years ago and have since invested their surplus capital largely in trade and construction in urban areas. They report being wary of government policies to control moneylending and of tying up too large a volume of capital in loans, particularly during the prolonged drought of 1985–87. Presumably, local lending by formal credit institutions, which increased in the 1980s partly due to the efforts of SEWA, has also displaced some portion of the Thakkars' moneylending.[61]

Over the past 10 to 15 years, the Bharwads have taken over a sizeable share of moneylending in the village thereby replacing the Thakkars as the main moneylenders in Maatisar. With the commercial-isation of milk, the Bharwads, who owned large herds, began generating a surplus. Some of this was invested in land, mainly by mortgaging in land for their own cultivation; with the additional surplus generated through agriculture, some of the Bharwads have become large money-lenders.[62] Indeed, one of the Bharwads is rumoured to be the largest moneylender in the village.[63] In all, nine of the 19 Bharwad households have extended loans against mortgaged land and eight are engaged in other forms of moneylending.[64]

From among the Koli Patel households, a sub-set of relatively prosperous farmers engage in moneylending: 23 out of a total of 144 households. Sixteen of these households have extended loans against mortgaged land, mostly to other Koli Patels. Only six out of 51 Vaghri households are reported to be engaged in moneylending. Of these, four have extended credit against land mortgaged by other Vaghris, and two have extended medium-term, high-interest loans to other Vaghri households. The other known moneylenders in the village

---

constructing a second building. He reports repaying the Rs 40,000 loan in monthly instalments of Rs 800 and receiving Rs 1,000 per month in rent: a net profit on his investment of Rs 200 per month.

[61] Official records indicate that about Rs 226,000 worth of loans from formal credit sources was disbursed in Maatisar during the 1980s. See Part II for more details on formal credit.

[62] Refer to the section on Land for a discussion of the Bharwad's acquisition of land.

[63] Another Bharwad is rumoured to be an even larger moneylender, but that with the exception of a few local loans against mortgaged land, he prefers to extend loans only outside the village. It is said that this Bharwad has extended a high-interest loan of Rs 100,000 to a Vaghri in the neighbouring Dumali village.

[64] It should be noted that not all Bharwad households have been able to generate a surplus and engage in moneylending. In fact, a few Bharwad households have been forced to mortgage the land they acquired to other Bharwads.

include two Brahmins, two potters, the Vankar postmaster, a school-teacher, and one of the two priests. Of these, only one potter-turned-shopkeeper offers credit sales and extends credit against mortgaged land. All the others give loans against pawned jewellery or utensils.

Weaving

Maatisar is home to the only community of wool weavers in the whole of Dholka *taluka*: elsewhere in the *taluka*, the Vankars weave cotton. The local Vankars weave a thick woollen shawl, called the *dhabla*, on a simple pit loom usually installed in the front veranda of their huts. Given the narrow width of the traditional loom, the *dhabla* is actually two strips of woven wool cloth hand-stitched together and finished with tassels.

Although only the men weave at the looms, weaving is only one step in the production of a *dhabla*, and the entire production process is decidedly a joint male–female venture. In fact, time–use data indicate that women in Vankar households averaged 4.5 hours in *dhabla* production, whereas men averaged only 3.3 hours per day.[65] Women perform many of the important operations in the production process, from carding and spinning the wool to preparing the starch to combing the threads and filling the bobbins and shuttles. While the dyeing and starching of the wool and preparing the weft is undertaken by both men and women together, men weave, stitch and tassel the shawls and handle all the marketing. The equipment used is simple and much of it is produced locally. Looms and other equipment are handed down from one generation to the next. When there is more than one son in any generation, older sons generally separate their residences, at which time they also acquire new, separate looms. At present, in the 22 households that declare weaving as their main source of income, there are 20 active, traditional pit looms.[66]

Both the buying of raw wool and the selling of the woven *dhabla* take place at any of several places: within the village to local residents

---

[65] It should be noted in this regard that some Vankar women have been trained to weave by SEWA and are now, therefore, more intensively involved in the weaving process than in the past.

[66] SEWA has introduced two new kinds of weaving to the village, merino wool and cotton weaving. Some Vankar households now operate only the new looms for these types of weaving; other households keep both traditional and new looms active; and some have not adopted new looms.

or to nomadic Rabaris (who come at a given time each year to sell wool and place orders for *dhablas*); at certain market towns in Saurashtra; or village-to-village.[67] All the market transactions are handled by men, even those which take place within the village. Traditionally, two shepherd communities, the Bharwads and Rabaris, bought *dhablas*. Some of the Rabaris tie–dye and embroider the *dhablas*,[68] while Rabari women stitch the *dhabla* into a skirt. In both the Bharwad and Rabari communities, the men wear the *dhabla* as a shawl. However, this pattern seems to be changing: some Rabari women have abandoned the *dhabla*-skirt for cloth skirts and some Koli Patel men have begun using *dhablas* as shawls or blankets.[69]

During our study year, the market for *dhablas* virtually collapsed and, for the first time in living memory, some households stopped *dhabla* production completely. It was difficult, therefore, to determine the average volume of production and sale for a normal year. Rough estimates indicated that weaving households average a net income of about Rs 1,000–1,500 per year.[70]

During the time of Shermia, the Vankar weavers performed three activities: their traditional weaving, their *veth* services and seasonal

---

[67] Raw wool is sold either by the sheep or by the kilogramme. The actual shearing is done either by the shepherd (who owns the sheep) or the weaver (who buys the wool). Black and white wool are sheared separately. To use Bharwad terminology, black wool is 'gold' and commanded a 1987 price of Rs 30 per kg; and white wool is 'silver' and commanded a 1987 price of Rs 22 per kg.

[68] The tie–dyeing is done in Surendranagar by the Khatri community at Rs 60 per *dhabla*; the embroidery is done by the Rabari women themselves.

[69] In years when there are many mosquitoes, the market for *dhablas* to be used as blankets expands.

[70] On the basis of figures provided by several weavers, the following rough averages for production costs and sale prices were calculated:

Production rate: Pre-weaving 2–3 days
Weaving 1–2 days
Costs per Dhabla:
Raw Materials:

Wool		89.50	(3.2 kg. per *dhabla*)
Dyes		15.00	
Starch		2.00	
Labour:		40.00	(4 days per *dhabla*)
		Rs 146.50	

Selling price per Dhabla: Rs 206.25
Net profit per Dhabla: Rs 59.75
Annual production: 20–25
Annual net income: Rs 1,195–1,494

agricultural labour (both local and migrant). As *veth* services, the Vankars collected firewood and fodder and acted as messengers for Shermia. Although there was more demand for their weaving at that time, the Vankars also participated in paddy planting and harvesting locally (in Maatisar and neighbouring villages) and migrated to Bavla or Koth (market towns in Dholka *taluka*) for two to five months of cotton-podding.[71] Over the past 10 to 15 years, some Vankars have begun to migrate, mostly to Kheda district, for paddy plantation and harvesting.

When Shermia transferred land to his former clients and tenants in the mid-1950s, six or seven Vankars were allotted land which they later sold to other caste groups in the village. However, eight years ago, some Vankar households lobbied for land under the Gujarat Agricultural Lands Ceilings Act. A total of 10 Vankar households were allotted two acres each. Four of these sold the land they were allotted. Of the other six, only three households cultivate their land themselves; the other three share-crop out their land. As a result, no Vankar household claims agriculture as a primary occupation and only three Vankar households claim cultivation as a secondary occupation.

Some Vankar households derive a supplemental source of income by flaying animals. As there are no Chamars (tanners) in the village, Bhangis and Vankars collect and flay dead animals. In return, they are able to sell the hides and bones of the animals to Chamars in a neighbouring village.[72] To carry out these activities, 17 Vankar and Bhangi households have organised themselves into two groups, which collect and flay animals by rotation. Rough estimates, based on information from several informants, indicate that each of the 17 households can expect to earn, on the average, just under Rs 120 per year from flaying animals.[73]

---

[71] The peak months for cotton-podding are Falgun, Chaitra, Vaishakh (March–May). Interestingly, until the last 10 to 15 years, almost all cotton-podding was done at cotton gins in small towns. More recently, as improved roads and increased numbers of tractors have facilitated transport, cotton-podding has increasingly shifted to villages. During the study year, a large Darbar landlord from the neighbouring Dumali village arrived with a tractor–trailer full of cotton and hired a large number of Vankars for four days of cotton-podding. Recently, a variety of cotton which does not require podding has been introduced, thereby reducing the demand for cotton-podders generally.

[72] In addition, although they are embarrassed to admit it, the Vankars eat the meat of the dead animals.

[73] These estimates were based on the following ranges of income reported:

Average income per animal: Rs 40, based on the following prices—

Pottery

Other than the Vankar weavers, the other artisan caste group in the village is the Prajapati (potter) caste. In the early 1950s, there were four potter households; at present, there are seven. Of the additional three, one is an immigrant household and two are headed by sons of the original four households. During Shermia's time, the potters were expected to provide the following *veth* services: fetching water, collecting fodder, supplying and replacing pots, and cleaning utensils. One of the Prajapatis, as a special client of Shermia's, was also expected to receive Shermia at Bavla town, accompany him on hunts, and act as a watchman.[74] During that time, all but one Prajapati household engaged in both cultivation and pottery. The exception was that of a full-time factory worker in Ahmedabad city.[75]

Like the service caste groups, the potters operate under the *jajmani* system, whereby they provide pots to designated patrons in return for fixed payments and concessions.[76] In the past, all potters prepared pots and were paid in kind at harvest for the supply of a stipulated number of pots. According to one report, the concession was 20 kgs of

	Skin	Bones
Cows	Rs 20–25	Rs 5
Buffaloes	Rs 40–45	Rs 10
Calves	Rs 10–30	Rs 3

Average annual mortality rate: 50
Number of households: 17
Average annual income per household: Rs 118

[74] According to that potter, he was kept so busy by Shermia that he only found time to make pots during the summer months when Shermia shifted his residence to Dholka town.

[75] His father was a famous pot-maker and his widow carries on a small trade in pots, buying pots in Bavla and selling them in Maatisar.

[76] According to McAlpin (1983: 103), in describing the parallel system of village servants (called *buletadar*) in Maharashtra, weavers 'were nowhere included among the village servants. There appear to have been two reasons for this. First, weavers were not necessary to the continuance of the agricultural process. Potters, blacksmiths, leather workers, and carpenters were. Second, weavers did not provide any service that could not be obtained through the market. Cloth was available from itinerant merchants or periodic fairs. Services provided by scavengers (rubbish and night-soil removal), washermen, brahmins (rituals for life-crises rites), barbers (not only haircutting and shaving, but frequently also marriage brokering) could not generally be obtained in periodic markets in pre-modern India.'

grain for 10 to 12 pots per household.[77] Also, each potter supplied pots only to a designated set of customer–patrons, his *garas*. For instance, one potter household supplied pots to one Koli Patel sub-caste neighbourhood and to all the Bharwads, Brahmins and Thakkars. These patrons or *garas* are passed down from one generation of potters to the next.

As I will discuss in the section on Caste Services, the *jajmani* system which supports the service and artisan castes is gradually eroding in the village. In the case of the potters, all the older generation of potters maintain their hereditary ties with patrons but some have stopped producing pots and most are paid in cash (on a piece-rate basis) rather than in kind (on a harvest-share basis). At present, only two households (those of a father and one of his sons) regularly produce pots; the other son is a farmer. One other household produces pots, but only for marriage and death ceremonies. These three households sell the pots they produce on a cash basis to their original *garas*; the other potter households buy pots elsewhere and sell them to their *garas*. All of the younger generation of potters, with one exception as noted above, have left pottery altogether. Three are engaged in cultivation and, occasionally, wage labour; another works exclusively as a wage labourer.

Caste Services

In earlier times, in order to meet the needs of the predominantly peasant population, different caste communities provided specific services to peasant households: carpentry, blacksmithy, barbering, etcetera. The centrality of cultivators or landholders to the *jajmani* system is seen by cultural anthropologists in largely cultural or ritual terms (Raheja 1988). In our study, we analysed the system in more economic terms: as a system wherein cultivators recognise the right of labourers and other service providers, to share and/or participate in agrarian production (Breman 1974). As such, we did not investigate *jajmani* transactions from the ritual perspective of giving and receiving

[77] According to this informant, the same concession rate persists until today. He finds that he incurs a loss if he supplies pots at the concession rate, so he has transferred to a cash payment system. Only one household still supplies pots at the old concession rate. Interestingly, that household has supplemental sources of income: the husband works as a peon in the *gram panchayat* office (at Rs 150 per month) and his wife fills bobbins at the SEWA weaving centre (at Rs 100 per month).

presentations, but from an economic perspective of providing goods and services in exchange for payments in (generally) kind, notably harvest shares.

In Gujarati, these service castes are referred to as *vasvayas*, or persons who 'settled' in villages. Historically, the service castes were recruited as needed to patron villages where they were given land to settle and cash allowances or grain payments in kind for their services.[78] Even in the past, only a few service caste households resided in Maatisar: carpenters (*sutars*), barbers (*naiks*), genealogists (*Barots*) and priests (*pujaris*).[79] Over the past decade, two of the three carpenter households have migrated to Ahmedabad city. At present, Maatisar has two Muslim barbers (one a *vasvaya*, the other a recent immigrant), five Barot genealogists, one carpenter, and two priest households (one for each of the main temples).

Of the two Muslim barbers, one is older in both age and residence, having been called to the village from his original home near Bhavnagar when the previous barber, who was childless, died.[80] He now engages in part-time carpentry as his son has taken over the barber trade. The other barber immigrated to the village around 1980. The older barber was recruited to the village by the Koli Patel *panch* (council of elders) and was offered a house and grain payments from each household every year.[81] In addition, he is entitled to frequent handouts of vegetables and potatoes from the shopkeepers and head-loads of dry fodder at harvest from Koli Patel farmers.[82] If he shaves the beards or cuts the hair of outsiders to the village, he charges a flat fee. The other

---

[78] These concessions or *inams* were regulated or curtailed by various laws: the Pensions Act of 1871, the Resumption Rules of 1908, and the Invalidation of Hindu Ceremonial Emoluments Act of 1926. Most recently, the Bombay Service Inams Useful to Community (Gujarat and Konkan) Resumption Rules of 1954 recognised some of these services as 'useful' and resumed the *inam* system (Government of Gujarat 1984: 582–3).

[79] As I discussed in the section of Weaving, no Chamars (tanners) ever lived in Maatisar. The traditional Chamar service of removing and flaying dead animals is carried out by local Vankars and Bhangis.

[80] The present barber had a relative in a neighbouring village who acted as middleman in the negotiation.

[81] According to different reports, barbers are entitled to 10–20 kgs of paddy and wheat per year from each household in exchange for weekly haircuts.

[82] As this barber is now quite old, his son has taken over the business. The old barber is currently engaged in part-time carpentry work. Even though he has essentially retired, both he and his son receive grain concessions. His wife is a traditional midwife who has received training from and is registered with the Primary Health Centre in Bavla town.

barber receives no concessions, as he immigrated to Maatisar on his own, and charges all customers a fixed amount.

In addition to the temple compounds where they live and the temple land which they cultivate, both priests in the village are entitled to a daily concession of grain from the households which worship at their respective temples.[83] According to one, he visits roughly 75 households each day to collect small bowlfuls of flour and grain. On average in a good year, he can collect 2.5 kgs of flour and 2.5 kgs of grain each day, that is, over Rs 3,500 worth of flour and grain each year. In addition, at each of the two main harvests, all 75 households gift him anywhere from two to 20 kgs of grain, depending on the crop yields and size of the individual household.[84]

The Vankar weavers are the only caste in the village which patronises the resident Barot genealogists. As a result, the Barots have acquired the status of the Vankars and live in the Vankar *vas*.[85] These professional bards and genealogists have hereditary relationships with specific households in a designated circle of villages. They visit each village every few years to update the genealogies, recording the deaths and marriages of the sons of their client families. These genealogies are recorded in a script known only to the Barots. In addition to maintaining genealogies, the Barots sing and narrate stories on special occasions. However, the demand for their specialised services is on the decline, so much so that four young Barots have migrated with their families to Ahmedabad city: three as skilled labourers (as a welder, mason and gardener respectively) and one as a cloth-seller.

In addition to the Barot bards, two men in Maatisar play drums, one man plays the flute, and one man sings at various festivals or ceremonies in the village. One of the drummers is a Bhangi who plays the drum (*dholi*) two or three times a year for other Bhangi and Vankars. He is paid Rs 125 each time. The other drummer, a Rawal (camel carter), plays for other caste groups in the village whenever he is called

---

[83] The Brahmins and Thakkars worship at the Swaminarayan temple, where a member of the congregation, rather than a priest, officiates. The various Backward Castes worship at the two other temples, each presided over by a resident Gosai priest. As elsewhere in India, payments to the priests are generally greater than to village servants (*kamins*) such as barbers or carpenters (Raheja 1988).

[84] During a drought year, the payment at harvest is lower than in normal years given the decreased yields or outright failure of various crops.

[85] As mentioned earlier, elsewhere in Gujarat, Barots are generally classified as a Backward Caste (Shah and Desai 1988).

upon. He is entitled to five kg paddy and five kg wheat per year from each patron household. Also, several men from different castes are recognised as *buas* (spirit possessors) and are called upon to sing, beat drums and officiate at rituals for the local mother–goddess.

Salaried Work

For a village of under 300 households, Maatisar has a significant number of individuals (23 in all) who hold government jobs, both part-time and full-time. Of these, five work outside the village: a bus-conductor, a headmaster and a teacher in neighbouring village schools, the supervisor of the government's Mid-Day Meal Scheme in a neighbouring village, and the *talati* (village accountant) of a neighbouring village. In terms of number of jobs, salaried work opportunities appear to be reasonably distributed by caste. The only large caste groups not represented are the Bhangis (scavengers), most likely because they are the lowest caste on the status hierarchy, and the Bharwads (shepherds), because they have a tradition of not working for others.[86]

However, in looking closer at the distribution of government jobs by individuals or households, certain patterns emerge. Other than the self-made Vaghri bus-conductor, the jobs which pay Rs 1,000 or more per month are held by outsiders: the schoolteacher, headmaster and *talati*. The majority of medium-pay government jobs (Rs 250–500 per month) have been given to (or captured by) individuals who are dominant, either economically or politically, in the village: the Vankar leader, two rich Thakkar traders and three rich Brahmins, two of whom are husband and wife. The Thakkars and Brahmins enjoyed economic and social dominance even before negotiating government jobs. And though, in the case of the Vankar leader, his appointment as postmaster confirmed his role as caste leader, it was his past political lobbying and networking that led to his appointment. The low-paying, part-time government jobs (Rs 50–100 per month) have been allotted by local supervisors to women, either young widows or the wives of political clients.

---

[86] Even during the prolonged and severe drought of 1986–87, when they were forced to migrate with their animals, the Bharwads (with one exception) did not participate in the local or migrant labour markets. Ultimately, in late December 1987, a few Bharwads joined the relief works which had been offered locally since April 1987. This was the first time in living memory that Bharwads had either migrated with their animals in search of fodder or been forced to join relief works.

In addition to the government, SEWA offers salaried work in the village. A total of 14 Maatisar residents work for SEWA. Of these, eight are women, a ratio which makes up in part for the low number of women in government jobs (six out of 17). Further, as a women's organisation, SEWA is committed to hiring and training women for leadership and management positions. Whereas no women have been hired to the middle-management and medium-pay government jobs (Rs 250–500), SEWA has recruited and trained women as local organisers, vocational trainers and dairy cooperative secretaries.[87] Also, SEWA has deliberately recruited staff from the Scheduled Castes.

Despite a seemingly high rate of local salaried work, no residents of Maatisar commute for salaried work to Bavla town or Ahmedabad city. Indeed, no residents of Maatisar are engaged in salaried work in the private sector. And, as will be discussed in the section on Mobility only one permanent migrant from Maatisar has been employed in full-time work in the formal sector (in a maize mill). The other permanent migrants to urban centres are casually employed or self-employed.

Self-Employment

There are five types of self-employment opportunities in Maatisar: traditional caste occupations (artisan and service castes), shopkeeping or vending, cotton spinning (introduced by SEWA), tailoring and unskilled self-employment. The first two categories have already been discussed. There are four tailors in Maatisar, all immigrants to the village. About 28 households, mostly Koli Patels, supplement their earnings with cotton spinning. SEWA supplies the raw cotton, collects and sells the spun yarn. Among these, about 12 elderly or disabled individuals live entirely on what they earn by spinning.

Unskilled self-employment consists mainly of collecting, processing and selling natural resource products. I will discuss the range of natural resource products which are freely collected in Part II. Although most of these are consumed or sold in unprocessed form, two are processed: cow-dung made into fuel-cakes or manure (by women) and a shrub grass used to make rope (by men). Although these activities generate only modest returns in monetary terms, they contribute significantly to the livelihoods of individual households.

---

[87] The dairy cooperative secretary in Maatisar is one of 10 women recruited and trained by SEWA for that position in various villages in the region.

Patterns of Mobility

As I mentioned in the Introduction, we reconstructed baseline data for Maatisar from fragmentary evidence gathered in life-histories, genealogies and informant interviews, taking the early 1950s as the baseline. From what we were able to learn about the village at that time, we have made two broad assumptions about household occupations. First, that in the early 1950s most households derived a reasonably secure livelihood in normal years from their hereditary caste occupation. But with increasing population density and division of property on inheritance or marriage—there are roughly twice as many people and households in the late 1980s than in the early 1950s—both land and occupations have become severely crowded. As a result, fewer households are now able to generate subsistence from only their hereditary caste occupation.

Our second assumption is that both forced entry into and increased levels of participation in the wage labour market are, generally, indications of downward mobility. Whereas the local economy has expanded, widening opportunities in both the local and migrant labour markets, the net impact on different households has not necessarily been positive. The local labour market remains small relative to the demand, and wages have not risen significantly. For individual households, therefore, entry into the migrant labour market (which involves harsh conditions of work and residence) represents a survival, not a mobility, strategy.

As a rough approximation of the general patterns of mobility, the current position of households in relation to their traditional caste occupations and to wage labour can be used to position them at one of three points on a mobility continuum. Taking the peasant caste of Koli Patels, for example, those who still engage primarily or exclusively in cultivation fall on the 'stability' mid-point of the continuum; those who must supplement cultivation with significant amounts of wage labour or abandon cultivation for wage labour or other low-status activities fall at the 'downward mobility' end of the continuum; and those who supplement cultivation with moneylending or some status activity (e.g., salaried work or local politics) are at the 'upward mobility' end of the continuum.

Table 11 presents the typology of households by caste and occupation on this mobility continuum.[88] As the table indicates, many of the

[88] The two higher caste groups, Brahmins and Thakkars, have remained relatively stable.

Table 11
Occupational Mobility of Different Caste Groups

Caste/group	Downward mobility	Traditional pattern	Upward mobility
Bharwad	Livestock + labour	Livestock	Livestock + cultivation (+ moneylending)
(19)*	2	10	7
Koli Patel	Labour + cultivation Labour or other	Cultivation + labour	Cultivation + moneylending
(142)	75	44	23
Vaghri	Labour + other	Labour[1]	Labour + cultivation
(51)	22	7	22
Vankar	Labour + weaving	Weaving + Labour[2]	Weaving + salaried work[3]
(28)	1	22	5
Prajapati	Cultivation + labour	Pottery + cultivation	Shopkeeping or salaried work
(7)	2	3	2
Service castes	Caste service + other	Caste services	Caste service + tailoring
(15)	2	6	1
Total:	**104**	**92**	**60**

* Numbers in brackets = total number of households in each caste group.[4]

[1] In the early 1950s, the one caste that came closest to being a 'labour' caste was the Vaghris.

[2] Even in earlier times, almost all weaving households engaged in some seasonal labour.

[3] SEWA has worked closely with the Vankar weavers, some of whom are on SEWA's payroll as trainees or trainers. The Vankar leader is on the government payroll as postmaster for the village.

[4] These totals do not include households which migrated permanently: five Bharwad, eight Koli Patel, five Vaghri, one Vankar, three Prajapati, and seven service caste. Refer to Table 12 for current occupations of these migrant households.

Bharwad shepherds now supplement their earnings from livestock with cultivation; a few also engage in moneylending. Some Koli Patel peasants also engage in moneylending. However, many Koli Patels must now supplement their earnings from cultivation with significant amounts of wage labour. Whereas in the past most Vankar weavers engaged in seasonal cotton-podding, a few now seek alternative wage labour for longer seasons in the year. Other Vankars have benefited from the SEWA programme in support of weavers, both as trainees and trainers, and the current Vankar leader serves as the government-paid postmaster in the village. To summarise, over the past 30 years, some households reversed the proportion of time spent on labour relative to their traditional occupations; some added activities to supplement their traditional occupations; but only a few made significant shifts away from their traditional occupations.[89]

In terms of primary occupations, the majority of households follow their hereditary caste occupations. The only two caste groups for whom there is much variation in primary occupation are the Koli Patels (the traditional peasant caste who now engage in labour in significant numbers) and the Vaghris (the traditional 'labour' caste who now engage in both cultivation and labour).[90] (Refer to Table 2 for the distribution of primary occupations by caste.)

In terms of secondary occupations, each household engages, on the average, in more than two secondary occupations. No clear pattern of secondary occupations by caste emerges, except that most of those engaged in petty vending are Vaghri women.[91] All caste groups rear livestock. At least a few households from each caste group engage in moneylending, albeit lending of different types and scale. All major caste groups, except Brahmins, Thakkars and Bharwads, engage in wage labour, including seasonal migrant labour. Table 13 in Part II presents the distribution of secondary activities by primary occupation.[92]

Given the broad patterns of mobility, the question arises as to why, within each caste group, some households do relatively better, some do relatively less well and some remain relatively stable. As groups of

---

[89] A few households made significant shifts in occupation when they migrated permanently out of the village. Refer to discussion of permanent migration which follows. A longitudinal study of Matar Taluka, Kheda District, in Gujarat over the period 1964-65 to 1974-75 (Shah et al. 1985) reports low occupational mobility. Mobility was lowest among agricultural labourers, followed by households engaged in trades or artisan production, and was highest among cultivators.

[90] In earlier times, whatever demand there was for labour was filled partly by Vaghris (who also engaged in hunting and fishing), partly by the Vankar weavers (who engaged in wage labour for only specific times in the year), and partly by Koli Patels (who were primarily farmers). The one caste that came closest to being a 'labour' caste, for whom wage labour was a major source of income, was the Vaghri.

[91] Throughout Gujarat, Vaghris are known as vendors. In Maatisar, vending by Vaghris is highly seasonal (mostly vegetables and melons), so that the Vaghris are primarily engaged in either cultivation or labour.

[92] In addition to primary and secondary occupations, most households engage in routine subsistence-oriented activities, notably the searching–gathering–collecting activities of women. I will discuss these subsistence-oriented activities in Parts II and III.

households, the Bharwad shepherds and Thakkar traders have done relatively well. Almost all Thakkar households have been able to build on their inherited wealth and expand their economic activities. In so doing, they have recently begun to divest in land and moneylending within the village to invest in property, trade and (presumably) money-lending in Bavla town and Ahmedabad city. The more prosperous Bharwads have diversified their activities beyond herding to include agriculture and moneylending.

The story of the Bharwad reported to be the village's largest money-lender within the village is an interesting case study in individual entrepreneurship. As the story goes, this Bharwad was one of three sons of poor parents, who owned a few animals and had been given a house by Shermia. He was educated up to Class V and married at age fifteen to the daughter of Bharwads from a village near Bavla who owned a herd of 40 cattle. As is the custom with Bharwads, his family paid a bride-price to the bride's family. Soon after his marriage, his parents died and he separated from his brothers. At that time, his share in the family property totalled nine goats, a rope bed and a few utensils. He sold the nine goats, purchased two cows, began selling milk, and got a part-time job with a dairy cooperative in Bavla town. After working with the dairy cooperative for five years, he began a private milk trade: buying milk from neighbouring villages and selling it to private traders in Bavla. With profits from the milk trade, he invested in additional cattle and in land. By 1987, he owned over 35 acres of land and 20 head of cattle, hired attached labour to assist in cultivation, and was reported to be the largest moneylender in the village.

However, not all Bharwads have prospered. One Bharwad has been forced to supplement earnings from his own herd of cattle by grazing cattle which belong to other households and by wage labour (paddy and wheat harvesting). He is the only Bharwad who regularly engages in wage labour; one of only two Bharwads forced to graze animals for others; and, other than an elderly widower, the poorest Bharwad in the village. He owns a small and inferior herd: 12 thin animals. In a normal year, he grazes 10 to 25 animals for others, the number of animals grazed and the fee charged for grazing varying by season.[93]

---

[93] Generally, he grazes more animals during the winter and summer seasons (when grass is scarce and cattle have to be grazed longer and further). For animals grazed in winter, he charges Rs 10 per month and one *maund* of wheat. For animals grazed in the summer and monsoon seasons, he charges Rs 10 per month. For animals which he grazes throughout the year, he charges two *maunds* of grains.

During the drought period, fewer households contracted his grazing services and he was forced to share-crop out eight of his own animals. If conditions in the post-drought period did not improve, he predicted that he might be forced to sell his herd and migrate to Ahmedabad in search of wage labour opportunities.[94] His parents are not in a position to help him. Since the untimely death of his elder brother (six days after his own marriage), his younger unmarried brother and his parents have lived with his elder brother's widow.

As groups of households, the mobility of Koli Patels, Vaghris and Vankars has been mixed. In the early 1950s, most Koli Patels and Vankars generated reasonably secure livelihoods from farming and weaving respectively, supplemented by varying amounts of wage labour. By the late 1980s, a livelihood based primarily on the traditional caste occupation no longer proved secure for all. In the case of the Koli Patels, this is due largely to increased pressures on the land (i.e., increased numbers of farming households, both Koli Patel and other castes) as well as fragmentation of holdings across generations. In the case of the Vankars, this is attributable largely to increased competition within the caste group (i.e., increased numbers of Vankar weaving households) and a shrinking market for the traditional *dhabla*.

The position of the Vaghris was, it would seem, always mixed. They traditionally pieced together livelihoods from a variety of short-term seasonal activities (e.g., hunting, fishing, wage labour, and vegetable–fruit cultivation and vending) and still derive their livelihoods from an equally varied, although different, mix of activities (e.g., standard crop cultivation, labour, vegetable–fruit cultivation and vending).

More than half of the Koli Patel households (75 out of 142) have been forced to supplement their earnings from cultivation with increasing amounts of wage labour or to abandon cultivation altogether. In a few cases, households have been forced to mortgage part of the land they inherited to raise money to cover marriage costs. In many cases, the household's decline can be attributed in part to the division of property, whereby each succeeding generation inherited a progressively smaller share of land or, in the case of indivisible assets such as bullocks, wells or pumps, either no share at all or a joint share which is difficult to access.

By contrast, over 15 per cent of Koli Patel households (23 out of

---

[94] Several more prosperous Bharwads have migrated to Ahmedabad to engage in milk trading. At least one less prosperous Bharwad migrated to Ahmedabad to engage in construction work.

142) have enjoyed upward mobility. Among the sub-sample house-holds, two Koli Patel households have done better than others. One is a large, joint household, with inherited wealth still jointly owned and managed. The head of that household was the only son of an influential father who served as the *mukhi* (or local police chief) under Shermia and himself exercises considerable influence as a caste elder. He is also one of the largest moneylenders and cultivators in the village, operating a significant amount of share-cropped or mortgaged land in addition to what he owns.[95]

The other is a small nuclear family, including the husband's mother. Their story is an interesting case study in upward mobility—from depending on wage labour to engaging in part-time salaried work, cultivation, artisan production and petty trading. The husband's father was a landless labourer who, some 30 years ago, immigrated to Maatisar, his wife's natal village, as an attached labourer. Eight years later he died, leaving his wife and a young son. For approximately 10 years, the mother supported herself and her son through wage labour. After studying up to Class V, the son became a wage labourer, alternating between local and migrant wage labour opportunities. Five years ago he was married, paying Rs 5,000 (taken on loan) as the bride-price. His luck began to change when he was hired to a government job in the local branch of the Forest Department, where he earns about Rs 250 a month as a forest guard. His wife, who often works as an agricultural labourer, was hired for one year to work in the Forest Department nursery and, more recently, has begun spinning cotton yarn under the SEWA-run scheme. In 1984, the husband rented a push-cart from his cousin for three months (at Rs 50 per month) to test the feasibility of operating a small-scale trading venture. A few months later, with two loans of Rs 500 each (one from a shopkeeper and one from a Forest Department official), he bought the push-cart from his cousin.[96] His mother now sells *bidis* (cigarettes), *paan* (betel-

[95] From among the total Koli Patel households, a sub-set of relatively prosperous farmers engage in moneylending: 23 households (16 per cent) out of a total of 144 Koli Patel households. Sixteen of these households have extended loans against mortgaged land, mostly land mortgaged by other Koli Patels. Twelve of these households are engaged in other types of moneylending: four have granted wage advances to attached labour; four have extended loans against pawned jewellery or utensils; and six have extended high-interest, medium-term loans.

[96] He repaid the loan to the shopkeeper within 10 days with an interest charge of Rs 15. He repaid the loan to the Forest Department official with his salary for the following two months.

nut preparation), and biscuits from the push-cart at the local bus-
stand.

Given the profits from this small· retail business, this Koli Patel
household has been able to share-crop in some land (with two other
partners who actually cultivate the land) and mortgage in a tape-
recorder (for Rs 250 from a Vaghri). In the words of the household
head:

> When my father came to Maatisar, we had nothing. Even one meal
> each day was difficult. No one trusted us enough to give us a loan.
> But somehow we came through. Unfortunately my father did not
> live to see it . . . . My mother should be appreciated. She sustained
> us for 12 years on her own through her manual labour. I've only
> begun to earn during the last 10 years. Now, she can enjoy some
> leisure while still earning.

Although no Vaghri household has left wage labour altogether, two
Vaghri households have fared relatively well. One household jointly
owns, with two brothers of the household head, four bullocks, one
pump set, and just under 25 acres of cultivable land which their father
was given by Shermia, making the father one of two large farmers
among the Vaghri community at that time. In the early years of their
marriage, the husband migrated seasonally for groundnut harvesting
and stone cutting, and currently both husband and wife engage in
local wage labour. In addition to their earnings from wage labour, they
earn a profit from their share of the joint agricultural production.

The other relatively prosperous Vaghri household migrated to
Maatisar, ancestral home of the household head, from another village
only 10 years ago. Claiming there is 'no *danda* (means of earning) in
Maatisar', the household generates a surplus by migrating for agricultural wage labour eight months each year. They invest this surplus
(roughly Rs 4,000–5,000 per year) in local moneylending and, occasionally, in utensil trading in Delhi.

Within the Vankar community of 28 households, one Vankar
household has fared relatively less well, five have fared relatively well,
and the others have remained relatively stable. The Vankar household
which fared relatively less well did so for primarily two reasons: the
division of family assets (looms and other weaving equipment) between
three sons, and the need to raise bride-prices for three successive

marriages by one of the sons.[97] As a result of this erosion of the family property, each of the sons and their families have been forced to seek wage labour opportunities both within and outside Maatisar.

Two Vankar households which fared relatively well did so in very different ways: one through hard work and diligence, the other through politics and patronage. For many years, the first household supplemented its earnings from traditional wool weaving with wage labour (cotton-podding in the winter season and paddy plantation and harvesting in the monsoon season), which is the traditional pattern of the majority of Vankar households. When SEWA began its program to train women as weavers in the village, the wife of this household became the first diligent trainee and was selected for specialised training at the National Institute of Design in Ahmedabad.[98] She now serves as a part-time trainer for SEWA and as president of the SEWA-sponsored Wool Weaver's Cooperative in the village. Both husband and wife weave daily on two looms in their recently-expanded house: weaving the traditional wool shawl plus merino wool shawls and cotton fabric marketed by SEWA.

The second household is that of the current Vankar leader. Like other Vankar couples, for many years of their early marriage the husband and wife combined wool weaving with wage labour. At one point, after a bad drought, they abandoned weaving and migrated for the better part of a year. Their luck turned dramatically when, in 1975, the husband was appointed postmaster of the village. Although the husband attributes his political leadership to this appointment, it seems clear that he would not have been appointed if he had not curried favor with local politicians and developed strong ties to a political patron in a nearby village.[99] In addition, his wife was hired by SEWA for several years as a part-time local organiser.[100]

[97] The son divorced his first wife after two years of marriage; his second wife died after 10 years of marriage, and he married for a third time during the study year. The household is said to have paid Rs 1,200, Rs 6,000, and Rs 7,000 respectively in bride-price for the three marriages.

[98] Traditionally, as I noted in the section on weavers, only men weave at the looms. Women carry out and assist in many of the pre-weaving and ancillary activities. SEWA has trained several successive batches of Vankar women to weave.

[99] His patron, a schoolteacher, is the political client of several regional Scheduled Caste politicians, including a Congress–I Member of the State Legislative Assembly.

[100] Data on earnings (cf. section on *Weavers*) indicate that those Vankars who have remained relatively stable can expect to earn, on the average, Rs 1,600–2,000 per year:

Through these political connections, the postmaster has emerged not only as the local Vankar leader but also as the acknowledged local broker of government loans (both those granted under the IRDP programme and those granted by the Gram Sewak, plus special loan schemes for Scheduled Castes). Under his patronage and leadership, some 15 to 20 Vankar households receive loan–cum–subsidy packages from the government each year, ostensibly for investment in weaving. The Vankar households pay back these loans quickly and regularly, sometimes without investing them, in order to, as local informants put it, 'eat the subsidies' from multiple loans.

The individual age, capacity or nature of household members, particularly the household head, can play a part in the gradual deterioration of a household. In one case, the household head suffers mild cases of alcoholism and lethargy.[101] His father was a *jividar* (peon) to Shermia. As a child, he worked as a servant in Shermia's house. Later, he himself served for 10 years as a *jividar* at a salary of Rs 50 per month. As a one-time salaried worker, he now refuses to hire himself out as a wage labourer and takes up part-time intermittent work as a tractor driver, a rice mill mechanic or a guard. Because he no longer earns a steady income, he has been forced to mortgage some of his land, sell one of his huts and his radio and watch. In another case, an asthmatic widower, who has no sons and only one daughter who is married outside the village, is addicted to opium and lives largely off charity from his daughter and kin neighbours.

One Vaghri household which fared poorly did so for primarily two reasons: first, the need to mortgage their land and sell their pump set to raise money to cover marriage costs; and second, the alcoholism and lethargy of the household head. The family inherited some land and a pump set, but was forced to mortgage the land and sell the pump set to raise funds to cover the marriage costs of the husband's brother. The husband drifts in and out of various mechanic and driver jobs. He is also recognised as a *bua* and gets called upon, occasionally, to sing, beat drums and officiate at rituals. While the mother bore and

---

Rs 1,200–1,500 from weaving, Rs 120 from animal flaying, and Rs 280–430 from wage labour (assuming four to six weeks of work @ Rs 10 per day). By contrast, the Vankar postmaster and his wife together earn Rs 5,940 per year in salaried income alone: he earns Rs 395 per month as postmaster; she earns Rs 100 per month as a part-time SEWA organiser.

[101] I hesitate to use what sounds like prejudiced references to characterise individuals. But these terms were used by the family and kin of these individuals.

nursed the two younger children, the father drifted in and out of part-time jobs, and the eldest son attended school. The only member of the family with a regular income was the eldest daughter, who worked at whatever local or migrant labour opportunities became available. Although her marriage was initially postponed when the monsoon rains failed in July 1987, she was married in December that year for a bride-price of some Rs 8,000. Her family spent half that amount on wedding expenses and planned to use the rest to redeem their mortgaged land.

Further, a particular set of events can also precipitate a decline in household status. For instance, one Koli Patel household was forced to migrate to Maatisar from its native village, after a major land and wage dispute there. Other than an initial attempt at share-cropping during their first year in Maatisar and a limited amount of milk from their one goat and one cow, that household has been exclusively dependent on the wage labour of its various members since immigrating to Maatisar in 1984.[102]

Finally, the absence of adult working males can have a negative effect on household income and welfare. According to our findings, the poorest of the poor in Maatisar are households in which there is no adult working male: households headed either by widows or elderly persons/couples. There are 20 households headed by women, of which 13 have no adult working males, and 24 households headed by elderly persons, of which the majority have no adult working males. Such households face problems in managing their own production, particularly in agriculture; are often forced to lease, mortgage or sell their land (if any); and find it difficult to negotiate the labour, tenancy and credit markets. Elderly couples without sons to help manage their land are often forced to share-crop out their land and subsist on whatever odd jobs or small gifts they receive.

Over the past 15 to 20 years, some 37 households (or just over 10 per cent of total households) have migrated permanently out of the village. Nearly one-third of the permanent migrant households were from the economically-dominant caste groups: eight Thakkar and five Bharwad households. Over 20 per cent were from artisan and service caste groups: four Barot, three Prajapati and one Vankar household. Another 20 per cent were from the main peasant caste, Koli Patel. Just

[102] In 1984, when this household first arrived in Maatisar, they share-cropped some land from which they earned 25 *maunds* of paddy as their share. From 1985–87, due to the prevailing drought conditions, they did not share-crop land.

under 15 per cent were Vaghris, a caste whose traditional occupations
(i.e., vegetable, cloth and utensil vending) involve some extra-village
contacts.

Of these 37 households, roughly two-thirds migrated to urban
centres, mainly Ahmedabad but also Bavla, and, in one case, Delhi.
The remaining third migrated to other rural areas within the state,
both within and outside the district. In terms of occupations and
trades, roughly one half negotiated options within new lines of
occupation: welding, masonry, carpentry, factory work. Nearly one-
fourth, all from the economically dominant castes, negotiated opportunities within their traditional occupation: milk trade and general
trade. The rest negotiated permanent positions where they had been
seasonal migrants: in brickfields, rice mills or agriculture.

The households which migrated to Ahmedabad, just under half of
the total permanent migrant households, appear to have done so
directly in one step. However, for roughly one-quarter of the permanent migrants, seasonal rural–to–rural or rural–to–urban migration
represented a first step towards final settlement in the area of destination. A common pattern was seasonal migration as a first step,
followed by migration on a semi-permanent basis (lengthy seasonal
migration every year for some years), and finally permanent migration.

Not all of the permanent migration was induced by poverty or
crisis; rather, both push and pull factors were involved. The economically-dominant households which migrated permanently did so in
order to reinvest surplus within the same trade but in a different
geographic location.[103] The Barot and Prajapati households which
migrated represent a younger generation opting out of the traditional
caste occupation as the economic base of these occupations has been
eroded. These younger households responded to long-term trends, not
to an immediate, short-term crisis. The one Vankar household which
migrated did so after an intracaste conflict in the village. Interestingly,
it returned to Maatisar during the 1987 drought and resumed weaving.
When the household members were asked why they had returned,

[103] One Thakkar informant reported that Thakkars generally favour reinvesting in
trade and construction rather than in land or moneylending. Disinvestment in land is
not a recent trend for the Thakkars; they have share-cropped or mortgaged out their
land for some time. Disinvestment in moneylending seems due to at least three forces:
one, the waiving of all debts and the inquiry into moneylending practices during the
political period in the mid-1970s referred to as the Emergency; two, the inability of
debtors to repay during the recent protracted drought; and, three, displacement by
formal credit institutions and the local Bharwads.

they reported that wage labour opportunities in Saurashtra, the area to which they migrated, had collapsed due to severe drought conditions.

Most households migrated permanently in response to increasing impoverishment over time. For some, permanent migration followed several years of seasonal migration. Other households appear to have assessed their opportunities locally and decided to make the shift in a single move. In general, for each of these groups, the mobility was of a geographic, not socio–economic, nature. Only one migrant crossed into the formal sector, as a permanent worker in a maize mill. The others still work under the same conditions that they did in the past:

Table 12
Permanent Migrants by Caste, Destination and Type of Work

Caste	No. of HHs	Destination	Type of work
Thakkar	3	Ahmedabad	Shopkeeping
	2	Bavla	Shopkeeping
	1	Bavla	Rice mill ownership
	2	Kheda District	Shopkeeping
Bharwad	4	Ahmedabad	Milk trade
	1	Ahmedabad	Construction
Koli Patel	1	Ahmedabad	Masonry
	1	Ahmedabad	Factory work
	1	Near Ahmedabad	Masonry
	2	Near Ahmedabad	Brickfield labour
	1	Bavla	Rice mill labour
	1	Sanand *Taluka*	Attached agricultural labour
	1	NA	NA
Prajapati	1	Bavla	Rice mill labour
	1	Sanand *Taluka*	NA
	1	Near Ahmedabad	Brickfield labour
Carpenter	3	Ahmedabad	Carpentry
Vaghri	1	Delhi	Utensil selling
	1	Junagadh District	Stone cutting
	1	Sanand *Taluka*	Agricultural labour
	1	Saurashtra	Agricultural labour
	1	Dholka *Taluka*	Attached agricultural labour
Barot	1	Ahmedabad	Welding
	1	Ahmedabad	Masonry
	1	Ahmedabad	Cloth selling
	1	Ahmedabad	Gardening
Harijan	1	Saurashtra	Agricultural labour
Total:	37		

either as self-employed in trade; casually employed in brickfields, rice mills, the construction industry or agriculture; or as farm servants in agriculture. Table 12 presents the distribution of permanent migrants by caste, destination, and type of work.

Interestingly, there has been permanent migration both from and to Maatisar. In addition to the service caste groups who were 'called' to the village (two priests and one barber), two schoolteachers, three tailors, and about 10 Koli Patel and Vaghri labourer households have migrated permanently to the village. When asked why he chose to live in Maatisar rather than in the village where he worked, one school-teacher replied, 'Maatisar has more facilities.' When asked what he meant, he explained, 'Maatisar has several shops, electricity, good drinking water and is on the main bus route.' The immigrants all live in rented space, mainly in brick huts built by the Vankars, Koli Patels and Vaghris under the Government of India's Twenty-Point Programme.

In Part I, I have discussed broad patterns of household mobility in response to gradual changes over the past three decades. In Parts II and III, I will discuss household strategies in response to recurring seasonal fluctuations and periodic drought-induced crises, respectively. Although these coping strategies have been developed largely in response to time-specific conditions, it is important to note that coping strategies are also determined, in part, by household mobility over time.

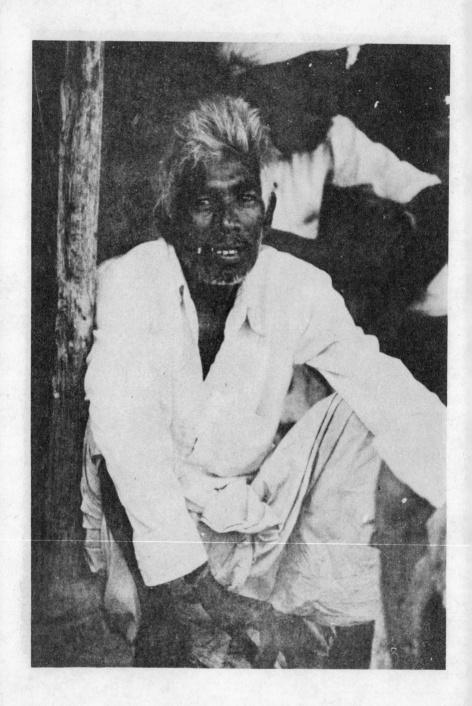

II

Coping with Seasonality

Seasonal Strategies

The local agricultural calendar is divided into three seasons: the *kharif* or monsoon season (June–October); the *rabi* or winter season (November–March); and the summer season (April–May). Each season can, in turn, be divided into periods of greater or lesser activity for those engaged in agriculture, either as farmers or labourers. The rhythms within seasons affect labourers the most as they find local employment largely at the beginning and end of the monsoon season, and at the end of the winter season; and their wages fluctuate within seasons. Farmers are affected by the sowing, interculture and harvesting requirements of specific crops, and their stocks of seeds and food fluctuate within seasons.

In normal years in Maatisar, the monsoon season is a period of intermittent hard work and increasingly low food availability. More households engage in cultivation during the monsoon, when all crops are grown under rain-fed conditions, than during winter when irrigation is necessary. Because of the labour requirements of the crops grown, particularly of paddy, more labourers are hired for both planting and harvesting in monsoon than in winter. A significant number of labourers are hired for monsoon sowing, the majority are hired during monsoon harvest, but very few are hired during the intervening two months.

Because the monsoon harvest comes a full six months after the winter harvest of wheat and barley and only a limited amount of sorghum is grown in summer, the monsoon season is a period during which food stocks are gradually, if not completely, depleted. The period just before monsoon harvest—which has been referred to elsewhere as 'the hungry season' (Longhurst 1986)—is one of considerable stress, especially for labourers but also for small farmers.

The monsoon harvest brings substantial relief to farm households but limited and brief relief to labour households. Because few farmers hire labour for planting winter crops, the month following the monsoon harvest is the time of peak migration by labourers in search of employment. Most migrants do not return before the end of the winter season. Farmers keep busy throughout the winter season, planting winter crops in November–December, harvesting the longer monsoon crops in January–February and harvesting winter crops in March–April.

After the brief flurry of activities around winter harvest, for which the majority of migrants return home, the village slows down for the summer. A few farmers grow a limited amount of sorghum as fodder. The remaining migrants return home to prepare for monsoon cultivation. These, briefly, are the seasonal rhythms in a regular agricultural year.

But Maatisar's economy is, of course, much broader than farming and there are marked seasonalities in non-farm, as well as farm, activities. For pastoralists, seasonality has as much to do with fodder, as with food, supply. Whereas the monsoon is the 'hungry' season for people, the summer is the 'hungry' season for animals: there is little wild grass, field waste or organic matter of any kind to be found, except for the small crop of sorghum. During the other seasons of the year, the pastoralists rotate their animals for grazing between the common pasture land (which is green during a normal monsoon) and private fallows (after both the monsoon and winter harvests), collect field waste and grow fodder as necessary (mainly in the winter).

The Vankar weavers rotate between weaving and wage labour according to the seasonal markets for their woven goods or their wage labour. The peak periods when they engage in wage labour are paddy plantation and harvesting. In the past, significant numbers of Vankars also migrated for cotton-podding from February to March. Other rhythms in the year include the season when the Barot genealogists undertake their annual round of client villages (usually winter), the times of peak demand for pottery goods (often before festivals), the seasons when labourers migrate in search of employment (predominantly winter but also summer and monsoon), and the periods when women are busiest collecting fuel and fodder (winter and summer).

The worst season in the year differs, then, by occupation. It becomes important, therefore, to track the timing of the worst season for each occupational group (Huss-Ashmore 1988). For subsistence farmers, the greatest resource stress appears to come in the period just before the monsoon harvest. The Bharwad shepherds experience greatest stress at the end of the dry summer season, when forage for herds is inadequate and water sources are depleted. Pure labourers, those who do not engage in activities other than wage labour, face chronic stress mitigated only by the three periods of peak local labour demand: monsoon planting, monsoon harvesting and winter harvesting. During the rest of the year, local demand for labour remains low.

Seasonality is further complicated by the fact that few households engage in only one occupation. Most households have to synchronise the seasonal opportunities or constraints of several occupations. Roughly one-third of the households in Maatisar attempt to synchronise cultivation with wage labour. For example, households which have access only to non-irrigated land (either as owners or tenants) often migrate for wage employment during winter, when cultivation requires irrigation. One-sixth of the households attempt to synchronise migrant wage labour with local wage labour, migrating during periods of low local demand for labour.

For most occupational mixes, the seasonal rhythms of different occupations do not overlap and, therefore, complement each other. The Vankar weavers are able to supplement wool weaving with wage labour without apparent conflict. A significant number of households combine rain-fed agriculture in the monsoon season with labour migration in the winter season. In some cases, however, the seasonal rhythms of different occupations do overlap and conflict. During the monsoon season, some households have to choose between local rain-fed agriculture, local wage employment or migrant labour opportunities.

These, briefly, are the seasonal rhythms in a *normal* year. But normal years are frequently interrupted by *unseasonal* years in which the onset, amount or distribution of rainfall differs from normal years. Less frequently, normal years are interrupted by *drought* years in which the rainfall falls far short of normal years.[1] Beginning with a

---

[1] Under this typology, normal years are seen as regular or average years in which rainfall follows predictable rhythms across and within seasons. Unseasonal years involve some variation in annual rainfall leading to distortions of the regular seasonal rhythms which, in turn, strain the capacity of indiviudal households and traditional social

shortfall of monsoon rains, unseasonal or drought years can throw regular seasonal rhythms out of gear (Longhurst 1986). With the uncertainties inherent in any given year, it is natural that different groups of households in Maatisar have evolved various strategies to cope with risk and uncertainty.

During normal years, households adopt strategies to help smooth known peaks and troughs across seasons; each season presents predictable peaks and troughs for each occupation and households adjust accordingly. During unseasonal years, given delayed or low rainfall, households adopt strategies to cope with unknown rhythms within seasons (mainly the monsoon season). Thus seasonal adjustments in unseasonal years generally involve mid-season adjustments in normal agriculture and related activities.

There is a small, but growing, literature on how households in India cope with seasonality and drought.[2] In Parts II and III, I present our findings from Maatisar within a framework which draws from, but also expands upon, these earlier studies. In Part III, I will discuss the coping strategies adopted in response to the 1987 drought conditions. In this Part, I focus on strategies developed to cope with seasonal fluctuations and on the institutions which govern access to village resources and, thereby, household strategies.

The coping strategies reported from various parts of semi-arid rural India do not differ significantly: these include growing a mix of crops and/or rearing a variety of livestock, entering the labour and tenancy markets as needed, drawing down stored goods or fixed assets, adjusting consumption, borrowing, and drawing upon traditional social security arrangements.[3] What differs from region to region and over time is the pattern of who adopts which strategies, in what sequence and under what circumstances.

What I describe and analyse here are the patterns by which different households in Maatisar, grouped by occupation, adopt various seasonal strategies and why. As part of the analysis, two important

---

security to adjust. Of course, normal years are also occasionally interrupted by good years, during which seasonal troughs are more easily smoothed and new seasonal peaks can be reached.

[2] Refer to Agarwal 1989; Behrman 1988a, b; Behrman and Deolalikar 1987, 1989, 1990; Caldwell et al. 1986a; Chambers 1986; Dasgupta 1987; Dreze 1988; Gupta 1988a; Jodha 1975, 1978, 1981a; Sen 1981.

[3] Similar strategies are reported from semi-arid Africa (Corbett 1988; Longhurst 1986; Jiggins 1986; Caldwell 1975, n.d.).

distinctions are drawn: between normal and unseasonal year strategies and between the seasonal strategies of different household groups. Different household groups experience seasonal phenomena in different ways and, therefore, make different seasonal adjustments. For example, households which depend on wage labour as well as agriculture may be less able than households engaged exclusively in agriculture to make mid-season adjustments in response to delayed or inadequate rains.

In analysing seasonality, several other critical dimensions of household livelihood systems will be discussed: the significance of *gender* as a basic variable in understanding household behaviour; the importance of recognising not only the *multiple* activities but also the multiple sectors, markets and institutions in which households are engaged; and the centrality of *non-market* activities, relationships and institutions to household livelihood systems.

In terms of the significance of gender, the data suggest that women's roles are central to livelihood generation in at least four ways. First, women work in most operations of all sectors of the local economy and for longer hours each day than men. Second, some of the component activities of livelihood systems are women's special responsibility, notably, the domestic and reproductive activities associated with household maintenance and the gathering, collecting and storage of free goods (especially fuel, fodder, and water). Third, women's roles and responsibilities cut across self-provisioning, income-conserving and market activities to a greater extent than men's. And, fourth, women operate effectively in most economic and social institutions, playing a significant role in networking caste and kinship relationships to help manage seasonal shortfalls and participating fully in both the local and migrant labour markets.

Normal seasonal adjustment involves a mix of primary, secondary and subsistence activities and a range of cross-seasonal strategies. In addition to their primary and secondary occupations, most households resort to one or more strategies to adjust to normal seasonal fluctuations. Although different household groups face different seasonal constraints and opportunities, certain common strategies predominate. These strategies are presented below in a rough order of preference.

1. Adapting or diversifying activities

Most households in Maatisar attempt to build flexibility into their basic livelihood system in order to be able to make mid-season or cross-season adjustments as needed: flexibility in their production plans and schedules, in their uses of different resources, in their deployment or recruitment of labour, and in their mix of different occupations and activities. Cultivators, for instance, mix crop and animal husbandry to varying degrees; mix and rotate crops with varying maturity and yields; mix family and hired labour in different ratios depending on the crop and the season; and combine cultivation with other activities as needed. Weavers produce intensively during the peak season for their woven products and seek wage labour in the slack season. Labour households seek local employment whenever it becomes available, combine cultivation or other activities in slack seasons, and migrate if necessary. Depending on the relative flexibility of their livelihood systems, individual households adjust more or less successfully to unseasonal rhythms.[4]

Engaging in multiple activities is an important way of promoting flexibility and countering risk and uncertainty. Normal and unseasonal fluctuations are most easily weathered by those who have access to one or more secondary activities; effective management of multiple activities can help smooth out seasonal troughs or even promote new peaks. Diversification is, therefore, a key dimension of livelihood systems. Almost all households in Maatisar are engaged in multiple activities.

When asked to declare their primary and secondary occupations during the preliminary census in the current study, only one-third of households declared one occupation; the remaining two-thirds declared two or more. Among those who declared a single occupation, many were later found to have overlooked secondary occupations in other seasons. Furthermore, almost all households overlooked various routine activities which do not generate income directly but help generate subsistence.

In discussing the multiple activities of households, then, I draw a distinction between primary, secondary and subsistence occupations or activities. As defined and used here, the *primary occupation* of any given household is that activity which occupies the major portion of the total time and attention of all working household members;

---

[4] Given that our study year followed two drought years and itself turned out to be a severe drought year, detailed quantitative data on normal year responses to seasonality could not be gathered. Instead, qualitative methods (notably, life-histories and informant interviews) were used to probe how the responses to drought differed from responses to seasonality in a normal year.

secondary occupations are the other activities that a household engages in either all the year round or seasonally; and *subsistence activities* are the routine subsistence-oriented activities (primarily the searching–gathering–collecting activities of women) that most households engage in daily.[5]

In terms of secondary occupations in Maatisar, the majority of peasant households engage in wage labour for some part of the year. More than 50 per cent of the shepherd households engage in agriculture. Almost all Vankar weavers engage in wage labour for specific agricultural operations, notably paddy plantation and harvesting. And nearly half of the Vaghris, who are otherwise engaged in wage labour, also engage in cultivation for one or two seasons of the year. Many households from all caste groups rear milch animals and a smaller number of households, mainly cultivators, rear draught animals. Some households are also engaged, seasonally, in the manufacture of rope from a local wild grass or, more regularly, in cotton spinning (introduced by SEWA).

In addition, virtually all households supplement their primary and secondary occupations with a significant daily volume of routine, primarily subsistence-oriented, activities, notably the gathering and collection of fuel, fodder and water, generally carried out by women.[6] Our close contact with a sub-sample of households in Maatisar indicates that households which are primarily engaged in agriculture or labour may be engaged in as many as five other activities across a given year. The range and number of secondary activities by primary occupation are shown in Table 13.

Individual household members, as well as household units, engage in multiple activities either sequentially or simultaneously. Time use data collected in six rounds over three seasons of our study year indicate that, on average, women work for longer hours (3.5 more hours) in a wider range of activities than men each day. The female-to–male ratio of participation in various spheres and sectors of activities is shown in Table 14.

---

[5] The concept of household livelihoods encompasses activities geared both to generating income and to conserving income. In this study, therefore, time spent in given activities, rather than income earned, is taken as a measure of which activities are primary or secondary.

[6] The few households, Brahmin and Thakkar, whose women do not themselves engage in these subsistence-oriented activities hire female labour to do so for them—most commonly, for fetching drinking water.

Table 13

Secondary Occupation by Primary Occupation

Secondary occupations	Cultivation	Livestock	Labour	Weaving	Trade	Others
Cultivation	(9)	1	4			2
Livestock/dairy	4	(3)	1		1	2
Labour	4	1	(8)	1		1
Weaving				(2)		1
Trade: Shopkeeping	1		2		(2)	
Vending	2	2	1			
Moneylending	1				1	1
Thresher on hire	1					
Share-cropping: In	1		2			
Out	3			1	1	4
Vaan-making	7	1				
Relief work	1		5		1	1
Bua-ship	2		5	1		
Migration	1					1
Ambar-spinning						
Grazing/herding						
Transport			2	1	2	(2)
Salaried work: Govt.						2
SEWA						
Driving			1		1	
Flour mill						

Driftter					(1)
Water fetching					1
Priest					(1)
Tailoring					1
Genealogist					(1)
Barber					(1)
Carpentry				1		1
Midwifery					1
Pottery					(1)
Total:	27	24	7	5	7	19
Average number of activities:	3	3	2.33	2.50	3.50	2.66

Source: Life-histories of 31 sub-sample households.

Note: Figures in parentheses indicate number of households in each primary occupation; these figures are not included in the totals or averages for secondary occupations.

Table 14
Female–Male Ratios of Time Use

1. Household maintenance	
Domestic activities	95:05
Reproductive activities	85:15
2. Family enterprise	
Animal husbandry	55:45
Agriculture	25:75
Gathering and collection	90:10
Manufacturing	35:65
Food processing	70:30
Construction	70:30
3. Local market[1]	
Wage work[2]	65:35
Salaried work	40:60
Trade	30:70
Caste services	15:85
4. Social maintenance and leisure	40:60
5. Education[3]	0:100

[1] Time use data for wider market participation was not available, as those participating in wider markets were not present in the village when time use data was collected.

[2] During the summer season, when very little cultivation was possible and relief work was available, the female–male ratio for wage work participation was 45:55. However, during the winter season (when wheat and barley were being cultivated) and when no relief work was available, the female–male ratio of wage work participation was 90:10. Presumably, in peasant and tenant households, men remained busy with family farm production and mostly women were deployed for whatever wage work was available. During the monsoon season, when attempts were made to grow the regular monsoon crops and relief work was available, the female–male ratio in wage work participation was 85:15.

[3] Among the 31 sub-sample households, no girls attended school during the study year.

2. Building Up or Drawing Down Inventories

To ensure year-round availability of various goods in normal years, most households attempt to build up inventories during peak seasons which they can draw upon during slack seasons. Many of these items are free goods collected from common or private land: dry grass for fodder; shrub grass for making rope; branches, brush and kindling for fuel; reeds for cleaning teeth; mud and clay for plastering houses; and cow-dung for fertiliser or fuel. Some of the items in these inventories are home-produced goods, notably foodgrains. A few are purchased goods, bought when prices are low and then stored. Most of these goods are stored for subsistence purposes, and a few for sale (rope, reeds for cleaning teeth, medicinal herbs).

However, not all households are able to generate or store surpluses. Obviously, non-cultivating households are less able than cultivating households to build up inventories of foodgrains. Less obviously, some farm households have to sell whatever they produce at harvest. Many households just build up inventories of free goods, notably fuel and fodder.

Running down or drawing upon stored inventories is a recognised seasonal strategy. In fact, these inventories are often built up specifically to fill in for seasonal troughs: for example, firewood and cow-dung cakes are routinely stored during dry winter months for use during the monsoon rains, when these goods are more difficult to collect and store. Because they are routinely drawn upon, these inventories generally do not last long under crisis conditions, such as drought.

It should be noted that most of the searching for, collecting of, and storage of free goods is carried out by women. Further, that women build most of the storage containers, notably the large clay pots in which grain is stored. One free good, shrub grass, which is used and sold in processed form as rope, is processed largely by men. Another free good, cow-dung, is used and sold in processed form as either dung-cakes or manure, and is processed largely by women.

3. Seeking Employment

Entering the labour market is a common way of dealing with the risks and uncertainty associated with seasonality. However, the demand for hired labour in and around Maatisar is limited. Our rough estimates indicate that, in years of good rainfall, a male labourer could be hired as local farm labour for a maximum of 220 days in the year and a female labourer for a maximum of 180 days. However, most labourers average fewer days of local agricultural wage labour: 175 days for male and 135 days for female labourers. Further, demand for attached labour (long-term farm servants) is low for men and virtually non-existent for women. Moreover, demand for non-farm labour is extremely low. A few labourers are hired locally for the following activities: women for fetching water, cleaning utensils, washing clothes and stitching mattresses; young boys to graze animals and run errands; and men for constructing houses and to graze and care for animals.

Just under 70 households in the village declared wage labour as their primary occupation; another 60 reported wage labour as their secondary occupation. It is difficult to estimate how many households would participate more regularly in the local labour market if the demand for labour were higher. Our findings clearly indicate that the local demand for labour does not meet the potential supply either in terms of total numbers hired, especially during slack agricultural seasons, or in terms of number of days hired.

4. Share-cropping

Entering the tenancy market as needed is one means through which households, both landed and landless, try to overcome seasonal constraints relating to their specific asset-base. Although the market for buying and selling cultivable land is rather inactive in the village, the tenancy market is quite active and consists almost exclusively of share tenancy. Interestingly, fixed-rent tenancy is practically nonexistent in the village.[7] During the winter season, in normal years, an estimated 15 to 20 per cent of households enter share-cropping contracts involving 10 to 15 per cent of the total cultivable land.[8]

A few of the general norms and practices in share tenancy in Maatisar relate to the seasonal coping strategies of households. First, the tenancy contract is predominantly a short-term one, generally for a specific crop in a specific season.[9] Second, the majority of share-crop contracts are negotiated for the winter season, when irrigation is required. Monsoon crops are grown entirely under rain-fed conditions and summer crops are relatively few in number and volume. Third, a household will decide to share-crop out land when it does not own or control one or more of the following factors of production (given in a rough sequence of importance): labour, capital, bullocks, pump sets or farm equipment.

[7] Only one case of land rental within the village, that of a Thakkar to a Koli Patel, was reported: the Thakkar leased out 10 to 12 *bighas* of normal land at Rs 3,000 per annum for three to four years. Reporting on data from a village in an adjacent *taluka*, Viramgam, Shinoda (n.d.) notes only one case of fixed-rent tenancy.

[8] During the 1986–87 winter season, affected by the droughts of 1985 and 1986, some 40 households (14 per cent of total households) share-cropped in land and another 40 share-cropped out land. Just over 10 per cent of the total cultivable land was share-cropped. According to village reports, the level of tenancy was lower during the drought than in normal years.

[9] Some short-term contracts are repeated between the same parties. In such cases, the implicit contracts may be for much longer terms than the explicit contract indicates.

In normal years, share tenancy corrects in part for the unequal distribution of land. Even during the winter of 1986–87, when the level of share tenancy was lower than in normal years, landless households operated nearly four per cent of the land cultivated (an average of just over half an acre per household).[10] The surplus households operated, on the average, almost six acres less than they owned. The small, medium and large farmers all operated, on the average, slightly less than they owned (refer to Table 7 in Part I for a summary of land ownership and operation by landholding strata). Of the total land taken on share tenancy, the landless households share-cropped in over 36 per cent, followed closely by the large farm households who share-cropped in over 34 per cent. However, the large households share-cropped out more than they share-cropped in. Among all landholding groups, then, it was only the landless households which generated a net increase in landholding from share-cropping.

Share tenancy allows households to make better use of their specific asset-base across the different agricultural seasons. For example, households which own land but have no pumps may choose to cultivate their land in the monsoon season, share-crop out their land in winter and migrate to return in time for preparing their land for the next monsoon season. Similarly, landless households can opt to share-crop in land in winter or summer if they own a pump set, or in monsoon if they own bullocks.

Although in general share tenancy appears to be a flexible and even progressive institution in Maatisar, female-headed households face specific disadvantages in the tenancy market, particularly those headed by young widows without grown-up sons. In Maatisar, young widows can and do claim use rights to their husband's share of land. However, when it comes to those productive assets which cannot be divided and which are often held jointly by the husband's family (such as pump sets, bullock-carts and bullocks), a widow has no legal claim. Her access to or use of these assets is at the discretion of her in-laws. As a result, if a young widow wants to share-crop out her share of land she cannot necessarily claim rights to her in-laws' pumps or bullocks when she negotiates the share-cropping contract.

Many studies on women in agriculture in India emphasise the fact that land is seldom registered in women's names and that, therefore,

[10] During the winter of 1986–87, 13 out of 118 landless households (11 per cent) operated land averaging 6.57 acres each. Interestingly, nine out of the 13 households were Vaghri, two Bharwad, only one Koli Patel, and one other.

women have limited access to formal sources of credit. Our findings suggest that the lack of land as collateral is not the main constraint for widows engaged in agriculture. Most widows inherit a share of land and most villagers negotiate loans for working capital from the informal credit market, in which women are quite active. The main problem widows face is that they often cannot gain access to or control over the indivisible means of production owned jointly with their husband's family. Consequently, they are at a disadvantage when negotiating a share-crop contract or they may be forced to mortgage their land.

5. Drawing Upon Common Property Resources

Common property resources (CPRs) in Maatisar are an important form of natural resource endowment and of collective subsistence, especially for the poor. Access to and use of CPRs display a marked seasonal pattern. With the onset of the monsoon rains in normal years, grasses on the common grazing land turn green, the village tanks fill with water, and the River Rodh begins to flow. Depending on the volume and timing of the rains, and on the intensity with which they are used, these resources wither or dry up by early or mid-winter (December to February).

Certain private property resources (PPRs) also become available for public use under certain conditions at certain times. In normal years, grass on field boundaries and stubble in fallow fields (both current and long fallows) are open to the public for free collection of fuel and fodder and for grazing. In normal years, there is also free and open access to cow-dung dropped in public spaces and in the fields (cow-dung dropped within the homestead area remains the private property of that home-owner).[11] In post-harvest periods, freshly-harvested fields are also open to the public for grazing: the only condition is that if the owner of the field has a large herd of animals, his/her herd has first rights to grazing. Further, at harvest, the poor are entitled to a bundle of crop residues from each farm household.

The benefits from CPRs are numerous and can be grouped into several categories, including physical products, supplemental income and employment, and certain community gains (e.g., drainage/recharge

[11] For a discussion of access to PPRs and CPRs under drought conditions, refer to Part III.

of ground-water, renewable resource supply, stability of farming systems).[12] In Maatisar, some 35 physical products were reported to be collected or harvested from CPRs. The largest number of products contribute to subsistence fuel and fodder supplies. Another set of products contributes to subsistence-oriented or locally-marketed artisan production. A final set is collected or harvested for strictly commercial reasons. Table 15 lists these products by source and by the purpose for which they are collected.

It is interesting to note that of the commercial products, two are no longer collected extensively. The time needed to collect *gokharu* seeds for oil is seemingly not worth the price received and the market for them is at some distance.[13] Until five years ago, *neem* berries, an ingredient for soap, were purchased by local Maatisar shops for sale elsewhere and by a local Muslim barber who used to manufacture soap. But the practice of collecting, marketing and processing *neem* berries appears to have died out.

Local trees and shrubs provide the largest number of physical products. They also represent assets which can be 'encashed' if the need arises. For instance, the *gram panchayat* is authorised to auction its trees if it needs to raise revenue. Similarly, privately-owned trees can be either share-cropped, mortgaged or sold when the owner needs cash.[14] Table 16 lists the uses of and benefits from trees and shrubs.

The benefits from CPRs flow largely to daily subsistence requirements for fodder and fuel and are tapped mainly by the poor who collect over 70 per cent of their fuel and 55 per cent of their fodder requirements from free sources (CPRs or open-access PPRs). Other households collect just over 50 per cent of their fuel and 25 per cent of their fodder requirements from free sources[15] (refer to Tables 17 and 18 for the source and average consumption per household of fuel and fodder). In practice, then, CPRs not only serve as a buffer against seasonal shortages, but also contribute to rural equity (Dasgupta 1987; Jodha 1983, 1985a).

[12] For a full list and discussion of CPR benefits in different parts of India, refer to Jodha 1986a.

[13] It was reported that 10 days' work yields 20 kgs of seeds which sell for Rs 70–125. The market for the *gokharu* seeds is in Kheda District.

[14] I will discuss the sale of trees during the recent drought in Part III.

[15] The 'poor' are defined here as landless labour, landless tenants and small land-holding households. 'Others' include medium, large and surplus landholding households and landless households not engaged in labour or tenancy.

Table 15
CPR Products: By Source and Purpose

Products	Source	Use
1. Fuel		
twigs and branches	6 varieties of trees*	subsistence & local barter/exchange
dung	public spaces, fields	barter/exchange
2. Fodder		
leaves	6 varieties of trees*	subsistence & local barter/exchange
pods	2 varieties of trees*	barter/exchange
berries	2 varieties of trees	barter/exchange
grasses	pastures, verges, fields	barter/exchange
stubble/residues	fields	barter/exchange
weeds	verges, fields	barter/exchange
dung	public spaces, fields	barter/exchange
3. Wood & Timber		
timber	4 varieties of trees*	commercial
wood—agric. equipment	2 varieties of trees*	
4. Fruits & Flowers		
flowers	1 variety of tree*	local liquor-brewing
fruit	2 varieties of trees*	commercial
5. Raw Materials		
clay for pottery	fields, pastures	local sale
reed for cleaning teeth	*dattan* plant	local vending
reed, fibre for rope-making, housing	*batha* shrub	artisan production: subsistence and local sale
straw for broom-making	*jinjua* plant	artisan production: local sale
6. Herbs and Oil		
medicinal oil	*gokaru* seeds	commercial
medicinal oil	*pilloo* seeds	commercial
herb	*peepal* leaves	commercial
oil for soap-making	*neem* berries	commercial
7. Manure		
cow-dung	public spaces, fields	subsistence; local barter/sale
8. Others		
fish	River Rodh	commercial

* Refer to Table 16 for list of local trees and shrubs.

Table 16
Trees and Shrubs by Use and Product

Species	Fuel	Fodder	Food	Others
Neem	twigs, branches	green leaves	berries	berries; hair oil; medicinal oil; oil for soap; timber
Mango	twigs, branches	dry & green leaves	fruit seeds	timber
Sami	twigs, branches	pods—goats	pods	
Piloo	twigs, branches	dry & green leaves—goats	berries	seeds: oil for soap
Desi Babul	twigs, branches	pods—goats & cattle		timber; *dattan*
Gundi	twigs, branches	berries, leaves	fruit	wood—agric. equipment
Peepal	twigs, branches	leaves—goats	fruit—cooked	ritual use; medicinal
Rayan	twigs, branches	berries, dry & green beans		wood—agric. equipment
Ber			fruit	
Bili/Bel				ritual use
Banyan			fruit	
Tamarind				flowers; liquor brewing
Mahowra				rope-making; housing material; binding for tobacco bundles; roofing; winnowers; comb for looms
Bhatha		green shoots		
Jingeri/Jinjua	kindling	green & dry leaves		straw-brooms
Gokaru		grass		seeds: Ayurvedic medicine
Grasses (18 varieties)				

Total: 13 varieties of trees
4 varieties of bushes and shrubs
18 varieties of grass

Table 17
Fuel Consumption and Source

Average daily consumption (kgs per household)	Poor*	Others**	Total
Winter	7.9	9.4	8.6
Summer	8.3	2.9	10.8
Monsoon	7.3	10.2	8.8
Total	7.8	11.1	9.5
Proportion (%) of fuel from different sources	Poor	Others	Total
Freely collected	71.4	51.7	59.5
Received as wages	0.0	0.1	0.1
Purchased	21.3	24.9	23.5
Home-produced	2.2	13.9	9.3
Not specified	5.1	9.4	7.7

Table 18
Fodder Consumption and Source

Average daily fodder consumption (kgs per household)	Poor*	Others**	Total
Winter	17.7	43.3	33.7
Summer	5.7	12.6	10.2
Monsoon	8.2	22.0	16.2
Total	9.6	23.5	18.2
Proportion (%) fodder from different sources	Poor	Others	Total
Freely collected	57.3	25.9	32.6
Received as wages	4.3	0.4	1.2
Purchased	33.7	23.1	25.4
Home-produced	3.8	48.6	39.2
Not specified	0.9	1.9	1.7

* Poor = landless labour, landless tenants, and small landholding households.
** Others = medium, large and surplus landholding households plus landless households not engaged in labour or tenancy.

However, as I have discussed in Part I, several forces have intervened to limit the capacity of CPRs to cushion seasonal fluctuations. First, some CPRs have been privatised. Second, they have been overused and, thereby, degraded because of increasing human and cattle populations and the lack of proper management or regulation. Third, the shepherds have exercised a priority claim on the common grazing lands, sometimes to the exclusion of others. Before the shepherds acquired land and began to grow fodder, they reared their livestock almost exclusively on the common pastures, thereby generating a surplus. Interestingly, whilst CPRs have provided an important source of subsistence for the poor, they have also served the commercial interests of the shepherds.

6. Drawing Upon Social Relationships

Several forms of traditional social security or informal insurance in rural India have been widely commented on, notably the patron–client relationships, intercaste *jajmani* relationships, caste and kinship support mechanisms, and public access to common property resources.[16] Much of the recent literature indicates a gradual erosion of these systems and relationships over time. This is attributable to several trends, including increasing demographic pressures on land, common property resources and traditional occupations; and the increasing commercialisation of labour and product markets.[17] Some of the recent literature also points to differences in the operation of these systems between peak and slack seasons and between normal and bad years.

Our data from Maatisar indicate that some of these systems operate differently between peak and slack seasons in normal years but all operate differently between normal, unseasonal and bad years. As yet, neither patron–client nor *jajmani* relationships have shown signs of fluctuation across seasons in a good year. However, long-term changes have eroded the capacity of these systems to minimise the effects of

[16] To name a few, Wiser (1936), Epstein (1967), Breman (1985a), and Dasgupta (1987) on patron–client and *jajmani* relations; Dasgupta (1987) and Caldwell et al. (1986) on kinship support mechanisms; and Jodha (1985a, 1986a) on common property resources. There is also a body of literature that discusses patron–client, kinship and other social relations in terms of a moral economy: for a review of some of these studies see Appadurai 1984.

[17] For example, the competition between labourers for limited wage employment in the casual labour market and the sale of goods which were earlier distributed free to labourers or clients.

drought or other crises and now threaten their capacity to cushion seasonal fluctuations. I will discuss the impact of long-term change on these systems below and I will discuss the operation of these systems during drought in Part III.

In analysing the seasonality of social support mechanisms, a distinction needs to be drawn, first, between family, kin and caste-based relationships and, second, between loans or reciprocal transactions and outright gifts or charity. In peak seasons in normal years, caste neighbours frequently loan each other small amounts in cash or kind and make outright gifts in cash or kind to particularly needy households. In slack seasons or in unseasonal years, the circle to which these reciprocal or charitable transactions are extended often narrows from caste neighbours to kinship networks.

The capacity of not only caste neighbours but also kin to extend these support services has been increasingly strained over time. Droughts, and more so famines, often bring these support systems to a breaking point, leaving individual families or even individuals to cope on their own. However, largely because of the effective presence of relief works, the 1985–87 drought did not precipitate the breakdown of family units in Maatisar.

7. Reducing or Modifying Consumption

Reducing or modifying current consumption, particularly food intake but also expenditure on social or religious commitments, are common strategies to deal with uncertainty and shortages. However, the reduction or modification of consumption varies between normal years and drought years. During the former, food intake has seasonal patterns both in terms of types of food eaten and total amounts eaten. The periods before harvests are typically times of lower intake than the periods immediately after. Households will further reduce normal seasonal levels only after other routine seasonal adjustments have been made. During the drought, as I will discuss in Part III, given that food stocks were low and options for other responses were greatly reduced, modifying and reducing food intake was a common and early strategy.

Given that most social and religious commitments have known seasonal rhythms, in that there are special seasons for marriages and auspicious dates for festivals, expenditures on these events remain reasonably constant in both normal and unseasonal years. However, as I will discuss in Part III, such expenditures were reduced or postponed during the drought.

8. Borrowing or Lending

Several types of informal credit and several sources of formal credit operate in Maatisar. I describe these in greater detail in the section on Credit Markets below. Briefly, there is a broad correspondence between the purposes for which loans are taken and the types of loans taken. The following types of loans are generally used for consumption and contingency: short-term, interest-free loans; barter or exchanges between kinship and caste groups; credit advances to casual labour; and credit sales at the local shops. Social costs, notably marriage costs, are most frequently met by mortgaging land and also by credit advances to attached labour. The capital for major investments (e.g., pump sets or bullocks) is raised either by mortgaging land, pawning ornaments, negotiating government bank credit, or through credit purchases in the market towns.

Working capital needs, notably for agricultural inputs, appear to be financed largely by informal sources of credit: by tenancy cost-sharing or local interest-bearing loans. Medium-term loans for working capital are often negotiated at Ekatrij to be repaid, with the interest paid in kind, at Diwali or vice versa.[18] Loans in kind for seed are also taken. The interest rate, also paid in kind, varies by crop. For instance, barley seeds must be repaid in double as the yield per kilo of seeds is high; wheat seeds are repaid in one-and-a-half times the amount borrowed as the yield per kilo of seeds is not as high.

Shortages of cash or stock (e.g., food, seed, fodder) are a common seasonal phenomenon. The seasonal search for cash or kind loans is, therefore, a dominant seasonal strategy, especially for poor households. Women are active negotiators of consumption and contingency loans, both credit purchases from shopkeepers (women and children are the most frequent shoppers at the local stores) or small, interest-free loans from kin and neighbours (the majority of small loans,

---

[18] To illustrate (although the typical size of loan would be greater), a loan of Rs 100 taken at Ekatrij would be repaid with Rs 100 and two to three *maunds* of paddy as interest at Diwali. And a loan of Rs 100 taken at Diwali would be repaid with Rs 100 cash and two to three *maunds* of wheat as interest at Ekatrij.

barters or exchanges in kind are negotiated woman–to–woman). Also, women frequently negotiate loans or gifts from their own parents or kin in their natal village, either at the request of their husband and his family or on their own. Several instances were reported of mothers and daughters making 'secret' loans or gifts to each other (e.g., bundles of fodder, foodgrains, a calf) without the knowledge of men in either the giving or receiving household.

Women are often actively involved in negotiating loans against pawned items, as the items pawned are typically assets owned and controlled by women: household utensils and jewellery. As Agarwal (1989: 54) points out, in 'addition to the importance of holding onto productive assets such as land and cattle, jewellery is a much more liquid asset than land, and unlike cattle less prone to price plummeting'. However, as Agarwal goes on to argue, the sale (or pawning) of such items has a special significance 'when we note that usually these are the only assets possessed by women'. Once these items are pawned, if they are not readily redeemed, women 'would be left with nothing to fall back on if abandoned or in case of a drought . . .' (*ibid.*).

Women are less actively involved in credit advances. They are not hired as attached labour for which half the contracted wage is typically paid in advance. In addition, in nuclear or extended families women are not usually involved in negotiating crop advances. And as female heads of households they have less access than men to production loans and even less so to crop advances. However, women are able to negotiate very small credit advances, to be deducted from their wages, if they work in other households. For instance, two young widows who fetch water for high-caste households reported that they were able to negotiate small credit advances (Rs 50–100) against their labour services.

Whereas there is limited segmentation of the informal credit market by gender, it is very marked in the formal credit market. In negotiating loans from formal credit institutions, the issue of landownership as collateral becomes critical. The only reported cases of institutional loans to women were those brokered by SEWA (for milch animals) and by the Vankar leader (for looms). In both cases, the women beneficiaries were members of the two cooperatives in the village (the dairy and the weaver's). SEWA is responsible not only for the actual presence of these two cooperatives in Maatisar but also for the fact that both are all-women cooperatives.

In addition to borrowing, women engage in several types of lending.

Two or three wives of known moneylenders themselves extend not only small-scale loans but also medium-size loans against pawned items. The wives of shopkeepers often take turns at running the shops and are engaged, therefore, in credit sales. And, as has been mentioned earlier, women are often involved in several forms of small-scale lending, exchanges or charity, usually in kind. These include mother–to–daughter or woman–to–woman loans and occur primarily within kinship groups, but also within caste groups. These women–to–women loans are frequently negotiated as stop-gap measures to overcome seasonal cash flow problems. Significantly, as Gupta et al. (1987) observed in Maharashtra and we observed in Maatisar, often these women–to–women transactions are known only to the women involved.

9. Building Up or Drawing Down Assets

Even in normal years, non-productive assets are often pawned as security for loans. In Maatisar, as elsewhere in India, the most common items to be pawned are jewellery and household utensils. However, even in drought years, people resist the mortgage or sale of productive assets. If forced to draw upon productive assets, households prefer to mortgage rather than sell them. Over the past 15 to 20 years, the number of reported land sales has been far lower than the number of reported mortgage transactions: 19 sales totalling 150 acres compared to 62 mortgage transactions totalling 235 acres.

Again, as a means of raising capital to meet marriage, subsistence or other expenses, mortgaging is greatly preferred over the outright sale of land.[19] Households are forced to mortgage land most frequently to meet marriage expenses; significantly, no households reported selling land for this purpose.[20] After marriage expenses, the next most common reason cited for mortgaging land is to meet subsistence needs

[19] Maatisar residents were reluctant to provide information on land transactions. We gathered much of our data on land transactions from third party sources, which we then cross-checked. Because the informants were often third parties, we were not always able to determine the actual reasons for the transactions in roughly half of the mortgaging cases and just under two-thirds of the land sale cases.

[20] Under the social norms of most castes in the region, each family is expected not only to cover the marriage costs of its own children but also to contribute to the marriage costs of children in the extended family (brothers, sisters, nephews and nieces).

or, as simply put by one respondent, 'in order to eat'. Again, even in this case, no household reported selling land.

As a category of households, the households headed by widows, especially young widows without grown-up sons, reported the highest rate of mortgaging and sale—either because they could not manage or cultivate their land single-handedly, or their in-laws put pressure on them to forfeit their husband's share back to his family, or they needed cash to maintain their families. Other cases of land sale included two permanent migrants. Other cases of land mortgage included a permanent migrant who mortgaged his land when he migrated, a local politician who mortgaged his land to cover electioneering costs, and a barber who mortgaged the land which he received as part of the 'concession' for his services because he did not take up farming.

10. Migration

As mentioned previously, a significant number of labourers from about 50 households migrate seasonally for rural labour opportunities to other areas. On the supply side, there appear to be two main reasons for this migration. First, the local tenancy and labour markets do not adequately absorb the pool of available labour. Second, many small farmers and tenant–farmers cannot afford the irrigation costs to cultivate crops in the dry winter and summer seasons. On the demand side also, there appear to be two major reasons for this migration. Cash-crop and non-farm employment opportunities in other parts of Gujarat attract migrant labour because both the level of wages paid and the level of employment offered are higher than in Maatisar. Migrant labourers are able to negotiate reasonably steady employment for five to eight months during the long, dry season when the local wage labour market offers, at most, 70 days of employment.[21]

A clear pattern of migration, with marked seasonality and strict segmentation by caste, has developed. Koli Patels, along with a few

[21] Seasonal migration is 'usually especially high from unirrigated semi-arid areas into more prosperous irrigated ones' (Agarwal 1989). Maatisar, a semi-irrigated village in a semi-arid area, offers a slight variation on this general pattern. Labourers migrate from Maatisar during the winter season, which is the one season in which the irrigation facilities of the village are operative. However, winter cultivation in the village is carried out almost exclusively by family labour; labourers are hired only for winter harvest. Labourers from Maatisar migrate, therefore, to irrigated cash-crop areas, where hired labour is required for labour-intensive cultivation and post-harvest processing.

Prajapatis, migrate for five to eight months to Bavla, the nearest
market town, for rice mill work and to the outskirts of Ahmedabad
city for brickfield work.[22] Most Vaghris migrate for five to eight
months to Amreli or Junagadh Districts for groundnut harvesting,
surgar-cane processing and supplemental agricultural wage opportunities, while a few households migrate to crush stones at Porbandar
in Junagadh District. Traditionally, some members of most Vankar
households migrated to the nearby towns for two to three months of
cotton-podding and to Kheda District for one to two months of paddy
plantation and harvesting. In recent years, a variety of cotton which
does not require podding has been introduced, thereby reducing the
demand for cotton-podders.

Not all migrants stay away for either the whole season or for only
one season. The study data indicates the following variations in the
duration of stay:

1. Workers who migrate for a *single agricultural operation* (e.g.,
   paddy harvesting or groundnut harvesting) lasting three to five
   weeks;
2. Workers who migrate for the *entire winter season* (five months)
   or the *combined winter and summer seasons* (eight months);
3. Workers who migrate *each year* for five to eight months on a
   semi-permanent basis;[23]
4. Workers who migrate to become *farm servants for a year.*

In addition to distance, a large number of other factors seem to
influence the duration of stay: whether the migrant group is composed
of single workers or a more complete family unit, whether they are
landless and whether they have seasonal work in Maatisar to which
they can return.

The season for longer-term (five to eight months) migration is the
dry season from Diwali (generally in October) to Holi (generally in
March), after which some households extend their migratory period

[22] One Vaghri household reported working at brickfields for a brief period between
agricultural labour opportunities during the winter of 1986–87.

[23] These migrants are not considered permanent migrants because they return each
year to Maatisar to engage in cultivation, local wage labour or some other activity. As I
discussed in Part I, 37 households have migrated permanently from the village over the
past 15 years.

either until Ekatrij (generally in April) or until the monsoon rains.[24] The main months for paddy plantation and harvesting are July and October respectively. The season for cotton-podding runs from the beginning of the cotton harvest in February until the énd of May. Although in the past Vankars migrated regularly for cotton-podding for two to three months, there has been a decrease in this type of migration.

Several aspects of seasonal labour migration from Maatisar do not fit conventional concepts about migration. First, only half of the migration is to urbanised or industralised areas; the remaining is to other agricultural, mostly cash-crop, areas. Second, the season for migration is relatively long. Third, agricultural migrant labour circulate through several villages and countless employers during the migration season. Fourth, most migrants move and work as family units. A total of 104 members from 42 households migrated in the 1986–87 winter season: of these only 10 individuals migrated singly, with the remaining 32 households averaging nearly three migrants per household. Not all migrants work (notably, young children and the elderly), but the majority do. Table 19 presents the distribution of migrant households in November 1987 by caste and number of household members.

Interestingly, the proportion of women migrants is just over 45 per cent. The proportion of women migrants was highest (50 per cent) among agricultural migrant households. Most commonly, married women migrate with their husbands and small children, especially for the longer migration period. Less frequently, girls and young women join work teams of boys and men of their own caste group, especially for single-operation migration such as paddy harvesting. In this case, as Breman (1985: 209) noted, 'they usually work under the protection of a male member of the group—a brother, brother-in-law or husband . . .' .[25]

[24] Most labourers prefer to return to Maatisar for Holi, to celebrate the festival at home and to seek work during the local winter harvest. Some return to their migrant work sites for an additional six to eight weeks of work. If they extend their migration season, they then return either at Ekatrij (which in 1987 fell on May 2), whe ı most land-lease and land-mortgage contracts are finalised, or in time to prepare the land for the monsoon season. According to informants citing the Hindu calendar, migrant labour return at the following months for the following reasons:

Chaitra—Holi festival + wheat/barley harvest
Jeth, Ashad—summer *juwar* harvesting + ploughing
Shravan, Bhadarvo—paddy plantation

[25] In other parts of Gujarat, work teams composed entirely of women can be found (Breman 1985).

Table 19
Households Which Migrated in November 1987 by Caste and Number of Migrants

Caste	Number of households		Number of persons	
	Total	Migrated	Total	Migrated
Koli Patel	142	16	830	73
Vaghri	51	11	316	42
Vankar	28	2	163	11
Barot	5	1	14	NA
Prajapati	7	1	43	2
Others	11	1	66	NA
Total:	**244**	**32**	**1,432**	**128**

These then are the common strategies in Maatisar for coping with seasonality. In addition, village households occasionally draw upon resources offered by the government and the local non-government agency, SEWA. But the external resources offered by government—including credit, extension and marketing services—are not synchronised to seasonal requirements. For example, government credit services have not been targeted at seasonal requirements for working capital but at longer-term, fixed capital requirements. Further, government employment schemes are generally operationalised only when drought is declared, not as a means of providing employment in slack labour seasons.[26]

SEWA's credit services have also not been targeted at seasonal requirements for working capital but for the purchase of milch cattle. But SEWA does offer two types of seasonal employment to certain households: cotton spinning (20 households) and cotton plus merino wool weaving (10 households).[27]

The strategies for coping with seasonality constitute a largely endogenous sytem, with the notable exception of seasonal migration (50 households) and employment from SEWA (30 households). This styem is regulated and facilitated by various local institutions, both

[26] In areas classified as drought-prone, more regular employment schemes are offered. Dholka *taluka* is not classified as drought-prone.

[27] The cotton and merino wool weavers are all from the Vankar caste, who generally weave the traditional *dhabla* during the seasons when a market is available, and cotton and merino wool items in other seasons. Fifteen of the cotton spinners are Koli Patels. Of the other six, two are Prajapatis, two Vaghris, one Bhangi, and one other. The majority (12) of cotton spinners are from landless households.

social and economic. In the following section, I describe the overall operations and seasonal dynamics of these institutions.

Institutions Which Govern Access to Resources

In coping with seasonality, and in generating livelihoods more generally, most households engage in both market-oriented and subsistence-oriented activities and operate through both economic and social institutions. Through social institutions they often gain access to resources over which through purely economic institutions they would command limited, if any, access—most notably, freely collected natural resources to meet fuel, fodder and other subsistence needs; and kinship or caste-based sources of loans, labour and assets.

In analysing livelihood systems, therefore, it is important to recognise that both economic and social institutions help to determine which households gain access to what resources. Further, that the customary obligations inherent in social institutions can be viewed as a form of common economic strategy: that of providing the goods and services required by one party while guaranteeing the subsistence needs of the other. As such, the distinction between economic and social institutions becomes somewhat blurred, particularly so in the case of patronage relationships which are often cited as a feature of traditional social systems but which were also important features in traditional tenancy, labour and credit markets. Although both types of institutions regulate economic behaviour, it should be noted that economic institutions operate largely on the principles of *competition* and *negotiation*, whereas social institutions operate largely on the principles of *trust* and *reciprocity*. In this section, I examine how both types of institutions operate to regulate access to resources in normal years. In Part III, I examine how drought conditions limit the scope for reciprocity and increase competition for free goods.

Social Institutions

In the literature on traditional social security in rural India, several types of social institutions have been widely commented on: patron–client relationships; *jajmani* relationships; and family, kinship or caste-based support mechanisms. In analysing these institutions in Maatisar, we focused on how they have been affected by long-term changes and how they operate during both seasonal fluctuations and drought-induced crises.

1. Patron–Client Relationships

The patron–client relationships which operate in Maatisar are of two basic types, familiar from other village studies. The first are economic-based patronage relationships: those between employers and labourers, landowners and tenants, land mortgagors and mortgagees, shop-keepers and customers, moneylenders and borrowers. The second type of patronage relationships are political in nature: those between politicians and their supporters or between factional leaders and their followers. Under a more closed local order in the past, patrons were expected to underwrite the subsistence needs of clients plus provide affection, generosity and protection in return for the services, respect and loyalty of their clients. For example, in return for readily available and cheap labour services, employer–patrons insured subsistence and protection to their employee–clients (Bardhan 1984a).

Unlike some parts of India where traditional patronage patterns still hold, economic-based patronage relationships in Maatisar have given way to competitive market forces in labour and tenancy markets. As a result of this process, three new patterns in employer–employee relationships have emerged: casual labourers are rarely 'tied' to patrons by credit or other transactions; few labourers are attached to patrons as regular farm servants; and the few attached labourers are rarely 'tied' to patrons for longer than a year at a time and do not necessarily receive credit from patrons. Whereas the fixed annual payment in kind to attached labour is supposed to guarantee a minimum subsistence, the annual renewal of the contract is not guaranteed and the credit needs of the labourers are not necessarily recognised.

Casual labourers are at a particular disadvantage in that their minimum subsistence is not guaranteed and that they must often resort to mortgaging their land, if any, to meet social obligations. In exchange for their freedom, as few are now 'tied' to patrons, casual labourers have lost the guaranteed subsistence that patronage was supposed to provide. In the past, to raise funds to cover marriage or other costs, labourers often 'bonded' their labour in return for both a fixed sum of money and a guaranteed subsistence. At present, to raise capital, labourers often 'bond' or mortgage their land in return for a fixed sum of money but a more vulnerable livelihood in that they have been alienated, at least temporarily, from an important means of production.

Our data indicate that the terms and conditions of tenancy contracts in Maatisar are not enmeshed in other economic linkages between the two parties: tenants are free to lease in land from more than one landlord, they do not generally render paid or unpaid labour services to the landlord, nor do they generally market their share of output through their landlords. Moreover, in Maatisar there is a fair amount of 'reverse' tenancy (whereby the landowner owns less land than the tenant in the contract) and cost-sharing (whereby the landowner and tenant share some, if not all, input costs). Given these characteristics, the current labour and tenancy markets in Maatisar do not appear to incorporate many of the features, both positive (i.e., guaranteed subsistence) and negative (i.e., exploitation), of the patron–client system as it operates (or operated) elsewhere in India.

2. Jajmani Relationships

Under what in North India is referred to as the *jajmani* system (Wiser 1936) and in Maatisar is referred to as the *vasvayas* system, certain caste groups render specified services to a fixed group of patrons (in some cases the whole village) throughout the year in return for a fixed payment in kind at harvest time and other concessions.[28] Although in the past there may have been a wider range of service castes in Maatisar, at present there are only one barber, five genealogists, two priests and one carpenter.

Over the years, certain of the service and artisan caste groups have opted out or been pushed out of their caste-based occupations: four Barots, three carpenters and three potters have migrated permanently and four potter households have abandoned pottery production. The gradual erosion of the economic basis of the *jajmani* system can be attributed to several forces, including the greater use of cash in transactions, increased opportunities for occupational and spatial

[28] 'The term *jajmani* is not used in Gujarat except in the case of the relation between the Brahman priest or the Bhat or Barot bard on the one hand and his patron (*yajaman*) on the other. That is the classical sense. For all other *jajmani* type relations different words are used in different parts of Gujarat, such as *sat, avat, gharaki, gharakvati, sukhadi,* etc.' (Desai in Shah and Desai 1988: 62).

mobility,[29] and the substitution of various *jajmani* goods and services by commercial goods and services, such as metal pots and utensils in place of clay pots and utensils.[30]

In the past, the relationship between patrons (*jajmans*) and their clients (*kamins*), who provided goods and services, was not purely contractual. Those who provided goods and services were assured not only regular payments but also periodic gifts and concessions (e.g., food and clothing). Given the greater restrictions on occupational and spatial mobility in the past, these benefits helped guarantee individual subsistence and general stability. At present, *jajmans* guarantee payments and offer occasional gifts or concessions only in normal years. In periods of overall shortages, such as the drought, many *jajmans* are forced to withhold payments.

3. Family, Kinship, and Caste Relationships

In most parts of rural India, several forms of traditional support systems exist along family, kinship and caste lines. The relative strength of these support systems depends on the region and on the 'times' (i.e., whether it is a period of seasonal shortages or more acute stress). In Maatisar, each caste group lives in its own residential neighbourhood (comprised of one or two kinship groups).[31] Although support is extended to fellow caste members during peak seasons in normal years, traditional support systems operate largely along kinship lines.[32] In peak seasons in normal years, caste neighbours frequently

[29] As I noted in Part I, of those who migrated permanently, only the three carpenters found employment in their traditional caste-based occupation. Three of the four Barot migrants are engaged in skilled labour (as a welder, mason and gardener respectively) and one in cloth selling. The three potters are engaged in non-skilled labour (in rice mills or brickfields).

[30] According to Dasgupta (1987), writing about a village in Haryana, the 'direct sources of income based on hereditary service relationships have become largely defunct because they have ceased to be valuable for the landowners' (p. 104).

[31] The Koli Patels live in four neighbourhoods or *vas*, each of which is comprised almost exclusively of one kinship group. The Vankar *vas* is divided into two sections, each of which is comprised of one kinship group. The Bhangis and Rawals are comprised of one kinship group each. And the Vagris live in three neighbourhoods, each of which is comprised of one kinship group.

[32] One formalised caste-based support mechanism should be noted. The Vankars operate a contribution system as a means of raising money to cover marriage expenses, by which one household makes a gift of cash to another with the expectation that it will be returned in double at the time of marriage in the donor household.

136 / Coping with Seasonality and Drought

loan each other small amounts in cash or kind, and, if a particular household is needy, make outright gifts in cash or kind. In slack seasons in normal years, the circle to which reciprocal or charity transactions are extended often narrows from caste to kin.

Kinship networks offer various mechanisms for adjusting to uncertainty in both production and consumption. To manage short-term consumption needs, women turn to other women in the same kinship group to borrow small amounts of foodstuffs, fuel, fodder, etc. and richer kin often extend charity to poorer kin. To manage seasonal production requirements, households from the same kinship group often loan, pool or exchange productive 'assets, including labour, pump sets, farm implements and bullocks. Also, if for any reason households are unable to tend animals or manage land, they generally share-crop these assets to kin who, according to kinship norms, will manage them responsibly on their behalf.

Reciprocal relations through gifts or loans or other types of assistance are not restricted to one village. Interestingly, women are active negotiators of cross-village exchanges. Although village exogamy and patrilocality are the norm in marriages, women seldom marry at great distances from their natal villages and make annual, if not more frequent, visits to their natal homes.[33] During those visits, they are known to seek support of their natal kin, especially in times of crisis. During our study year, many households reported receiving support of various kinds from the women's family or kin. Several women reported small, but frequent, gifts of foodstuffs, fodder and fuel from their mothers. Several households reported taking loans from the wife's kin. Significantly, several households reported migrating for large parts of a year to the wife's home for casual labour opportunities, and two or three reported migrating to the wife's home for attached labour opportunities. Further, as I will describe in the section on Migrant Labour Markets, a significant number of migrant labourers seek seasonal employment each year largely through caste- or kinship-negotiated recruitment channels.[34]

[33] Most caste groups in the village belong to a small endogamous units, which comprise households of the same caste living in a designated circle (gol) of villages and/or towns, within which they are supposed to marry (Shah and Desai 1988). The designated circle of villages for all caste groups in Maatisar falls within Dholka or neighbouring talukas, except for the Thakkars whose circle of villages extends outside Ahmedabad District to Kheda District.

[34] In most village studies, caste dynamics are discussed in vertical or hierarchical terms—that is, in terms of intercaste relationships and reciprocities (Shah and Desai 1988). More attention needs to be given to caste as a horizontal entity. For example, our

Several forms of traditional social security exist within the family itself. Elderly parents are expected to live with and be supported by the youngest son. Other than in the Brahmin and Thakkar castes, young widows are allowed to remarry: among the Bharwad shepherd community, they are expected (but not forced) to marry the younger brother or cousin of the husband. Among all caste groups, if young widows choose not to remarry, the husband's kin are expected to help support them until such time as the widow's own sons, if any, can support her. Should the husband's family and kin fail to provide support, young widows may return to their natal village and seek support from their brothers or parents.

However, these family support systems do not always operate according to customary norms. Many widows complain of no longer receiving the support of their husband's kin. Indeed, as I discussed in Part I, young widows are often forced by their in-laws to forfeit their use rights to their husband's share of his family land. Some elderly widows complain of no longer receiving the support of their own sons. As a group, widows without adult males to support them are particularly vulnerable to seasonal fluctuations and drought conditions.

To illustrate, one elderly widow lives with her daughter-in-law, widow of her younger son, and two grandchildren. They live in one room adjacent to her elder son and his family. The elder son has denied his mother her share of the family property and has appropriated most of his sister-in-law's share.[35] In return, the two women are given a small share of grain at harvest and no other support throughout the year. The younger widow pieces together their meagre joint livelihood from a variety of sources, as the mother-in-law is too old to do much more than gather firewood.[36] For a period of time during the 1985–87 drought, the younger widow reluctantly insisted that her mother-in-law manage on her own and cook separate meals as she was simply not able to support her. At a later point, the daughter-in-law was able to invite her mother-in-law to rejoin her and the children for meals. Throughout this time, they continued to share the one room and the one mud stove.

data point to the importance of intervillage caste relationships as a recruitment channel for migrant labourers and as one form of traditional social security.

[35] Shortly after her husband's death, the sister-in-law mortgaged two *bighas* of the land she inherited to a caste neighbour.

[36] The sister-in-law earned about Rs 13 per day (less than US $1) from a variety of activities: fetching water for others (Rs 3), spinning cotton (Rs 4), selling milk (Rs 3), and part-time work at the child care centre (Rs 3).

Many villagers reported that family support systems have eroded over time, but it is unclear to what degree family support systems operated according to custom in the past. Our findings suggest that demographic pressures on land and occupations have strained the capacity of many families to support all members equally. Certainly, we observed that many sons, when they separate from the joint family, cannot claim their inheritance until the father dies and cannot always claim a share from joint production in the interim; that some elderly widows are not supported by their sons; and that many young widows are not supported by their husband's families.

4. Village or Community Rights

As I have aldready said, certain resources are the common property of the village: permanent pasture land, forest groves, nine village tanks, the local river, the village well, the community threshing grounds, village-owned trees and the boundaries along public roads. As citizens of the village, all residents are entitled to open and free access to these resources. Although these CPRs are not well-maintained or regulated by the *gram panchayat* and some of them have been privatised, they remain an important form of collective subsistence, especially for the poor. And although often CPRs literally dry up, leading to conflicts over access to what remains, the principle of common village rights is upheld.

The principle of common or village rights also applies, with the notable exception of one caste group, to four caste wells, located in or near the residential centre of Maatisar (see map of Study Village Lands). These wells are the main sources of drinking and domestic water supply in Maatisar. With the exception of the Scheduled Castes who use their own well, three of the wells are commonly used by all other caste groups.

Also, as I described in Part I, certain private property resources (PPRs) are made available for public use under certain conditions during certain seasons in normal years: grass on field boundaries, stubble in fallow fields and crop wastes in freshly-harvested fields. However, unlike CPRs to which villagers have *rights* as citizens of the village, these PPRs are offered as *concessions* to the public by their owners only under certain conditions and at certain times. Generally, private owners withdraw these concessions whenever there are short-ages, often in unseasonal years and usually in drought years.

Economic Institutions

1. Land Markets

The land market in Maatisar operates largely through tenancy, partially through mortgage transactions and rather infrequently through outright sales or purchases. Over the past 15 to 20 years, the number of reported land sales have been far fewer than the number of reported land mortgage transactions: 19 sales compared to 62 mortgage transactions (an average of about one sale per year). The volume of land exchanged in sales has also been lower than the volume of land exchanged in mortgage transactions: roughly 150 acres compared to nearly 235 acres.[37] It seems clear that most households prefer to mortgage land when in need of capital, with the hopes of redeeming it, rather than to sell it outright. Exceptions include a few permanent out-migrants and the Thakkar traders who are consciously disinvesting in land.[38] However, it is not clear how many households have actually been able to redeem land or to foreclose on mortgages.[39]

There are two systems of mortgage. Under the first, the original owner or mortgagor forfeits to the mortgagee his/her use rights to the land. This system, referred to as *giro*, is the most common, and is the system by which the Bharwads have accumulated so much land. Under the second system, the original owner can retain (under the

[37] It should be noted that data on land transactions were difficult to obtain. These data were collected from multiple informants and cross-checked repeatedly. For some transactions a range of figures, taken from two to three different sources, was reported. In such cases, the average amount reported has been used. In 15 cases of mortgage, figures for the actual amount of land transacted were not available. For these, the average amount per transaction of the other 47 cases was used.

[38] Reporting on data collected in 1975–76 in four states of India (West Bengal, Bihar, Uttar Pradesh and Orissa), Bardhan (1984a: 95) notes: 'Even with full property rights in land, the market for buying and selling cultivable land is often rather inactive. Unless forced by extremely difficult circumstances, a resident villager does not usually sell his land. One possible reason is that land prices do not fully compensate for the very high risks in parting with this secure asset as evaluated by the farmer. In the absence of integrated financial markets, the transaction costs of investing the sales proceeds in alternative ventures is also far too high. Besides, the externalities of landownership in terms of social status and credit collateral for the owner may not be fully reflected in the land prices in the market. Land-lease markets, on the other hand, are quite active, at least until recently, before land reforms legislation abolished tenancy in some areas or drove it underground.'

[39] Some households report having mortgaged and then redeemed land several times.

terms of the original contract) or reclaim (when the contract is renewed) rights to share-crop the land. This system is less frequent and is referred to as *bhare* or *giro haath*. Traders, rich Koli Patels and a rich potter are known to mortgage in land under this sytem. The right to grant share-cropping rights rests with the mortgagee who must trust the owner to be a responsible tenant. In such cases, the mortgagee decides whether or not to share in expenses.

Despite the fact that the mortgage rate for land is generally lower than the prevailing market price of land and despite the uncertainty of whether one can ultimately redeem the land, the terms and conditions of mortgaging are perceived to be favourable. The mortgage contract can range from two to 10 years depending on the negotiation between the two parties: the average term is five years. If the term of the contract lapses, the owner can renegotiate with a second mortgagee and transfer the land. The transfer of mortgaged land, whether from one mortgagee to another or back to the original owner to share-crop, is referred to as *giro haath*. The revenue tax, *vighoti*, is paid by the party that uses the land, normally the mortgagee. Although the owner generally forfeits his use rights to the land, the mortgage loan is perceived to be 'interest-free'.[40] Finally, there are provisions for renegotiating the mortgage contract once a year, either to lengthen the term of the contract, to refinance the loan, or to negotiate tenancy rights to the mortgaged land.

Every year at Ekatrij, all new mortgaging and share-cropping contracts are settled and all old contracts are reviewed.[41] Mortgage contracts generally involve written, signed and stamped agreements which state the names of both parties, the amount, type and registry number of the land given on mortgage, and the amount and terms of the loan taken. If the term of a mortgage contract lapses and both parties agree, the original agreement can be renegotiated for an additional term. If the original owner wishes to take an additional loan

[40] According to a saying or *kahavat* in Gujarati, 'There is no interest on land.' The implied meaning is that the use rights to land are, in fact, the interest.

[41] There are two days in the year which are considered particularly auspicious in Gujarat: Dussehra and Ekatrij. It is thought that there is no need to consult astrologers for transactions on those days, that these days are auspicious 'for every good thing'. On Ekatrij, for example, fishermen are said to take to the sea and farmers to begin tilling the land. Ekatrij falls on the third day (the day of the small moon) in Vaishakh of the Hindu calendar (personal communications, Ela Bhatt and Niru Bhai Desai). In 1987, for instance, Ekatrij occurred on May 2. In some years, one or both parties will delay finalising a mortgage contract until the first rains to determine the risk of or potential for cultivation.

against his/her land, he/she can do so up to the market price of the land. If the market price for land has risen over the previous year, the owner can refinance the loan accordingly.[42]

Either at the end of or mid-way through the mortgage period, the owner can decide unilaterally to transfer the land to another mortgagee by paying off the original loan. Like other transactions, this transaction must be registered at Ekatrij. For instance, if the owner suspects that the original mortgagee may attempt to claim the land, he/she can transfer the land by taking a second loan, paying off the first mortgagee and transfering the land to a second mortgagee. If the mortgagee should want to buy or 'claim' the land, he/she would have to pay the owner an additional sum of money and pay the *talati* (village accountant) a fee of Rs 500–2,000 to re-register the land.

Given the flexibilities in the mortgage market, there is a general perception that mortgaged land can be redeemed. Two frequent responses to our questions about the possibility of redeeming land were: 'In good years, people will take back their land' and 'If I work hard, I can redeem my land'. Contrtibuting to this optimism is the fact that people seldom mortgage all their land, retaining some for cultivation. In practice, given the general awareness in Gujarat of ownership and caste rights, there is reported to be little, if any, actual foreclosure on mortgaged land.[43]

2. Tenancy Market

In the literature on share-cropping, there are two basic alternative assumptions about crop shares. The first is that the crop share is uniform for all tenancy contracts in a village. The second is that the crop share varies from one contract to another depending on the relative bargaining power of individual tenants and owners, on their differential risk aversion, or on some other factor. Neither of these neat theoretical alternatives seems to fit our study data.[44] There is

[42] The ceiling rate for a mortgage is the market price at the time of the initial negotiation or any subsequent renegotiations; the floor rate reflects the needs and demands of the owner. In 1987, informants reported that the maximum mortgage rates were Rs 1,000 per *bigha* for dryland and Rs 2,000 per *bigha* for irrigated land but that, in practice, the normal amounts taken were Rs 100–300 per *bigha* for dryland and Rs 500–600 per *bigha* for irrigated land.

[43] Personal communication, Sudarshan Iyengar. There is a local term, however, for when the mortgagee claims the land without registering it: *pachavi padu*.

[44] These alternatives have also been substantially challenged by the 1975–76 large-scale study of contractual relationships in four states in northern and eastern India by Bardhan and Rudra (Bardhan 1984a).

certainly no uniform crop share for all tenancy contracts, nor is there an infinite variety of crop shares. Crop shares cluster around three simple ratios: 33:66, 50:50 and 66:33.

The real complexity and variability in the contracts are to be found in the allocation of input costs (Robertson 1987). In roughly half the contracts, costs are shared.[45] The relative proportion of cost shares assumed by each party does not seem to depend on farm size, on risk aversion capacity or on the crop/season but rather on the relative endowment of each party in land, labour, water resources and bullock power.

The asset endowment of each party serves as a set of feasibility constraints or options which are weighed against the feasibility set of the other party in determining who contributes what resources under the contract and who gets what share of the crop. The decisions with regard to whether and how to share the input costs of seeds, fertiliser and diesel oil appear to take place only after a decision has been reached with regard to assets and to affect only secondarily how shares are divided.[46]

A significant variety of share-cropping patterns were reported in the village.[47] As noted, these variations have more to do with how input costs are shared than with how output or crops are shared. Indeed, although the crop share ratios are the most conspicuous aspect of the share-cropping contract, they are also the least flexible and tend to cluster around the three simple ratios mentioned above.[48] The most common type of contract is that which entitles each party to half the

[45] According to Bardhan (1984a: 116), the 'widespread prevalence of the cost-sharing arrangement as a part of the tenancy contract is a strikingly new phenomenon in Indian agriculture.'

[46] It should be noted that, on occasion, the role of owner or tenant is shared by two parties. In one case reported during the study year, the co-tenants jointly owned a pump set and shared equally the tenant's share of costs and crops. In another case three co-owners jointly owned a plot of land and shared equally the owner's share of costs and crops.

[47] The following analysis is based on 43 cases of share-cropping reported during the study year.

[48] Such ratios are so common that they provide the names for the share-crop contracts:

Triju or Trija Bhage = one-third
Ardhu or Ardha Bhage = one half

crop.[49] Under it, the owner and tenant pool assets and share input costs in what is perceived by both parties to be roughly equal proportions. However, under this basic contract, at least seven variations were reported, including:

1. Owner provides land and irrigation;[50] tenant provides all inputs and labour;
2. Owner provides land and shares irrigation and input costs; tenant provides labour and shares irrigation and input costs;
3. Owner provides land, shares input costs and labour input; tenant provides irrigation, shares input costs and labour input;
4. Owner provides land, shares cost of diesel oil, input costs and labour input; tenant provides pump, shares cost of diesel oil, input costs, and labour input.

Another common type of contract is that which entitles the tenant to a two-thirds share and the owner to one-third. Under this type of contract, the owner generally provides only land and the tenant provides inputs, irrigation and labour. However, several variations on this basic contract were also reported, including:

1. With poor quality land or low value crops, the tenant's share becomes three-fourths;

[49] Reporting from a village in Viramgam *taluka*, a neighbouring *taluka* also in Ahmedabad district, Shinoda (n.d.) observes: 'In all the cases of share-cropping, both lessor and lessee enjoy 50:50 share of the produce including by-products and generally share equally the capital input such as fertiliser and pesticide. Besides land tax and other cesses, expenditure on manure·is met by lessor while seeds and hired labour charges are met by lessee. Lessors are afraid of court cases, so generally they do not lease out their land to the same lessee continuously for more than three years except when both parties are relatives.'

[50] Although the terms 'owner' and 'tenant' are used here, as they are standard terms in the literature on share-cropping, they should not be taken to signify 'landowning' and 'tenant' classes. Indeed, as the analysis will show, in any given season individual households often enter more than one share-cropping contract, sometimes as tenant in one and owner in another. Further, there is a fair amount of 'reverse tenancy' under which the tenant owns more land than the owner. Reporting from a dry grain farming region in Karnataka, South India, Hill (1982: 172) observes that the institution of 'landlordism' has been stood on its head: 'most of those who rent out land being widows and other small landholders, who are quite right in thinking that the rent they would receive from a tenant is greater than the potential net return from own-cultivation.'

2. If the owner provides land and a pump set, the tenant provides the diesel oil, inputs and labour.

There were a few instances of a third type of contract as well. Under this, the tenant provides only his/her labour and receives one-third of the crop while the owner provides everything else (land, irrigation and inputs) and receives two-thirds of the crop.

In Maatisar, we identified several general practices in share-cropping. The first is that the tenancy contract is predominantly a short-term one, generally for a specific crop in a specific season.[51] Second, the majority of share-crop contracts are negotiated for the winter season when irrigation is required. Third, the initiative to negotiate can be taken by either party. Fourth, landowners prefer share-cropping out to farm neighbours as they can then supervise the tenant.[52] Landowners also share-crop to others, in the following order of preference: those from the same kin group or residential neighbours (largely coincident), outside relatives, and others. Fifth, tenants can deal with more than one landlord in a given season or year, and a single household can be engaged simultaneously in owner cultivation, tenant cultivation, and/or wage labour during any given season. Finally, contract terms are generally honoured by both parties.[53]

[51] In some cases, when the land would otherwise lie fallow, contracts for several seasons or years are negotiated. Most commonly, unirrigated land which lies fallow in the winter season is share-cropped out for two to three successive winter seasons. In some cases, when the landowner is unable or unwilling to cultivate his/her land, it is share-cropped out for two to three years. For example, the Vankar leader, who weaves and holds a salaried job (as the village postmaster), has share-cropped out his two acres of land under two three-year contracts to one Koli Patel farmer. However, generally, the land rotates after each season either back to the owner or to another tenant or to the same tenant under another contract.

[52] Our data confirm, with one exception, what Bardhan observed from the large-scale study of contractual relationships cited above: 'The landlord quite often (though certainly not always) gives production loans to the tenant, shares in costs of seeds, fertilisers, etc., participates in decision making about the use of these inputs, and in general takes a lot of interest in productive investments on the tenant farm (as well as on his self-cultivated land), quite contrary to the prevailing image of rentier or usurious landlords.' The one exception to Bardhan's findings is that, according to our data, landlords in Maatisar rarely give production loans but often share in input costs.

[53] One Brahmin landowner has a reputation for repeatedly violating the terms of the contract and insisting on a higher share. One informant claimed that in the future, given the bad reputation of this Brahmin landowner, only a confident, powerful tenant would share-crop with him, commenting, 'If we were in the tenant's place, we would not grow even 200 grams of wheat.'

We also identified certain general patterns with regard to when and why share-crop contracts are negotiated. The first is that a household will decide to share-crop out land when it does not own one or more of the following factors of production, presented in a rough sequence of importance: labour, capital, bullocks, pump sets and equipment.[54] Second, more land is generally share-cropped out in winter than in other seasons, and more for wheat than for other crops. Third, more land is share-cropped out with field neighbours than with others.

Contrary to the literature which emphasises feudal or semi-feudal relationships between the tenant and the owner (Bhaduri 1973; Bharadwaj 1974), our findings indicate that the terms and conditions of tenancy contracts in Maatisar are not generally enmeshed in extra-contractual relations between the two parties. Tenants are free to lease in land from more than one landlord, and they do not generally provide paid or unpaid labour services to the landlord. Further, landlords are not the principal marketing channel for their tenant's share of the crop. Rather, most sales are handled unilaterally by tenants. Finally, landlords are more likely to share in the costs than they are to extend production credit to tenants.

In summary, our findings confirm some of the emerging patterns in share tenancy reported by Binswanger and Rosenzweig (1981) in their review of tenancy arrangements in India. The first is that tenancy markets are highly flexible, with sharp seasonal variations. Second, contracts are determined in a bilateral bargaining process that allows the parties involved to make better use of specific asset endowments. Bullocks, pump sets and labour, not just land, are important factors in the negotiation of tenancy contracts. Also, both parties often partici-pate actively in cultivation and input decisions.[55] Third, there is no clear pattern of which households become tenants or landlords: there are fewer pure tenants (i.e., that own no land) than owner–tenants; some households may simultaneously be tenants, landowners and wage labourers during any given season; and small farm households

[54] Reporting from a village in North India, Bliss and Stern (1982: 131) contend that 'the major function of tenancy is to bring land to its co-operating inputs in a situation in which the opposite method, bringing inputs to the land, works nothing like as well.'

[55] Reporting from a village in Viramgam *taluka*, Shinoda (n.d.) notes: 'Type of crop and amount of capital input, if any, is jointly decided by both parties at the time of contract.' Reporting from a village in North India, Bliss and Stern (1982: 131) report 'fairly close supervision by the landlord'.

frequently share-crop land to larger farm households (i.e., reverse tenancy).[56]

3. Labour Markets

Local Labour Market: The local labour market in Maatisar is of moderate size, providing primary employment to approximately one-fourth of the households and secondary employment to another one-fourth. The vast majority of labourers are employed as casual rather than as permanent or attached labourers. Among those households which declare labour as their primary occupation, the ratio between casual and permanent labour households is 60:15.[57]

The terms under which casual labourers are employed in Maatisar can be broadly distinguished as either daily or contract employment. Under the time-rate or daily wage system (*dari*), labourers are offered a specified wage for a fixed period of time, usually some portion of a day's work. Under the piece-rate or contract system (*udhad*), they are offered a specified lump sum payment for performing a specific task. Within these broad frameworks, labourers are recruited and paid under a variety of arrangements. The key variables are whether they are recruited individually or in a group, and whether they are paid in cash or in kind.

Daily wage labourers are usually recruited individually. While recruitment can be initiated by either party, generally employers contact labourers. Among the Brahmins and Bharwads, who do not hire out their labour and do not use their women as family labour, preference is given first to Koli Patels.[58] Among the lower castes, preference is given first to kin, then to members of the same caste group, and only then to other castes in the village. Occasionally, labourers contact employers, either directly when the employer lives within the same caste neighbourhood, or indirectly when the employer is from another caste group. Also, occasionally, an attached labourer may be asked to 'recruit' labourers from among his kin when his employer requires casual labourers.

[56] Again, reporting from a village in Viramgam *taluka*, Shinoda (n.d.) notes: 'The cases that the holding of lessor is relatively smaller than that of lessee (share-cropper) are nearly half of the cases of tenancy contract. With these reasons, lease market is not monopolistic but quite competitive.'

[57] In a survey of 27 villages in Gujarat, Shah (1978) found the ratio between casual and permanent labour households to be 84:16.

[58] The Thakkars do not farm but share-crop or mortgage out their land.

There is a common understanding throughout the village as to the prevailing daily wage rate, as well as how many hours is meant by a 'day's work', at any particular time in the year, even though wages vary by task and crop both across and within seasons.[59] Wages appear to be sensitive largely to one or more of the following demand factors: interfarm needs during peak demand periods, wages in neighbouring villages during peak demand periods, and other local wage opportunities (e.g., government relief works). In Maatisar, the range of variation was between Rs 5 per day and Rs 15 per day. Most commonly, wages were lower at the beginning of a season and increased toward the period of peak demand at the end of the season.[60] In addition, for any given wage under any given conditions, the relationship between the labourer and the employer can also influence the wage level.[61]

In Maatisar, the labour-force is remarkably unsegmented by caste or gender. All labour is supplied by Backward or Scheduled Castes. There is little segmentation of the labour market along gender or age lines. At the time of peak labour demand, employers can exercise little choice between labourers on the basis of skill or manageability. The only exception to this general rule is that for paddy plantation, preference is given first (after kin) to Vankars, then to Vaghris, and lastly to Koli Patels. In times of slack labour demand, the employer can be more selective, choosing labour either on the basis of skill, ease of supervision or some other criteria.

There are three main castes which engage in agricultural wage labour in the village: Vankars, Vaghris and Koli Patels. At least three reasons were cited for giving preference to Vankars and Vaghris in paddy plantation. First, paddy plantation is considered arduous and

[59] Dreze and Mukherjee (1987: 11) argue that in India task-specific wages tend to circle around a 'standard wage' that appears 'to be, to a great extent, rigid over time (in money terms)'. The 'standard wage' is found to be particularly rigid downwards in slack periods, so much so that the 'standard wage' will not, they argue, crash.

[60] For instance, the wage rates during the wheat–barley harvest in 1987 started at Rs 5 per day (a lower–than-usual wage ascribed to the prolonged drought in the area) but rose to Rs 11 a day during the period of peak demand for labour (in response to the wage rate offered in a neighbouring village).

[61] We were told that when labourers are hired by kin they are sometimes paid a rupee more per day than if they are hired by someone outside their kinship network. One landlord reported, for example, that during the 1988 winter harvest he paid Rs 9–10 to labourers from his own *vas* (neighbourhood) whereas he paid Rs 8 to labourers from other neighbourhoods. The neighbourhood or *vas* to which he belongs is comprised almost exclusively of a single extended kin group.

demeaning (as one informant put it, 'The work is muddy and dirty.') and may, therefore, be either allotted to or pre-empted by the low-caste Vankars. Second, Vaghris are reputed to be fast workers and paddy plantation is a particularly time-bound activity. Third, Vankars are not available as labour throughout the year as they are primarily weavers, but the slack season in weaving coincides with the peak period of demand for paddy plantation. One additional supply factor may explain the predominance of Vankars and Vaghris over Koli Patels in paddy plantation: very few Vankars are engaged in culti-vation, only half of the Vaghris are, whereas over two-thirds of the Koli Patel households remain busy in their own fields during paddy plantation.

Under the contract or piece-rate system (udhad), labourers are generally recruited as a team (toli). Each team designates a scout or leader, referred to as the agewan, from among its members. The agewan is the contact person for employers who scouts for labour opportunities, negotiates the contract and collects and distributes payments. He is chosen for his knowledge of the labour market and his bargaining power and often receives a commission or takes a 'cut' for his advance work.[62] Unlike the mukadam or jobber who is often used to hire migrant labour (see below), the agewan is from the same caste as the team and works with them. Agewans scout for and negotiate employment opportunities both in the local and in the migrant labour markets.

Most labourers prefer the piece-rate system as they can generally negotiate higher wages for the same operation than on the daily wage basis.[63] As one informant stated: 'If you work hard, you can earn more. We don't even take time out to drink water.' Given that there are no time restrictions under the udhad system, labourers who might earn

[62] In Maatisar, we were not able to obtain information on the agewan's commission or cut. In a personal communication, M.D. Mistry reported two systems of agewan payment from other parts of Gujarat: some agewans charge the employer a commission (e.g., Rs 0.50 per labourer per day); others take a 'cut' from the wages paid (e.g., by paying each labourer a rupee less than the wages collected from the employer).

[63] We were told that often the udhad system works to the advantage of the employer who can avoid paying the minimum wage (personal communication, M.D. Mistry). The Minimum Wage legislation is thought to be less precise and less enforceable for piece-rate work than for daily wages. We were also told that the udhad system can serve to strengthen the bargaining power and latent organising of labour. Our data suggest that the udhad system does strengthen the bargaining power of labourers and offers them higher wages.

Rs 10 per day in daily wages can earn as much as Rs 25 per day under the contract system. A variation on this system, generally referred to as a harvest-share contract, is when a team is contracted to harvest a specific unit of land in exchange for a specified share of the harvest. Piece-rates vary by crop and are calculated either by unit of weight (e.g., as with cotton-podding) or by unit of land (e.g., as with rice plantation and harvesting).[64] They can also vary from contract to contract, even for the same crop.[65]

Although they entail serious problems of quality control (Dreze and Mukherjee 1987), piece-rate contracts appear to be preferred by employers when a great deal of work must be carried out in a short space of time as with plantation and, particularly, harvest operations. Despite the general preference for piece-rate contracts by both employers and labourers, there appears to be no significant shift in this direction in Maatisar. Labourers for paddy plantation and harvesting have been recruited under the *udhad* system for at least the last 30 years. The plantation and harvesting of other crops, including the main winter crops (wheat and barley), are still carried out largely on a daily wage basis.[66] The harvesting of two crops, summer sorghum and monsoon *guar*, are handled under either system depending on the constraints of the employer. By contrast, in areas where migrant labourers are recruited for plantation and harvesting, the trend towards contractualisation is more marked (Breman 1985).[67]

Whether under the time-rate or piece-rate systems, labourers for harvest operations are generally paid in kind as the landowner has a surplus of grain at harvest. Labour for plantation, however, is usually paid by a combination of cash and food. Ploughing is paid either on a

---

[64] Migrant labourers report that groundnut harvesting is most often paid on the basis of the unit of weight completed.

[65] In Maatisar, the piece-rates for planting paddy varied from Rs 100–150 per *bigha* and the piece-rates for planting wheat varied from Rs 25 (with food) to Rs 100 (without food) per *bigha*. Dreze and Mukherjee (1987: 14) argue that one distinguishing feature of piece-rate contracts is that they are more negotiable than daily wage contracts, leading to 'the strong flexibility (over time and across individuals) of *both* earnings per task and—more importantly—earnings per day'.

[66] The harvesting of winter wheat and barley is less time-bound than the harvesting of paddy. This is because the winter crops are grown on the same land as monsoon paddy whereas the main summer crop, sorghum, is planted on different land than winter wheat and barley. Some cases of piece-rate contracts for harvesting wheat were reported.

[67] Migrant labourers from Maatisar reported that groundnut and sugar-cane harvesting is predominantly contractualised in the area to which they migrate, Saurashtra.

piece-rate or daily wage basis and either in cash or kind, while workers for irrigation operations are generally contracted on a seasonal or a monthly basis and paid by a mix of daily food and a fixed amount of the crop. While most of the labour arrangements in Maatisar are casual, four boys and eleven men are employed as regular farm servants.[68] Unlike in the past, when farm servants were generally 'attached' for specified tasks and indefinite periods of time, present-day farm servants work more standard working hours at increasingly specified tasks, enter annual or other fixed-term contracts, and turnover regularly. In return, relative to 'attached' labourers in the past, they receive fewer loans or advances on wages (Breman 1985).[69]

In Maatisar, two main reasons are cited for deciding to become a farm servant. The first is the need for a lump sum, advance payment: most farm servants negotiate half of the annual wage as an advance payment to be paid back without interest by six months' work. As reported, this advance payment is used either to pay back a debt, to cover marriage costs or as investment capital. The second is that under the farm servant contract the servant's daily subsistence needs for food, drink and clothing are taken care of.

All of the regular farm servant contracts include an annual wage, two to three meals a day, and two to three sets of clothing per year; some are also provided lodging. In one or two exceptional cases, farm servants are offered use rights to some agricultural land. For child servants, the annual wage ranged from Rs 450–500; for adults, the annual wage ranged from Rs 900, paid to a servant who had worked in the same household for six years, to Rs 3,000. In Maatisar as well as in the surrounding area, the annual wage averages between Rs 1,500 to Rs 2,000. The differences in annual wage can be attributed in part to differences in age or physical capacity. Farm servants in Maatisar do not necessarily live at the employer's homestead but do work full-time. As a rule, they receive advance payment, but not interim small loans.[70]

Demand for attached labour is low for men and virtually non-

[68] Two of the men, outsiders from neighbouring villages, are kin of their employers.

[69] According to Breman, attachment 'for an indefinite period, severance of the relationship only in exceptional cases and often its prolongation into following generations, work obligations for the servant's whole family and finally the nonspecific and exchangeable nature of the services were the chief elements of servitude in the past' (Breman 1974: 41).

[70] Generally, when farm servants are able to negotiate interim small loans, the loans which are less than Rs 200 are extended interest-free and those which are greater than Rs 200 are extended with an interest rate of five per cent per month.

existent for women. A few women, mostly young widows or girls, work as maidservants: this service is contracted independently and unilaterally by the women, not as part of the attached labour contracts of men. Most maidservant contracts are short-term (four to six months) and part-time. The working hours vary, depending on the size and requirements of the household, as does the wage. Maidservants are generally not entitled to the in-kind benefits they might have received in the past. Reporting from south Gujarat, Breman (1985) observes that there is no longer the possibility of credit to maidservants. However, in the study village, two young widowed maidservants reported they were able to negotiate small, interest-free loans (Rs 50–100) from their employers.

Significantly, wages do not vary by age or sex for the same operation in any of the labour arrangements discussed. Because wage rates for men and women vary in many parts of India, this particular aspect of the labour market was discussed at length with male and female informants of various ages and castes. Everyone seemed to agree that women and men have 'always', at least in living memory, been paid equally. This could be attributed to several reasons. Gujarat is recognised as a state with a relatively high female labour-force participation rate, and elsewhere in Gujarat women are reported to be paid equal wages to men. Moreover, the labour-force in Maatisar is comprised exclusively of Backward and Scheduled Castes, whose women traditionally work alongside men.[71]

The perceived equality of wage rates may mask more subtle forms of gender differentiation: for example, occupational segmentation by gender or 'hidden' wage differentials. While the wages for men and women under the piece-rate contract system are reported to be the same, the possibility of 'hidden' wage differentials for women within the piece-rate system is higher than within the daily wage system. It is easier to hide whether or not women are allotted different shares within a work team than it is to hide whether or not women are paid different daily wages. Similarly, wages are consistently lower for certain operations typed as 'women's work' (notably, pulse and sweet potato harvesting) presumably because women are willing to work for low wages.[72]

[71] It should be noted that all of these Backward Castes pay a bride-price at marriage; the custom of bride-price is most often associated with regions where female manual labour is highly prevalent and valued (Miller 1981).

[72] It should be noted that very often children work alongside women in these operations, for which they receive wages that are as low or lower than women's.

In addition, the rural labour market exhibits different patterns of male–female recruitment and payment. Women are absent from certain segments of the labour market, notably ploughing and long-term farm servant contracts. Higher caste women, because of caste and related status considerations, do not perform field (or other manual) labour. Finally, women have access to contract work and migration opportunities only through men, generally male members of their family or kinship group (Binswanger et al. 1979).

Migrant Labour Markets: A significant number of labourers, both individually and as household units, migrate seasonally to other areas for rural employment opportunities. Some informants claim migration began only after Shermia's time, which lasted until 1957. Others say migration became possible only after the public transport system reached the area in the late 1950s. Still others maintain that migration started after the *gram panchayat* system was introduced in the early 1960s. Whichever account is true, local labourers began migrating only 25 to 30 years ago.

A clear pattern of migration, with marked seasonality and geography and strict farm and non-farm segmentation by caste, has developed. Migrant labour appears to be recruited by four or five basic systems, which correspond closely with the type of work. I will describe below the different types of employment available to migrant labour and the recruitment system for each type of labour.

Koli Patels, together with a few Prajapatis, migrate for five to eight months to work in brickfields. The nearest brickfields are located on the outskirts of Ahmedabad city. Unlike in south Gujarat, where Breman reported that brickworkers were recruited as gangs by a jobber (*mukadam*) on the owner's commission, local brickfield migrants respond to general word-of-mouth notification that brickfield work is available, or send scouts to determine when there is a demand for labour. They migrate as household units whose members work in pairs, averaging 1,200–1,500 bricks per day. The migrant labourers seem to work, invariably, at actual brick-making, not at brick loading or unloading.[73] They are paid on a piece-rate basis,

[73] This pattern confirms what was observed by Breman (1985: 289): 'Most work is carried out at night and in the morning, from midnight to 9 a.m. or from 4 a.m. to midday. The preparatory work for the following night—the mixing and kneading of the clay—which takes several hours, is done in the afternoon, after which the gangs go to sleep. Only the labourers who carry head loads of dried bricks to the oven (*bhata*) or who unload bricks from the oven onto lorries, come from the surrounding villages.'

Rs 30–40 for every 1,000 bricks. In addition to their piece-rate wages, the brickworkers are provided with a 'room', a partitioned space within a camp hut in which to live.

The rice mills to which local labour migrates are located in the nearest market town, Bavla. Like the brickfield workers, the rice mill migrants are primarily Koli Patels plus a few Prajapatis, and respond to a general word-of-mouth notification that rice mill work has resumed. They, too, move as household units rather than as gangs. They are paid either on a daily or monthly wage basis, ranging from Rs 7–12 per day to Rs 400 per month, and are also provided with a place to live.

A few Vaghri households migrate to stone quarries at Porbandar in Junagadh District to work at the crushing yards. These households report that they have been migrating for stone-crushing for the past 10 years. They have direct contact with the owners, who give them advances and open an account for them with a local shopkeeper, from whom they buy their daily necessities. They are paid either on a daily basis (Rs 10–15 per day) or on a piece-rate basis (Rs 50–60 per truck-load or Rs 5 per ton).[74]

There are several significant aspects to migration for sugar-cane harvesting and processing. The migration season is long, generally five to eight months, as it involves both a primary operation, harvesting, and a second operation, processing. In addition, the nature of the labour process in harvesting dictates group migration (Agarwal 1989). As reported by Breman (1985) from a sugar-cane area in south Gujarat, the labourers work in teams—the male cutter followed by a helper (usually a wife, sister or daughter) to clean the stalks of leaves, followed, in turn, by a child to bind the cleaned stalks together. Recruitment for cutting and processing sugar-cane is tightly organised by a jobber–foreman, the *mukadam*, who acts as an intermediary between the owner and the workers. The labourers are paid either on a daily (Rs 12 per day) or on a monthly basis (Rs 350–450 per month). In addition, they are generally provided jute cloth with which they are expected to construct their own lean-to shacks.

Some Vaghri households have migrated annually for the past 20 years for groundnut harvesting and other agricultural wage labour in Amreli and Junagadh Districts in Saurashtra. Recruitment for these

[74] Breman (1985) reports a particular problem faced by the stone-crushers. In order to crush the rocks, an air-compressor is needed to make holes in the rocks. Often, the workers have to wait days on end for their turn with the compressor. While they wait, they generally earn nothing.

types of agricultural operations is organised largely along caste or kinship lines, without mediation by a *mukadam*. Caste or kinship teams move out along established routes in search of work, or household units maintain established ties with regular employers, negotiating contracts at the end of one season for the next. If any change in the pre-negotiated contract is required, the employers contact the migrant households directly.[75] Migrant farm labourers are paid either on a time-rate or piece-rate basis, with paddy harvesting contracted by unit of land. Like sugar-cane workers, these migrants live in lean-to shacks made of jute cloth.

In addition to these dominant patterns, a few households migrate each year to other destinations for different labour opportunities. Two or three Vaghri households migrate to Ahmedabad for seasonal work as masons or for selling vegetables. One Vaghri household migrates occasionally to Delhi to sell utensils, and about six Vaghri households migrate each year to other villages in the area, often where their in-laws live, to work as attached labour. A few Koli Patel households migrate to other villages in the district for agricultural wage labour, either on a seasonal basis (e.g., wheat or guava harvest) or on an annual basis as attached labour. Traditionally, some members of most Vankar households migrated to the nearby towns for two to three months of cotton-podding and to Kheda District for one to two months of paddy plantation and harvesting. In recent years, however, a variety of cotton which does not require podding has been introduced, thereby reducing the demand for cotton-podders.

Whether more or less tightly organised, the movement of labour follows highly personalised or caste-based contact and control mechanisms. The jobber organises gangs based on primary loyalties— caste, kinship or neighbourhood (largely coincident in Maatisar). The more loosely structured teams are also composed of members from one or more neighbouring households. Overall, the preference is for familiar routes, where several of the migrants have worked in previous years, or contracts have been negotiated by scouts (*agewans*) from Maatisar or relatives resident in the migrant area, or where arrangements have been confirmed through written or verbal communication (Breman 1985: 329).

Some workers, notably brickfield workers, are not paid fully until

[75] For example, in 1987, groundnut production dropped to only 20 per cent of normal years. Those households which normally migrate for groundnut harvesting were notified by the landlords in Saurashtra whether or not their labour was required in 1987.

the end of the contract period but are paid a weekly subsistence allowance.[76] Other workers, particularly those recruited by a *mukadam*, are given advances at recruitment which serve to bind them to a specific employer but also to cover their costs before their first payment. Most migrant households are able to save a sizeable portion of what they earn;[77] some are forced to save given their employers' policy of deferring full payment until the end of the contracted work season. Voluntary savings are either stored or sent back to the village as remittances. Many single migrants remit an average of Rs 200 per month while most family units remit between Rs 100 and Rs 200.

In most migrant households, these savings are used primarily to meet basic needs during the lean summer months. However, at least one household, a Vaghri household, invests some of its savings in moneylending in Maatisar.[78] According to what we were told, no migrant household has been able to accumulate enough savings to consolidate their holdings or invest in capital assets.

In the migrant labour market, as in the local labour market, women labourers reported receiving wages equal to those of men. Questioned at length with regard to wages, the only migrant labour market in which they reported wage differentials was the urban construction market, where women are said to be paid Rs 18 per day and men Rs 20 per day.

In writing about tribal migrants in south Gujarat, largely from the perspective of the *area of destination*, Breman (1985) notes a regional specialisation, whereby migrants are allotted different types of work according to the regions from which they come. In our study of Maatisar, an *area of departure*, a segmentation of the migrant labour

---

[76] Some brickfield workers reported they had to return to the work site after Holi, which they celebrated in Maatisar, in order to collect their final, full payment. This confirms what Breman also observed in regard to brickfield and stone quarry workers: 'Every week the labourers receive for their living expenses a sum far below the wages they earn. In this way they gradually build up a balance, with which the employers bind them until the end of the season' (Breman 1985: 256).

[77] Generally, migrant labourers earn more per day and are employed for more days per season when they migrate than they would earn or be employed in any season in Maatisar.

[78] In discussing relief works earnings with labourers in the village, it became clear that those who migrated regularly would calculate quickly how much to consume during the earning period and how much to save for the lean period. They were adept at calculating daily food requirements and at remembering daily food intake, even after several months had lapsed.

market by caste is noted: that is, specific castes, undifferentiated by skill-levels in the local labour market, follow different migration circuits, both geographically and occupationally.

However, the study data confirm two other observations made by Breman in regard to the marked segmentation of migrant labour markets. First, that there is little or no overlapping between the different migration circuits and there is little or no likelihood that the different labour groups will change over from one work sphere to the other, unless some crisis precipitates a change.[79] Second, that the segmentation has 'little to do with real differences in training or specialisation by area, but goes back to the accidentally established migration channel along which labour has since been recruited' (Breman 1985: 234); or, as we observed, that the markets for migrant labour are determined more by their personal or caste-based *contacts* than by their individual or caste-based *skills*.

Credit Market

Seven types of loans from informal credit sources were reported in Maatisar:

> *Giro* (land-mortgage loans): I described the terms and conditions of mortgage loans in the previous section on Land Markets.
> *Mandi didu* (house- or asset-mortgage loans): No cases of mortgaged house property or productive assets were reported during the study year.
> *Udhar* or *Nama* (credit sales): In offering credit sales, shopkeepers 'tie' certain customers to their shop and, in lieu of interest, charge slightly inflated prices. Some shopkeepers extend a line of credit for a fairly long time (up to six months); at least one, the Marwari, restricts the

[79] Because of the shift to a different variety of cotton, and the subsequent decline in demand for cotton-podding labour, some Vankars began migrating in the early 1980s to Saurashtra for groundnut harvesting. Vankar relatives in Saurashtra, known to local large farmers (Patels or Patedars), negotiated the initial link for these labourers. Because the prolonged drought also reduced the demand for paddy labour, one group of labourers from seven Vankar households went for groundnut harvesting in Saurashtra for the first time in 1986. In contrast, because the prolonged drought also reduced the demand for sugar-cane and groundnut labour, a few Vaghris migrated to Kheda District in search of paddy harvest opportunities for the first time during the 1985–87 drought.

line of credit to one month. When the sale is made, the customer's name (*nama*) and the due date for payment is written down. If the customer defaults on these loans or defers repayment for too long, the shopkeeper may close that customer's account.[80]

Rakhai (pawning): Pawning is also referred to as *gahena par dena* (literally, 'giving against ornaments'). In extending loans which exceed Rs 500, moneylenders generally insist on a pawned item as security. Most commonly jewellery or household utensils are pawned. Each type of commonly pawned item commands a 'standard' amount of loan with interest.

Byaj (interest-bearing loans without collateral): For loans between Rs 200 and Rs 500, if extended without collateral, the moneylenders generally insist that the loan be paid back within a month and charge an interest rate of five to 15 per cent for that month.

Uchina (short-term, interest-free loans): Small temporary loans (of less than Rs 100 to be repaid in less than a month's time) generally carry no interest charge. Small short-term loans (of less than Rs 200 to be repaid in one or two months) generally carry a low interest rate of two to five per cent per month.

Upadh (credit advances): Credit advances are made against either labour services or expected crop yields. In the past, before loans from the Integrated Rural Development Programme (IRDP) or through the Gram Sevak became available, more Thakkar shopkeepers provided crop advances of as much as Rs 10,000 if needed. By 1987, only two shopkeepers in Maatisar were reported to extend crop advances. Two types of advances against crops were reported. One is the total advance sale of the crop, whereby the shopkeeper and the farmer calculate the yield and estimate the harvest price. The shopkeeper advances the calculated value of the yield and the farmer must repay the calculated value in kind. If the yield exceeds the estimate agreed upon, the

[80] If customers default repeatedly, their line of credit will be closed. At that time, the customers may want to open an account at a different shop but find their reputations as defaulters have preceded them.

farmer is entitled to sell or keep the excess. The other is, simply, a negotiated advance which the farmer repays in kind. It was difficult to estimate the normal volume of crop advances because our study year was a drought year (in which both lenders and borrowers were averse to risk) and because the shopkeepers were particularly hesitant to discuss this type of moneylending.

Moneylenders also extend loans of over Rs 500 without insisting on security, but charge a slightly higher interest rate. The interest for both secured and unsecured loans varies according to the caste of the lender: Brahmins and Thakkars (the higher caste groups) charge as much as 15 per cent interest per month; Bharwads, Koli Patels and Vankars charge a more standard 10 per cent per month; and other caste groups charge as low as five per cent per month.[81] Loans which exceed Rs 2,000 are generally given only against mortgaged land.

A limited amount of credit advance is interlinked with labour contracts—routinely with attached labour contracts and only occasionally with casual labour. Most attached labourers or farm servants negotiate half of their annual wage as an advance payment to be paid back without interest by six months' work. Indeed, the advance payment is what attracts most labourers to farm servant contracts. A few farm servants are also able to negotiate interim small loans, of which those that are less than Rs 200 are extended interest-free and those greater than Rs 200 are extended with an interest rate of five per cent per month. Unlike in areas where casual labour is more closely 'tied' to regular employers, the possibility of casual labour obtaining small loans from employers is not great in Maatisar. In some cases, at the beginning of a labour season, labourers can obtain small, interest-free loans of Rs 100–200, which they repay in daily deductions from their wages. However, no cases of such loans being extended by employers to casual labourers during lean seasons were reported.[82]

[81] A five per cent monthly interest rate, or 60 per cent per annum, is not, of course, low relative to commercial bank rates. However, given the transaction and 'hidden' opportunity costs plus the rationing of commercial credit, the informal credit market remains very active.

[82] In their 1979 survey of labour contracts in rural West Bengal, Bardhan and Rudra found that in 78 per cent of their random sample of 110 villages, a system of loans against commitment of future labour exists: that is, 'there is a large class of labourers who take loans from the employer during the agricultural lean period, when there is little farm work, in exchange for a commitment to provide labour services during peak periods, when labour demand is high' (Bardhan 1984a: 86).

In addition to these more *contractual* forms of local credit, several forms of *reciprocal* credit operate in Maatisar. The term 'contractual' is used here to refer to forms of credit negotiated primarily as market transactions; 'reciprocal' is used to refer to credit transactions negotiated primarily through mutual social obligations. Reciprocal credit, including small gifts given with the unspoken understanding that the gift will be reciprocated and small, interest-free loans, is most common between relatives or kin, but also between members of same caste group. At least one form of reciprocal credit within one caste group has been formalised. At Vankar weddings, relatives and friends are expected to make cash contributions. Each contribution is returned in double the amount at the next wedding in the donor's house.[83]

The informal credit transactions discussed above did not operate solely within the boundaries of Maatisar. In fact, most types of informal credit cut across neighbouring villages or extend to market centres. Three cases of land share-cropped out to and one case of land share-cropped in from neighbouring villages were reported. Credit purchases in market towns for items ranging from marriage clothes and ornaments to agricultural inputs to agricultural equipment (notably, pump sets) were reported. As with local credit sales, the moneylender in these instances is the shopkeeper. In the case of pump sets, farmers often negotiate a local loan for Rs 1,000–2,000 to use as the downpayment to purchase a pump on credit.[84] Outside loans are also taken from moneylenders (e.g., Thakkar shopkeepers) in market towns, from moneylenders in neighbouring villages or from relatives (most commonly, the wife's parents or kin) in nearby villages. Loans are also extended to nearby villages—by the large moneylenders to non-relatives and by a number of households to relatives. It should also be noted that the Thakkars, the professional moneylenders of Maatisar, are known to borrow money from outside which they loan out at a slightly higher rate of interest within the village.

In addition to these informal sources of credit, loans from several sources of *formal credit* have reached the village: cooperative credit through a now defunct Farmer's Service Cooperative; loans and subsidies from the Integrated Rural Development Programme (IRDP); loans for milch animals and pump sets from the State Bank of India; and loans for pump sets and wells from the Land Development

[83] Srinivas (1976) refers to a similar system of reciprocal cash contributions at non-Brahmin weddings in his classic study of a village in Karnataka state, South India.

[84] Most of the pump sets are purchased directly from Rajkot, the city where they are manufactured.

Bank. The largest number of formal sector loans have been IRDP loans-cum-subsidies, made primarily to women members of the SEWA-organised dairy cooperative for the purchase of buffaloes and cows.

The first recorded bank loans (seven in the 1960s and eight in the 1970s) in Maatisar were to Koli Patels to sink wells, purchase pump sets and (in one case) buy a tractor.[85] In the 1970s, the rural labour branch of the Textile Labour Association in Ahmedabad (TLA) nego-tiated two batches of loans for the Vankar weavers from the nationalised banks.[86] Since 1982, the State Bank of India has distributed 48 loans in Maatisar: 24 to Koli Patels, seven to Vaghris, five to Bharwads, three to Rawals, one each to Bhangis and Vankars.[87] Between 1980 and 1986, 96 IRDP loans were distributed in Maatisar: 28 to Koli Patels, seven to Vaghris, seven to Bharwads, 19 to Vankars, and the balance to other caste groups[88] (refer to Table 20 for the distribution of formal bank loans by purpose and by caste).

A Farmer's Service Cooperative covering three villages, including Maatisar, was active for some 15 years from roughly 1965 to 1980. The first and second presidents of the cooperative were from Maatisar: a wealthy Koli Patel farmer and the current Koli Patel *sarpanch*. For some years, a large number of small loans were taken and repaid regularly. However, the third president of the Cooperative, who was from one of the other villages, stole nearly Rs 700,000 from the cooperative. Then, some 10 years ago, a group of powerful cooper-ative members took a few large loans totalling roughly Rs 80,000 which they deliberately did not repay. Eventually the Cooperative was declared bankrupt with a total loss of nearly Rs 800,000, and has never been reactivated.

[85] *Source*: Officer, Land Development Bank, Dholka. At present, no tractors are owned in Maatisar.

[86] Under the auspices of the TLA, 20 Vankar households received loans of Rs 1,000 each in 1973 and another 20 Vankar households received loans of Rs 1,000 each in 1978 through nationalised banks in Ahmedabad, the State Bank of India (SBI) and the Central Bank of India (CBI) respectively.

[87] *Source*: Bank Manager, State Bank of India, Dholka. Other banks, such as the District Cooperative Bank, the Kalupur Cooperative Bank, the Nagarik Cooperative Bank and the Punjab National Bank, have not disbursed any loans in Maatisar.

[88] *Source*: Officer, IRDP Office, Dholka. No official records were available for 1987 and 1988. According to village reports, 12 Vankar households received IRDP loans in 1987 and three Vankar and three Bhangi households received IRDP loans in the first half of 1988. According to official records, the Harijan Development Corporation has not distributed any loans in Maatisar during the past 10 years.

Table 20
IRDP and Bank Loans by Caste and Purpose [1980–88]

Caste	Purpose												
	Milch animals		Diesel pumps		Trade		Working capital		Equipment		Others		Total	
	#	Vol.	#	Vol.	#	Vol.	#	Vol.	#	Vol.	#	Vol.	#	Vol.
Koli Patel	47	61,084	2	14,494	1	1,100	—	—	—	—	2	630	52	77,308
Vaghri	14	45,000	—	—	—	—	—	—	—	—	—	—	14	45,000
Harijan	11	14,480	—	—	—	—	7	5,195	1	630	—	—	19	20,305
Bharwad	12	19,906	—	—	—	—	—	—	—	—	—	—	12	19,906
Prajapati	—	—	—	—	—	—	—	—	—	—	—	—	—	—
Brahmin	—	—	—	—	—	—	—	—	—	—	—	—	•	—
Thakkar	—	—	—	—	1	830	—	—	—	—	—	—	1	830
Bhangi	6	9,721	—	—	—	—	—	—	—	—	2	900	8	10,621
Barot	3	3,300	—	—	—	—	—	—	—	—	—	—	3	3,300
Rawal	6	9,333	—	—	—	—	—	—	1	2,500	—	—	7	11,833
Other	17	20,737	1	5,886	—	—	—	—	8	3,281	1	500	27	30,404
Total:	116	183,561	3	20,380	2	1,930	7	5,195	10	6,411	5	2,030	143	219,507

Note: Official records were available for IRDP loans: 1980–86; State Bank of India: 1982–88; Land Development Bank: 1980–86.

Water Markets

There are two broad types of water resources: ground and surface. In Maatisar, all surface water resources are common property but are sometimes 'appropriated' for private purposes. By contrast, ground water resources are private property but are sometimes 'conceded' for public use under certain conditions.[89] Therefore, although not all households in the village own ground-water resources, in practice most village households have relatively free access to ground-water resources for the purposes of drinking water, domestic water supply and watering animals.

Irrigation is the only use of ground-water for which a private water market operates. Water for irrigation is transacted both on hourly rental terms and as part of seasonal share-cropping contracts. The hourly rental of water can be paid in cash or kind. The prevailing market rate in 1987 for one hour of irrigation water was Rs 9–10 in cash or a share of the crop in kind. In a few cases, the pump-owner provided irrigation in return for 33 or 50 per cent of the crop, the share depending on the irrigation requirements of specific crops. More often, the pump-owner provided land and irrigation in return for 50 per cent of the crop. In another common arrangement, the landowner provided land, irrigation plus 50 per cent of the labour and/or inputs in return for 50 per cent of the crop. Under such an arrangement, the tenant shared the costs of inputs and labour and provided the bullock- and man-power for ploughing.

Livestock Markets

One-third of cultivating households do not own bullocks. For plough-ing their fields, these households are forced to contract bullock, plough and/or labour services. The rates and arrangements for con-tracting ploughing services vary but, like irrigation services, are contracted in two basic ways: on a piece-rate basis or on a share-crop basis. On the piece-rate basis, bullocks, ploughs and/or labour are contracted to plough a specific unit of land. The rate for ploughing a given unit of land varies with the season, the crop and the soil

[89] As used here, ground-water resources refer to wells and pump sets. Actually, underground water itself is a CPR and 'its unrestricted exploitation is likely to result in inefficient use and inequitable distribution' (Rao et al. 1988: 135) plus undesirable effects on the environment.

conditions. Payments can be made either on a fixed fee basis in cash or on a fixed share basis in kind. Under share-cropping contracts, various arrangements for ploughing services are negotiated depending in large part on the asset-base of the two parties, but also in part on the season, crop and soil conditions.

Some households share-crop their cattle to other households. One common practice is the 'salvaging' of non-productive animals, whereby rich households share-crop their sickly or 'dry' cattle to poorer households, often in the same kinship group. The share-croppers are permitted to cut grass from the owner's fields for fodder. After several months or years, usually once the animal regains its health or productivity, the animal is returned to the owner. The share-cropper is given, as his/her share, half the animal's added value as estimated by the owner. For example, if a pregnant animal is share-cropped, the share-cropper is given half the value of the calf or calves born.

Summary

This analysis of village institutions suggests that, in Maatisar, kinship ties remain a significant factor in the allocation of labour and credit, in the access to free goods, in various exchanges both for production and consumption, and in traditional social security. Those related by kinship can expect to receive credit from, to be hired by, or to exchange labour with their kin. A few political clients receive credit from their political patrons in exchange for their loyalty; most notably, the Vankar leader arranges government loans on a regular basis for his factional supporters.[90] However, the flow of credit from economic patrons to clients is not as significant as reported elsewhere (Bardhan 1984a; Binswanger and Rosenzweig 1981). In at least three markets— the tenancy, labour and product markets—patronage relationships have given way to market forces.

A limited amount of credit advance is interlinked with labour contracts, routinely with attached labour contracts and only occasionally with casual labour. Most attached labourers or farm servants negotiate half of their annual wage as an advance payment to be paid

---

[90] The only individuals in Maatisar who can offer significant political patronage are the current Vankar leader, and the ex-*sarpanch*, who have ties with regional power centres; and, to a lesser degree, the current *sarpanch*. These political patrons, unlike earlier economic patrons, do not recognise the right of labourers to share and participate in agrarian production but offer patronage for new political ends (Breman 1974).

back without interest by six months' work. A few farm servants are also able to negotiate small interim loans. Unlike in areas where casual labourers are more closely 'tied' to regular employers, the possibility of casual labourers obtaining small loans from employers is not great in Maatisar.[91] At the beginning of a labour season, some labourers are able to negotiate small, interest-free loans from their employers. However, during lean seasons, few, if any, casual labourers are able to obtain such loans from past or future employers.

Further, simultaneous contracts between two parties in more than one market are uncommon, other than the limited interlinkage between the credit market and the labour market mentioned above.[92] Our data suggest that if two parties are involved in a share-cropping contract the tenant is not likely to receive employment or credit from the landlord or to sell his/her share of the produce through the landlord. In Maatisar, the landlord is more likely to share costs with than extend credit to the tenant and the tenant most commonly sells his/her produce directly. Similarly, our data suggest that if two parties are involved in a mortgage contract, the original owner is not likely to be employed by the mortgagee.

In summary, it appears that market forces have replaced traditional modes of transactions to a significant degree in the tenancy, labour and credit markets in Maatisar. This is not to say that traditional transactions were not sensitive to market stimuli or did not involve calculated economic behaviour, but that traditional transactions, unlike modern market transactions, also involved the practice of underwriting subsistence needs (Herring and Edwards 1983). Although competitive market relationships provide open access and flexibility and reflect an expanding economy, they do not guarantee subsistence across slack seasons or other periods of uncertainty.[93]

[91] Bardhan (1984a: 73) describes labour-tying as follows: 'In the beginning of the year the employer contracts with some tied labourers, feeding them at a steady rate across the seasons (i.e., giving them consumption credit to survive the lean season) in exchange for their delivering committed labour supply in the peak season . . . .'

[92] Bliss and Stern (1982) report that in Palanpur, a village in Uttar Pradesh (North India), simultaneous contracts between two parties in more than one market are rare.

[93] According to Jodha (1989: 7), all adaptation or adjustment mechanisms 'that derive their strength from social sanctions and community's collective approach are less feasible' now than in the past. The major factors contributing to this change, according to Jodha, include increased differentiation of rural communities, introduction of formal institutions, the legal and administrative framework, and individualism injected by market forces.

In a study of changing agrarian relations in south Gujarat, Breman (1985: 444) argues that 'the breaking down of vertical dependence mechanisms does not in itself lead to a better existence for those being freed from them'. Similarly, in a review of several studies relating to the moral economy of South Asia, Appadurai (1984) argues that the loosening of patron-client ties, together with other political and economic forces, has led to partial emancipation for the poor without entitlement to a guaranteed subsistence. Therefore, as Jodha argues in his paper comparing quantitative approaches to the incidence of poverty in two villages of Rajasthan (1988: 2424), poor people give up exploitative arrangements with patrons 'only when they become economically more independent'. In Maatisar, our findings indicate that patrons, more often than poor people, give up patronage ties and that the erosion of patronage ties has contributed, together with demographic and economic forces, to the loss of routine entitlements for landless labourers and land-poor farm households.

Because competitive market relationships even in an expanding economy do not guarantee subsistence across slack seasons or other periods of uncertainty, except to households which are able to generate significant surpluses, the poor must find alternative guarantees of subsistence. During slack periods in normal years, *jajmani*, joint family and kinship relations still provide some degree of social security. But the provision of social security requires the presence of real resources and the absence of collective risk. During unseasonal years, when peasants are affected by low, short or untimely rains, they are less able to provide social security to others. And, as I will discuss in Part III, during periods of widespread or prolonged crises, particularly in drought years, even kin-based relations often break down.

III

Coping with Drought

Dimensions of the 1985–87 Drought

> *During the* chappanu *drought, people feared death.
> This year there is no fear of death, because of the relief
> works.*
>
> Bhangi Elder

Reporting in 1925, the Royal Commission on Indian Agriculture described the Indian economy as a 'gamble on the monsoon'. Even today, in the non-irrigated areas of India, the harvest of coarse grains remains a gamble on the monsoon. High rainfall variability and drought are common phenomena; as much as two-thirds of the cultivated area in India is subject to drought (Rao et al. 1988). During the 1960s and 1970s in Gujarat, there were eight widespread droughts, which affected more than 20 per cent of inhabited villages, and localised droughts in one or more arid areas every year. The worst droughts, which affected more than half of the villages, occurred in 1968–69, 1972–73, and 1974–75 (Government of Gujarat 1982). What constitutes a 'real drought' in many semi-arid areas, then, is not a single dry year but a succession of such years (Caldwell 1975). The drought of 1985–87 was just such a 'real drought' in much of Gujarat.

From 1985 to 1987, many parts of Gujarat suffered a shortfall of the southwest monsoon rains, which last from around June until October.[1] In Maatisar, according to village reports, each monsoon was

---

[1] Gujarat gets the bulk of its rain during the southwest monsoon. The levels of rainfall vary significantly across time and space. The following average levels of rainfall (in

progressively poorer, culminating in an almost total failure of the 1987 monsoon rains. In the state of Gujarat as a whole, rainfall from June to September 1987 was almost 54 per cent below normal (Rao et al. 1988). State-wise estimates of foodgrain production reflect the progressively poor monsoon rains. Before the drought, in 1983–84 and 1984–85, Gujarat state produced 5.7 and 5.3 million tons respectively of foodgrains. During the drought, state-level foodgrain production dropped dramatically to 2.7 million tons in 1985–86, 3.1 million tons in 1986–87, and 1.4 million tons in 1987–88 (Government of India 1989).

In Maatisar, according to village reports, the 1985 monsoon rains were poor but the paddy harvest was reasonable.[2] In 1986, the rains were poorer still—the village received only 10 to 12 inches in five brief showers—so that paddy yields dropped and the River Rodh and nearby Nalsarovar Lake dried up completely for the first time in recent decades. In 1987, it rained only five times: for 20 minutes in mid-July, lightly and briefly on three different days in mid-August, and lightly for an hour-and-a-half in the third week of August. What distinguished the 1985–87 drought from others in the near past was that it lasted for three years and that the shortfall in monsoon rains was severe, especially in third year.

Everyone in the study village agrees that the 1985–87 drought was the worst in living memory. But the elderly in the village recall their elders discussing a comparable drought, that of 1899–1900.[3] During that drought, there was apparently an acute shortage of food and fodder. Animals were fed leaves of the *ber* tree. People ate *rotla*

---

millimetres) were reported in Dholka *taluka* (Dholka Taluka Panchayat Office) and Ahmedabad District (Directorate of Agriculture):

	Taluka	District
1984	644	722
1985	199	686
1986	310	392
1987	374	222
1988	1,245	837

[2] Another source reported that, by the end of August 1987, the monsoon rains in Dholka *taluka* averaged 253 millimetres instead of the normal average of 762 millimetres (Government of Gujarat 1987a). But *taluka*-level averages are deceptive, as levels of rainfall can vary significantly even within *talukas*.

[3] In the year Samvat 1856 of the Hindu calendar: hence the local name for that drought, *chappanu* (literally, 'fifty-six').

(unleavened bread) or gruel made by mixing barley and *dodi* leaves. According to the elders, the suffering in 1899–1900 was greater than in 1985–87 for several reasons. At that time, people did not have pumps to extract ground-water, nor did they migrate for employment opportunities or, with their animals, for fodder.[4] And, most critically, the government did not offer relief works.

In her study of food crises and economic change in Western India between 1860 and 1920, McAlpin (1983) reports that the Gujarat region was free of food crises of famine magnitude for much of the nineteenth century. No famine was declared in Gujarat until 1899–1900. However, 'the mortality experience in Gujarat in the famine of 1899–1901 is the worst on record for western India in the British period' (*ibid.*: 196)—about 15 per cent of the population died over a two-year period. McAlpin suggests that the very high death rates in that famine resulted from a combination of factors, including the severity of the drought and the harvest failure; an unfamiliarity on the part of both the people and the civil servants with coping with such severe conditions; and a shortage of alternative sources of income and employment for the distressed population.

In this section I argue that the 1985–87 drought in Maatisar was characterised by sharp declines in production but relative stability in consumption and no excess mortality, attributable in large measure to the effective presence of relief works. I begin by describing the impact of the 1985–87 drought on the local economy, then detail public and private responses to it, and conclude with an analysis of how social security systems, both private and public, operate under drought conditions.

In his analysis of poverty and famines, Sen (1981) draws attention to the importance of distinguishing between declines in local food output, declines in overall food availability, and declines in the capacity of groups (or individuals) to command food. It is important, he argues, to distinguish between what *exists* and who can *command* what. In terms of what existed in 1985–87, although food output was greatly reduced during those years, food was made available throughout (first from government stocks and then from government imports). The mechanisms for making government food supplies available at the village level included the Public Distribution System, relief works and

---

[4] According to one informant, people had 'no knowledge of migration' at that time—that is, people did not regularly migrate in search of employment and, therefore, did not know where to migrate.

price controls. As will be discussed below, prices did not escalate dramatically (except the prices for fodder and fodder seed); the Public Distribution System was taxed beyond capacity in transporting, storing and distributing foodgrains when labourers at relief works were paid in kind (during the first half of 1987); and relief works were undertaken in many parts of the state for large parts of the drought years, particularly in 1987–88. The discussion will focus, therefore, on which households commanded access to food (and other commodities) and how they were able to do so rather than on the levels of food output or availability at the state or local level: in Sen's terms, on who commanded what rather than on what existed.

Impact of the Drought on the Local Economy

In analysing droughts, it is important to keep in mind that the problems which arise and the responses which people adopt vary according to specific conditions at different stages of each drought. For instance, during the period covered by this research (November 1986 to June 1988), local conditions and responses changed with each season:

Winter 1986–87:
> Shortfall in grain and capital due to poor monsoon rains in 1986;
> Reduced migrant labour opportunities due to reduced regional paddy, groundnut and sugar-cane yields;
> Near-normal local wheat and barley cultivation due to pump sets and adequate ground-water supply;
> Near-normal local labour opportunities but decreased wages due to overall drought conditions.

Summer 1987:
> Reduced local summer cultivation due to earlier shortfalls;
> Resumption of government relief works.

Monsoon 1987:
> Repeat planting of coarse grains and pulses;
> Greatly reduced cultivation of paddy;
> Substitute planting of sorghum on paddy land under irrigated conditions;
> Reduced local and migrant labour opportunities due to reduced cultivation;

Continuation of relief works until monsoon harvest;

Forced migration of shepherds with animals due to lack of fodder.

Winter 1987–88:

Reduced local wheat and barley cultivation due to shortfall of capital;

Reduced migrant labour opportunities due to low paddy, groundnut and sugar-cane yields and decreased brickfield and rice mill operations in the region;

Reduced local labour opportunities due to reduced cultivation and lack of capital;

Resumption of government relief works after six–week break;

Sinking of tube-wells and cultivation of cash crops by outside share-croppers.

Summer 1988:

Above-normal local sorghum cultivation due to tube-wells sunk by outside share-croppers;

Above-normal local labour opportunities due to above-normal cultivation;

Continuation of government relief works.

Monsoon 1988:

First rain on 12 June;

Above-normal rainfall.

In the following section, I discuss the accumulated effect of these changes on the major resources and occupations of the village. Later, I will discuss their effect on and the responses by different groups of households.

Cultivation

If there is a loss of 30,000 maunds of paddy in a single village then what will be the situation overall? No one is giving this any thought. No one is helping the cultivators.

Thakkar ex-Sarpanch

When monsoon rains do not arrive on time or are inadequate, rain-fed cultivation is directly affected. In response to reduced or untimely rainfall, farmers may adopt one or more of the following strategies: reducing or eliminating cultivation of one or more crops; adjusting the time of plantation to match the rainfall pattern (including repeat plantings if necessary); planting substitute crops (either drought-resistant or irrigated); or planting under irrigated conditions. Households generally adopt these strategies only as needed, depending on when and for how long the dry spell occurs, leaving their options open as early, mid-season and late droughts affect crops in different ways (Jodha 1981a).

In Maatisar, all monsoon crops are grown under rain-fed conditions. In years when the monsoon rains fail (either partially or completely), monsoon cultivation is directly affected. In 1987, when the drought was early and pervasive, Maatisar farmers resorted to all the strategies just listed. Many farmers planted at the regular time in late June and were forced to replant after the first rain in mid-July. Some deferred planting until after the first rain in mid-July, and only a few planted paddy, as paddy requires substantial flooding of the fields. In the second half of August, after it was too late to grow paddy even if the rains arrived, some farmers irrigated their paddy land to grow *juwar* (sorghum) as a fodder crop.[5] Despite these adjustments, all but three of the replanted and late-planted crops failed totally. Only 10 per cent of the cultivated area under the other three crops was harvested: a local variety of sorghum (*juwar*), red gram (*muth*) and *guar*, a variety of bean.

During the 1985–87 drought, the water table in Maatisar did not fall as low as it did in regions to the west.[6] By November 1987, some wells

[5] In 1986, the bulk of paddy land lay fallow as farmers kept hoping for adequate rainfall. Given the 1986 experience and the greater failure of the 1987 rains, farmers gave up on the prospect of planting paddy sooner. It should be noted that paddy has been grown in Maatisar only during the past two to three decades. Previously, a coarse, reddish grain, *bunti* or *kodara*, was cultivated on low-lying paddy land. When asked in August 1987 if he might consider planting *bunti* instead of paddy, one farmer explained that there is no late-variety of *bunti* whereas a late-variety of paddy can be planted as late as early September provided there is adequate rainfall.

[6] The situation in which rains do not arrive in time or in adequate quantity is technically only one form of drought, the *meteorological drought*. There are, in addition, two forms of *hydrological drought*: those conditions under which the surface water (e.g., rivers) dries up and those under which the ground-water or underground aquifers (except deep, geological aquifers) dry up. *Agricultural drought* is a shortage of water for crop growth, often defined as a deficit of soil moisture. To these three basic types of drought, Mortimer (1989) adds *ecological drought*, when the productivity of a natural ecosystem (e.g., common pastures) falls significantly. According to this classification.

(both dug-wells and tube-wells) needed to be deepened but none had gone absolutely dry. Given that winter crops are invariably irrigated and that ground-water was available, a few households purchased new pump sets in order to cultivate barley, wheat and lucerne as extensively as possible. Other households were, however, constrained by significant losses in the monsoon season not only of 1987, but also of 1986. They did not have enough capital to afford the irrigation and land-lease costs, and/or the input costs to plant winter crops as extensively as others.[7]

As no baseline data is available, we cannot compare crop yields in the drought year with crop yields in a normal year. However, we collected data for comparing the area planted with the area harvested for various crops in three seasons: winter 1986–87, summer 1987 and monsoon 1987. During the winter of 1986–87, the green gram and melon crops failed totally and 25 per cent of the area under lucerne failed. The other winter crops (barley, wheat and castor) did well. During summer 1987, 10 per cent of the area under sorghum failed. During the monsoon, as noted above, the majority of crops failed totally, and over 90 per cent of the area under the remaining crops (sorghum, *muth* and *guar*) failed.

These losses affected the various landholding groups in different ways. During winter 1986–87, the landless suffered significant losses of melons and green gram and a few large farm households suffered minor losses of lucerne. But in summer 1987, the surplus farm households suffered an over 50 per cent loss of sorghum. By monsoon 1987, the landless withdrew from cultivation altogether and all farm size groups suffered major losses: only the medium and large households managed to salvage some sorghum, *muth* and *guar*. Table 21 presents the land cultivated and lost by landholding group.

The uncertainty surrounding cultivation affected the local tenancy market as well. At Ekatrij in early May 1987, fewer share-cropping

---

the 1985–87 drought in Maatisar started as a metereological drought, led to the first form of hydrological drought, and resulted in both agricultural and ecological drought. However, it did not assume the characteristics of the second form of hydrological drought. Although the ground-water table fell by some 10 to 20 feet, the ground-water did not dry up.

[7] People reported selling trees in order to raise capital for the second planting during monsoon 1987 (all seed stock having been used for the first planting) and for cultivation of winter crops. Others took loans to purchase seeds and other inputs.

Table 21
Area Cultivated and Lost by Landholding [in Bighas]

Landholding	Winter 1986–87		Summer 1987		Monsoon 1987	
	Cultivated (Bighas)	Lost %	Cultivated (Bighas)	Lost %	Cultivated (Bighas)	Lost %
Landless	10	20	3	0	0	0
Small	2	0	0	0	6	100
Medium	108	0	29	0	203	91
Large	221	6	43	5	370	95
Surplus	77	0	9	55	135	100
Total:	**418**	**4**	**84**	**8**	**714**	**95**

contracts were negotiated than normal. For example, whereas some landless households had share-cropped land during the preceding two seasons, no landless households share-cropped land during the monsoon season in 1987. After the first planting of monsoon crops failed in early July, many tenants returned share-cropped land to the owners to avoid compounding their initial loss with predictable future losses.

But although the number of share-cropping contracts between Maatisar residents was lower than in normal years, the number of contracts with outsiders increased suddenly in late 1987. Some 15 groups of outsiders, together with their pump sets and bullocks, arrived in Maatisar from regions to the west where the water table had dropped sharply (the Nalsarovar area and Saurashtra). These outsiders negotiated land-lease contracts for winter 1987–88 and summer 1988: seasons in which all crops are grown on irrigated land. These contracts differed from normal land-lease contracts in three significant ways. First, the outside tenants were willing to share-crop normal unirrigated land and sink tube-wells on this land at their own expense. Second, they proposed to grow cash crops new to the region: cumin and groundnuts. And, third, three of the outside tenants negotiated fixed rent contracts (at Rs 300 per *bigha*), which are rare in Maatisar. In summer 1988, because they had sunk 15 new tube-wells on normal land where sorghum is grown, these outside share-croppers cultivated sorghum more extensively than local farmers do in normal years.[8]

---

[8] During summer 1988, because of the extensive sorghum cultivation, some labourers left relief works for the higher wages they could earn harvesting sorghum.

Given the state-wide shortage of fodder at the time, some of this bumper crop of sorghum was sold outside the village.[9]

Water

> In this area, it is not like Saurashtra. There is water, although not as much as last year. If one puts in the effort, applies oneself, anything is possible.
>
> Koli Patel Landowner

> If a household owns a well, they can, during a drought, borrow a pump set from a neighbouring farm at no charge. But if a household does not own a well, they cannot plant anything.
>
> Brahmin Landowner

The surface water resources in Maatisar, which had dried up in 1986, remained dry throughout 1987. However, most of the ground-water resources remained usable, although the water table dropped and the water turned brackish or saline in several wells.[10] By the end of 1987, due to the prolonged drought, the Koli Patel well had completely dried up, the Vankar well had only a few inches of brackish water left, and the water in the Vaghri and Brahmin wells had turned cloudy and begun to smell.

Fortunately, the *panchayat* tube-well, with its adjacent animal trough, and the SEWA well are both outfitted with pumps, located within the village proper and, as a matter of policy, freely open to all caste groups. Although, as I described in Part I, the *panchayat* well was operated only intermittently, SEWA deepened its well in mid-1987 and operated its pump several times each day. In addition, SEWA built an animal trough alongside the main road which was filled each day from the SEWA well, and hired an elderly widow to sit next to the trough and supply drinking water to passers-by.

[9] A Brahmin rice-mill owner made a significant profit as a middleman, buying sorghum at Rs 300–400 per 100 bundles from local farmers or outside tenants and selling it for Rs 700–800 per 100 bundles in Saurashtra.

[10] Refer to Part I for a list of the ground-water resources. During the 1987–88 drought, 10,402 out of the 18,275 inhabited villages in Gujarat were reported 'to have been affected by acute scarcity of drinking water' (Rao et al. 1988: 136).

All the private dug-wells and tube-wells are located in the fields which encircle the village proper. In normal years, when the pumps are on and water is flowing from these wells, all villagers are entitled to fill their pots and water their animals. Also, with the owner's permission, villagers are allowed to wash clothes or rinse fodder in the water channels. Fortunately, private pump-owners continued to permit such use throughout the drought.

As the ground-water level continued to drop, many of the dug-wells had to be deepened and many new tube-wells were sunk. Before the drought, wells averaged 50 feet in depth. By the end of 1987, many of them had been deepened to an average depth of 62 feet. During 1987, 20 households sank 26 new bore pipes, some to deepen old dug-wells and some as new tube-wells.[11] Two other households excavated new dug-wells. Of these 22 households, 10 had never owned a well or tube-well and nine owned no pump set. And six households bought new pump sets in the second half of 1987.

Labour Markets

If enough work is available, we can manage all else.

Elderly Widow

After the harvest of the winter crops in March–April 1987, the local labour market virtually collapsed. Other than a few men hired for ploughing before the rains were due, no labourers were hired for monsoon cultivation.[12] Even in normal years, very few labourers are hired for planting winter crops; fewer still, if any, were hired for planting barley and wheat in late 1987.

The migrant labour markets, both agricultural and non-agricultural, were also affected by the drought. After Diwali 1986, 42 households migrated to other rural locations for wage labour opportunities.[13] It was therefore reasonable to predict that additional households would be forced to migrate during the 1987–88 winter season. However, the demand for migrant labour dropped because of the drought, especially

[11] As noted above, 15 of these new bores were sunk at the expense of non-Maatisar tenants who had leased the land for the winter 1987–88 and summer 1988 seasons.

[12] In normal years, significant numbers of labourers are hired for paddy plantation and harvesting and a few are hired to work on other monsoon crops.

[13] Diwali is the Hindu festival of lights, which occurs in October or November.

for agricultural labour.[14] In normal years, the sugar-cane factories in Saurashtra recruit labour for five months. In late 1986, they recruited labour for only two months. In late 1987, these factories sent word that they had been forced to close because most of the sugar-cane crop had been sold as fodder, as per the directives of the state government. As an alternative, some households which normally migrate to Saurashtra migrated to Kheda District for paddy harvesting in late 1987, where they found employment for only four to six weeks.

The demand for migrant labour in brickfields and rice mills also dropped. The volume of rice milling declined sharply after the partial failure of the paddy crop in 1986 and fell further still after the even greater failure of the paddy crop in 1987. One of the indirect consequences of the drought was that the construction industry overall, including the manufacturing of bricks, slowed down.

During early November 1987, 32 households migrated for wage labour opportunities and another 24, which had migrated to rice mills or brickfields in 1986, were waiting for recruitment messages from their previous employers.[15] Among those who migrated in late 1987, half were landless, one-quarter were small landowners, and the remaining were medium and large landowners. Table 29 presents the migration pattern by landholding groups.

The state government operated relief works at a large number of sites in Gujarat during the summer and monsoon seasons of 1987. The relief works schemes in or near Maatisar remained active from mid-March through June, providing 64 days of employment. During this period, men and women from 140 households worked at the relief works, with half their wages being paid in cash and rest in kind. After the rains failed, these schemes remained active only intermittently, providing 35 days of employment from July through October. During this period, men and women from nearly 150 households reported for work and wages were paid in cash.

According to our estimates, the relief works provided as many days of employment during the summer and monsoon seasons to a significant number of labourers as the local labour market provides to the

[14] Assuming an output loss of nearly 50 per cent in Gujarat and Rajasthan during 1987–88, Rao et al. (1988) expected an income/employment loss in those two states of nearly 30 per cent.

[15] Government relief works were suspended indefinitely in mid-October, reportedly for the duration of the Diwali holidays (roughly two weeks), and were not resumed until early December, thereby adding to the anxiety of those waiting for migration opportunities.

average wage labourer during those seaons in normal years: about 100 days.[16] Labourers are normally paid Rs 8 per day for sorghum harvesting in the summer, Rs 10–15 per day for paddy planting and harvesting, and Rs 8–10 for planting and harvesting other monsoon crops. At the relief works, they were paid Rs 8–10 per day.[17] During the summer and monsoon season of 1987, therefore, labour households fared reasonably well not only in terms of the number of days employed but also in terms of wages. In addition, they received employment at relief works during the following winter, a season when the local labour market virtually collapses in normal years.

The drought affected attached labour in different ways. One attached labourer did not have his contract renewed, presumably because his employer did not want to spend extra money in a year of low yields. Another had his fixed annual payment lowered until his employers could determine the volume of crop yields. He was paid only Rs 600 of his Rs 1,100 annual wage and was promised another Rs 200 if his employer's winter crops did well. A third attached labourer decided not to renew his contract, opting for employment at the government relief works.

Livestock

> *God is punishing us. Men can go anywhere, but what about cattle?*
>
> Dairy Cooperative President

Residents of Maatisar characterised the 1985–87 drought as primarily a 'fodder drought' and claimed that fodder had never been in such short supply. Due to the accumulated effect of three years of low rainfall, the wild grasses that normally grow on the common pastures during the monsoon season virtually failed in 1987. Only a few green

[16] The relief works provided 64 days of employment in summer and 35 days of employment in monsoon 1987 to over 300 men and women. No data were available on how many labourers are employed in the local labour market during those seasons in normal years. However, we asked a large number of labourers how many days they could expect to be employed in different operations for each crop in a normal year. The average response was 15 days in summer and 83 days in monsoon for all operations and all crops. Refer to Part I for a breakdown of these averages by crop and operation.

[17] In 1986, the Government of Gujarat issued a notification raising the maximum that workers could be paid at relief works from Rs 7 to Rs 11 per day. The actual wages paid are tied to the volume and nature of the work completed. In Maatisar, labourers were generally able to earn between Rs 8 and Rs 10 per day.

shoots of one variety of shrub grass, *batha*, sprouted. Moreover, given the near-total failure of monsoon crops, only a limited amount of grass or weeds from the fields and virtually no crop waste or residues were available. Cattle were taken to graze the plots of failed monsoon crops but competition over rights to individual plots led to several conflicts.

Furthermore, village stocks of dry fodder were unusually low due to decreased crop yields in the previous two years. As a result, the price of fodder increased. Grass, which in normal years sells for Rs 6 per 100 bundles, began to sell for Rs 40. The price of sorghum, which in normal years is Rs 25 per 100 bundles, rose to Rs 70. And the price of lucerne seeds rose from Rs 400 per maund in June 1987 to Rs 1,000 per maund in October 1987. Moreover, the terms for purchasing fodder changed. Whereas in normal years women can purchase dry fodder on credit from kin, neighbours or co-members of the village dairy cooperative, during 1987 they were required to purchase dry fodder with direct cash payments (see Table 22 for the sources of fodder during the three seasons in a normal year and in 1987).

During the drought, the rules governing free collection of fodder and fuelwood also changed. When interviewed in early 1987, all groups of households claimed that fuelwood and fodder could be collected freely from all public and private sources, except, of course, fields of standing crops. Only one unspoken rule seemed to govern access: if a landowner also owned animals, permission should be taken to collect fodder from his/her fields. Otherwise, access to fuelwood and fodder was, seemingly, free and open. As one villager put it, 'If we deny people fuelwood or fodder, we have lost our humanity.'

But these are the norms in good years, not bad ones. In 1987, as fodder and fuelwood became increasingly scarce, the rules changed. Farmers no longer permitted other villagers to collect grass or weeds from their cultivated fields or to graze animals on their fallow fields. One widow was denied the right to collect weeds from the boundaries of her brother-in-law's fields. As the price of cow-dung cakes rose,[18] women began to quarrel over rights to collect dung from public spaces in the village. Shepherds grazed their animals at night on private fields. Many villagers lopped twigs and branches from both private and public trees at night. Although the Forest Department guards appeared lenient and turned a 'blind eye' on illegal cutting, private tree-owners tried to restrict unauthorised cutting.

[18] Because so many Bharwads migrated with their animals in 1987, the price of cow-dung cakes doubled from Rs 3 per 100 to Rs 6. The Bharwad migration will be discussed in more depth below.

Table 22
Fodder Sources: Normal Year and Drought Year (1987)

Season	Fodder type	Fodder source	Terms of Access	
			Normal year	Drought year
1. Winter	Green	Field waste	Free	Failed
		Grass/weeds	Free	Controlled
		Lucerne	Grown or purchased	Grown or purchased
	Dry	Paddy stalk	Grown or purchased	Failed
		Leaves	Free	Controlled
	Grazing	Common pastures	Free	Failed
		Harvested fields	Free	Failed
2. Summer	Green	Sorghum	Grown or purchased	Reduced yield
		Gokharu leaves	Free	Controlled
	Dry	Wheat straw	Grown or purchased	Reduced yield
	Grazing	Harvested fields	Free	Controlled
3. Monsoon	Green	Grass/weeds	Free	Failed
		Sorghum	Not grown	Substitute crop.
	Dry	Leaves	Free	Controlled
	Grazing	Common pastures	Free	Failed

But not all ways of dealing with the fodder shortage were illegal. During 1987, women went farther and spent longer collecting grass and weeds each successive season, averaging three hours per day during winter and four hours per day during monsoon. In normal years, grass and weeds are more readily available during the monsoon than in winter. Some households fed wild fodder to their animals: *bid*, a kind of water chestnut which in late 1987 could be purchased for Rs 9 per maund from a tribal caste in the Nalsarovar area; and *gokharu*, a medicinal herb which could be collected free of charge. Animals were forced to eat dry shoots of *batha*, whereas normally they eat only the green shoots.

Four major conflicts over grazing rights, some ending in physical violence, were reported. In two cases, the 'guilty' cows were beaten or stabbed so that veterinary doctors had to be called from the *taluka* headquarters to treat the animals and arbitrate the conflict. One of the cows eventually died. In another case, Bharwads from a neighbouring village grazed their animals at night on the irrigated sorghum fields of three Maatisar landowners but were not caught or fined. In the fourth case, a cow owned by landless household grazed on the cultivated field of a peasant household. The incident led to a fight between a son of the landless household and the owner of the field, during which the son of the landless labourer bit the ear of the landowner. The land-owner took the case to court, though eventually the case was settled out of court after the landless household paid Rs 1,700 in fees and penalties. The household raised this sum by selling the foodgrains they had earned from relief works. They were then forced to 'gift' the cow to a Bharwad, as they were no longer able to maintain it. In discussing the incident, the owner of the cow and father of the hot-tempered son, quoted a Gujarati saying, 'A bad cow has more ticks.'

Almost half the Bharwad shepherd households, all those owning more than 20 heads of cattle, migrated with most of their animals to a green belt in south Gujarat. Those who owned land left one or more family members behind to care for the farm. The landless shepherds migrated in whole family groups. Only one Bharwad with a large herd remained in the village, a surplus landowner who planted more than 10 acres of his land, primarily with sorghum for fodder, and sank a new tube-well during the monsoon season in 1987. This was the first time in living memory that the Bharwad shepherds of Maatisar were forced to migrate in search of fodder for their cattle, a phenomenon which I will explore in greater detail below.

Given the severe fodder shortage caused by the drought, livestock did not suffer as much as might have been expected due to various measures taken by those who owned animals. At least 30 animals died between November 1986 and October 1987,[19] but reportedly nearly as many animals die in normal years. Two Barot women sold their buffaloes.[20] One remarked that she had two goats, one pregnant and

[19] Our study sample of 59 households reported the sale of two buffaloes and the death of one cow, four buffaloes and one goat kid during the study year. The figure of 30 animal deaths was arrived at by extrapolating from that figure for the total number of households in the village. This figure does not include deaths, sales or other losses among the large number of animals taken to Umarpara by the Bharwads, as no reliable figures were available. Over 300 animals were taken to Umarpara, roughly one-third of the total village herd.

[20] At least two factors may have contributed to this sale of productive assets by Barots. First, many of the Barots did not undertake their annual round of patron villages during 1987, because the prevailing drought conditions reduced the demand for their services. Second, the Barots did not participate in relief works, because they have no tradition of engaging in manual work.

one newly-delivered, which would supply milk for her family. Two or three households which had share-cropped animals returned the animals to the owners. Interestingly, some households share-cropped out cattle to kin in more irrigated areas while other households share-cropped in cattle from kin in more saline areas.

No cases of outright abandonment of animals seem to have occurred. Residents of the village reported that people from other villages had abandoned animals on the road, after applying a ritual *tikka* (colored marking) on the forehead of the animal. One outsider abandoned a buffalo calf within Maatisar, which was adopted by a well-off Koli Patel household. Gujarat has a long tradition, associated primarily with the Jains, of running cattle camps for sick or dying animals. During drought years, existing camps are reorganised and new camps established to handle drought-affected animals. In 1987, hundreds of cattle camps were set up, largely by local religious trusts or political parties. However, no animals from Maatisar were handed over to a cattle camp.

Weaving

> *Do not bother to come sell shawls, as there is no one to buy them.*
>
> Message from Market Town

According to the ex-leader and oldest member of the Vankar weaving community, 1987 was the worst year for weavers that he could remember. To illustrate their predicament he recounted his own situation. During 1986, he had continuous work and orders. These orders kept him busy until May 1987. In early May, he received an order for two more *dhabla* shawls (at Rs 200 each), which kept him busy until late June. After that, he slowed down his weaving. In August, he received word from Vadhvan, a major market in Saurashtra for the traditional wool shawl, that Maatisar weavers should not come to sell shawls as the market had collapsed.[21] So, in mid-August, he made a round of the villages near Bavla where he sells some *dhabla*

---

[21] The traditional *dhabla* is sold primarily to Bharwads and Rabaris from Kutch and Saurashtra, two regions of Gujarat severely affected by drought for four consecutive years.

each year. He returned without selling or receiving an order for a single *dhabla*, something that had never happened to him before. In late August, for the first time in his life, he stopped weaving altogether.[22]

To make matters worse for the Vankar weavers, the demand for their wage labour also dropped. In normal years, most of the 26 Vankar households participate in paddy plantation and harvesting, both locally and in Kheda District. In 1986, only 15 to 20 Vankars were recruited to Kheda District for paddy plantation and harvesting. A few others migrated for the first time to Saurashtra to shell groundnuts (only seven to 10 days of work were available). By 1987, both the local and migrant labour markets were even further depressed.

Because of the decline in demand for both their weaving and their wage labour, the Vankar households concentrated on other activities. It should be noted that prior to the 1985–87 drought, due to the interventions of SEWA, 10 Vankar households had shifted from weaving traditional wool shawls to weaving cotton fabric and merino wool products. The SEWA-organised market for these goods was slightly reduced during the drought but the households were able to keep weaving. In addition, like the other Vankar households, these households participated in relief works.[23]

Fifteen Vankar households participate in and benefit from another occupation: the removal and flaying of dead animals. As I noted in Part I, each household is able to earn on the average about Rs 120 per year from flaying animals in normal years. During 1987, animal mortality was as high or higher than in normal years (local estimates vary). Therefore, this particular activity of the Vankars did not decline, and may have increased slightly, during the drought.[24]

[22] Seven Vankar households stopped weaving in mid-1987. After a bad drought some 15 years ago, two Vankar households migrated for the better part of the year for agricultural wage labour. One other Vankar household migrated permanently. Other than these isolated cases, Vankar households have never been known to stop weaving.

[23] Only one household did not send any members to the relief works: the one which first adopted non-traditional weaving and currently weaves cotton, merino wool and the occasional *dhabla*. The wife is president of the local weaving cooperative and the husband is the leader of the lower *vas* (neighbourhood) of Vankars.

[24] It should be noted that although there were probably more animals to handle and flay during the drought, the demand for hides and bones probably went down. In early 1988, two Chamars (tanners) from neighbouring villages were observed begging flour from Vankars in Maatisar.

Service and Artisan Castes

> *Those who depend on the village—barbers and priests—will die fifteen days before, we will die fifteen days later.*

> Group of Villagers

A few households in Maatisar live primarily on payments in kind, paid twice a year at the winter and monsoon harvests, for various caste services they provide: one barber, four genealogists and two priests. Also, seven potter households supply pots to specified clientele in the village. However, during the 1985–87 drought, the demand for these non-essential services and goods dropped as their patrons adjusted to the drought conditions. In 1987, these households were paid their semi-annual shares after the winter crop harvest in April but received no shares after the failed monsoon harvest. In normal years, these households also rely on charity or dole, such as vegetables and other small handouts given to the barber by shopkeepers and grain collected each day by the priests. These donations also dropped in 1987. For example, one priest reported that he collected 50 grams of grain each day from 70 households during 1986. Assuming that 50 per cent of the grain he collected was in the form of flour and rest in whole grains, his earnings from grain donations totalled about Rs 4,000. In 1987, only 25 to 30 households donated 50 grams of grain each day, so that his earnings from grain donations dropped to about Rs 1,700.[25]

The Barot genealogists also reported a reduced demand for their services during the drought, so much so that some decided not to undertake their annual round of patron villages. Those that did, claim they were paid in cash, not kind, which to them represented a drop in real earnings.[26] The potter households reported a drop in demand for pots, and the two potter households which still produce pots faced a shortage and subsequent rise in price of fuel and raw materials.

---

[25] These calculations are based on the assumption that, during both 1986 and 1987, flour averaged Rs 4 per kg and whole grains averaged Rs 2.50 per kg.

[26] The drought may have triggered a further decline in an already shrinking occupation: sons from three (out of a total of five) Barot households have abandoned their hereditary occupation and migrated permanently to Ahmedabad city.

Trade

Conventional wisdom suggests that traders, especially those engaged in moneylending, tend to benefit from the increased prices (due to presumed shortages), moneylending and distress sales generally associated with droughts. Our findings suggest, however, that the trader–moneylenders may not have enjoyed these benefits during the 1985–87 drought in Maatisar.

The traders reported a decreased volume in trade, as low in some cases as 25 per cent of normal volume. Moreover, except for fodder and fodder seeds, prices did not rise sharply. Table 23 compares retail prices in October 1986 and October 1987. The data also suggests

Table 23
Comparative Retail Prices: In October 1986 and October 1987

Commodity	Unit	Price in Rupees		Change %
		October 1986	October 1987	
1. Cereals				
Wheat	20 kg	50	55	+10
Paddy	20 kg	50	50–60	+10
Rice	20 kg	65	80–100	+38
Sorghum	20 kg	42	45	+7
Pearl millet	20 kg	41	52	+27
Barley	20 kg	30	52	+73
2. Lentils				
Chickpea—Channa	20 kg	105	120	+14
Pigeonpea—Tuar	20 kg	140	220	+57
Green Gram—Mugh	20 kg	100	120	+20
3. Oils				
Groundnut oil	1 kg	20	29	+45
Groundnut pods	20 kg	105	135	+29
Dalda	1 kg	20	28	+40
Ghee	1 kg	50	80	+60
4. Vegetables				
Potato	1 kg	4	5.50	+38
Onion	1 kg	3	6	+100
Bean—Guar	1 kg	1.5	4	+67
5. Others				
Castor seeds	20 kg	122	150	+23
Mustard	20 kg	100	200	+100
Cotton	20 kg	100	140	+40

Table 23 (Continued)

Commodity	Unit	Price in Rupees		Change %
		October 1986	October 1987	
Sugar	20 kg	130	150	+15
Tea	1 kg	40	45	+13
Tobacco	1 kg	6.5	14	+115
6. Fuel				
Kerosene	1 litre	2.25	2.25	0
Firewood	20 kg	12	10	−20
Cow-dung cakes	100 cakes	3	9–10	+216
7. Seeds				
Wheat	1 kg	3.25	3.25	0
Paddy	1 kg	3.50	3.50	0
Sorghum	1 kg	2.50	3	+20
Pearl millet	1 kg	n.a.	25	n.a.
Barley	1 kg	1.75	2.50	+43
Pigeon pea	1 kg	n.a.	10	n.a.
Green gram	1 kg	6	10	+67
Muth	1 kg	6	10	+67
Bean—*Guar*	1 kg	5	8	+60
Lucerne	1 kg	20	50	+150
Castor	1 kg	6	6.50	+8
8. Fodder/feed				
Millet straw	100 bundles	100	200	+100
Sorghum-Dry	100 bundles	125	300	+140
Groundnut cake	20 kg	140	180	+29
9. Fertilisers				
Urea	1 bag	122	122	0
Dap	1 bag	183	187	+2

that the volume of moneylending did not increase. In addition, only half of the loans reported during the drought were taken from the known moneylenders in the village. Finally, there were few cases of distress sale, or even mortgaging, of productive assets. All these factors will be discussed in greater detail below.

Official Responses to the Drought

Relief Works

Ever since the Famine Codes were promulgated by the British Administration towards the end of the nineteenth century, India's famine relief system, particularly the scarcity relief works, have payed 'an undeniable and crucial role in averting large-scale starvation' (Dreze 1988: 73–74).[27] In the non-irrigated, semi-arid parts of India like the region around Maatisar village, where the frequency of droughts appears to be increasing, the need persists for an extensive and responsive relief system. Relief works, offered by the Gujarat state government, played an undeniable role in averting increased impoverishment, if not starvation, of large numbers of people in Maatisar during the 1987 drought.

Relief works schemes were operative during all three years of the 1985–87 drought. During 1987 alone, they provided well over 100 days of employment to over 300 people:

Season	Employment Days	Number Employed	
		Individuals	Households
Summer	65	329	140
Monsoon	35	320	142
Winter	NA	332	152

As under most drought conditions, landless labourers and artisan castes participated actively in the relief works. As under other severe drought conditions, large numbers of peasant households, from all landholding categories, also joined the relief works. In fact, a larger percentage of landed than landless households participated. However, labour households were engaged in significantly more days of relief works on the average than cultivator households. A few shepherds, who normally do not engage in wage labour, joined the relief works at the very end of the year. Only the two higher caste groups, the Brahmins and the Thakkars, and two small caste groups, Rawal and Barot, did not (see Table 25 for the participation rates and the average number of days employed by different household groups).

While highlighting the effective role of relief works, two weaknesses of the system should be noted. The first is that the coverage of relief works is seldom as extensive as the scarcity conditions they are intended to address. In early August 1987, there were 76 active relief works schemes in Ahmedabad District, employing about 30,500 people: not nearly enough employment to meet the demand (Government of

[27] The public works schemes, designed to provide mass employment for a subsistence wage during periods of scarcity, are referred to variously as famine relief, scarcity relief, or simply, as here, relief works.

Gujarat 1987b). Even in the Maatisar area, where relief works schemes were active for the major part of the 1987–88 drought period, conflicts between workers from different villages over the allotment of work were common.

The second weakness is the almost predictable corruption in the actual operation of the schemes. In Maatisar, the *sarpanch* and his cronies (in collaboration with government clerks assigned to the relief works) charged illegal fees in distributing implements to be used (shovels and baskets), allotted the contract to supply drinking water at the relief works sites to a crony, and made false entries in the relief works registers. In mid-1987, they recorded a week of work at a site where no worker was actually given work. By collecting the wage payments against this false entry, each collaborator was able to 'earn' at least Rs 1,000. A delegation of villagers, with legal advice from SEWA, filed and won a corruption case at the *taluka* headquarters.

The local *sarpanch* used his illegal 'earnings' to expand and renovate his ration shop, as mentioned in Part I, and to refinance in his own name a significant amount of land mortgaged by his caste neighbours to the Bharwads. Interestingly, the *sarpanch* was able to maximise his gain by taking advantage of people who had suffered losses in the drought: the Bharwad shepherds had suffered significant production and asset losses, in that half of their cattle had been taken to south Gujarat and many of their cattle had taken ill or died. The long-term impact of such drought-induced gains and losses needs to be monitored and analysed.

Much has been written about such abuses in the relief system. In Maatisar, the positive role of relief works in providing social security to large numbers of people (the total wage bill during the summer and monsoon seasons alone was just under three lakh rupees)[28] outweighed the abuses or leakages in the system (the amount embezzled in the false entry case was, allegedly, between Rs 15,000 and Rs 20,000). This is not to argue that the abuses should be ignored but to acknowledge the crucial role of relief works in averting hunger and starvation.

Other Government Relief Measures

In addition to scarcity relief works, the Gujarat Scarcity Manual (1987

---

[28] This estimate of the wage bill is based on the following calculation: 99 days of employment @ Rs 9 per day × an average of 325 workers per day = Rs 289,575.

edition) clearly describes an integrated drought relief programme, including gratuitous relief in the form of free food or cash for persons who cannot participate in relief works; cattle camps; low-interest credit in the form of cooperative credit society loans and *taccavi* emergency loans; provision of seeds; supply of drinking water; and the public distribution system, functioning through a network of fair price or ration shops. On paper, these measures form a 'coherent whole designed to face the crisis in a comprehensive and decided manner' (Dreze 1988: 74). However, in practice, as Dreze (*ibid.*) also reports, these measures are often not uniformly or comprehensively offered.

Official data for Dholka *taluka* as a whole and our data from Maatisar village reflect a less than uniform or adequate coverage of these measures. During 1987 in Maatisar, according to official records, 12 people (two Vankars, 10 Koli Patels) received a cash dole of Rs 4 per day for an average of 243 days.[29] Although some *taccavi* loans for purchasing seeds were reported in the *taluka* as a whole, no *taccavi* or other loans were offered in Maatisar.[30] Cattle camps were opened and fodder was sold by the government in some parts of the *taluka*.[31] However, no cattle camps were opened near Maatisar and only SEWA, not the government, offered fodder for sale. Between October 1987 and August 1988, the Dholka Taluka Panchayat Office deployed eight tankers filled with drinking water to 38 villages. Maatisar did not face a drinking water crisis but at least five nearby villages did and received drinking water supplies. Although each village was supposed to receive water once a day, roughly one day in five they did not, due to technical problems with the tankers or to inadequate water supply where the tankers were filled.

Finally, during the 1987 summer season, when all relief works

[29] Among the 31 sub-sample households, four households were unable to participate in the relief works due to age or disability. These households received no gratuitous relief or other official assistance and were forced to live off the charity of their kin or, at least in one case, from begging.

[30] During 1986–87, in Dholka *taluka* as a whole, Rs 2,010,618 were provided as *taccavi* loans for the purchase of seeds. During 1987–88, no loans were given (Dholka Taiuka Panchayat Office). As another relief measure, during 1986–87 in the *taluka* as a whole, Rs 27,000 worth of land revenue tax payments were written off and another Rs 1,130,000 worth of revenue tax payments were deferred (Dholka Taluka Panchayat Office).

[31] During May and June 1987, the Dholka Taluka Panchayat Office sold 72 truckloads of dry grass and 88 truckloads of green grass at different places in the *taluka* (Dholka Taluka Panchayat Office).

payments were made in kind, the public distribution system was taxed beyond its limits. By the monsoon season, the state government had passed a ruling that all relief works payments be made fully in cash rather than half in kind and half in cash, as was done earlier. It is not clear whether this decision was made because government reserve stocks of grain were quickly being depleted, or because the public distribution system was not able to transport, store and distribute the vast amounts of food involved, or due to both these factors. For whatever reason, stocks at the local ration shop remained low during the second half of 1987, a period of peak demand for food grains.

SEWA

Throughout the drought period, SEWA staff played an informal but significant advocacy and monitoring role: lobbying for relief measures with local government officials; covening a consortium of non-government organisations (NGOs) who lobbied at the state level; and generally monitoring both the drought conditions and the official response. In addition to this indirect role, SEWA took three direct actions to help ease the local drought situation: arranging the transport and sale of fodder from south Gujarat to several villages in our study area; constructing a cattle trough (*avedo*) along the main road near Maatisar which was filled daily from the SEWA well; and providing subsidised seeds, fertiliser and fuel to grow lucerne during winter 1987–88.

After the state government put out a directive in mid-1987 that all sugar-cane should be cut green as fodder, SEWA purchased and transported four truckloads (nine tons each) of green sugar-cane from south Gujarat to Maatisar and nearby villages. The staff of the SEWA-managed local dairy cooperative handled the distribution and sale of the sugar-cane. Members of the local dairy cooperative were entitled to purchase the cane at a slightly lower rate than non-members. SEWA established norms that permitted each household to purchase a certain amount of sugar-cane for each animal owned up to a maximum amount. On at least one occasion the SEWA staff who went to purchase the sugar-cane returned empty-handed from south Gujarat because trucks (not sugar-cane) were not available. However, SEWA was able to maintain a reasonably steady supply of cane from August through October 1987 and an intermittent supply until the monsoon rains in 1988. In addition, SEWA arranged to sell 25 bags (65 kg each) of concentrated cattle feed from the District Cooperative Dairy through the dairy cooperative in the village.

Although none of the village wells dried up completely, the water in many of the wells became discolored or slightly salty in taste. To provide a steady source of good water to all caste communities in the village, SEWA deepened its well which is equipped with a pump. To supply water to local and migrating animals, SEWA constructed a cattle trough on the main road which it filled each day from its well.[32] To supply drinking water to passers-by, an elderly widow was hired to draw water from the SEWA well and sit near the animal trough. On the main road from Viramgam to Bavla (a distance of over 30 miles), the SEWA cattle trough was the only free, public source of water. As one villager reported, 'In all of the Nal Kantha area, SEWA's name has become famous because of the water trough.'

SEWA also took steps to promote extensive cultivation of lucerne during the 1987–88 winter season by providing subsidised inputs. Its staff drew up a list of beneficiary households, including those who did not own cattle but expressed interest in growing lucerne for sale. The plan called for partial subsidy (50 per cent) of fertiliser, seeds and fuel costs to 100 small farm or tenant households to cultivate lucerne on 500 *bighas* (285 acres).[33] The plan was implemented in late 1987.

Household Responses to the Drought

Households adopt various coping strategies in response to drought conditions. A growing body of literature on these coping mechanisms, both from Africa and Asia, focuses on the differences between seasonal and crisis coping strategies, the sequence and timing of these strategies, and the objectives (and constraints) which influence the choice of strategies. In the Indian context, in a well-known debate with Morris (1974, 1975), Jodha asserts that the primary concern of rural families when faced with drought conditions is the protection of productive

[32] Maatisar is on a regular migration route from Kutch and Saurashtra to Kheda District.

[33] The subsidy per household was Rs 450 for an estimated total cost of Rs 900:

Fuel: 7 waterings × 18 litres × Rs 2.20 per litre = Rs 277
Seeds: 5 *maunds* @ Rs 60 per *maund*
Fertiliser: 1 bag urea @ Rs 122
1 bag DAP @Rs 187

assets to guarantee future streams of income, not, as Morris claimed, the protection of a certain standard of consumption.

The pattern of response to drought in Maatisar confirms Jodha's assertion: namely, that households will attempt to preserve their holdings of key productive assets for as long as they can. In order to do so, they take the following broad sequence of measures. Households respond initially by tightening their belts and consuming less food, drawing upon inventories which they have stored for contingencies as needed. If necessary, they dispose of non-productive assets such as utensils, jewellery or other household items. When no other options remain open, they dispose of key productive assets, preferring mortgage to outright sale. Under extreme shortage conditions, some households are forced to take drastic measures, such as migrating in search of food or abandoning a spouse or children. As noted by Jodha (1975: 1613), the 'sale or mortgage of assets or recourse to out-migration becomes operative at a late stage when other devices have by and large already been exhausted and should be regarded as true indicators of distress in a given scarcity period.'

What follows is an analysis of actual responses to the 1987 drought in Maatisar by various household groups. Not all households adopted the same responses in the same sequence, and some responses were adopted simultaneously rather than sequentially. For the purposes of this analysis, however, I present these responses in a rough order of preference and sequencing.

1. Adapting or Diversifying Activities

In normal years, as I discussed in Part II, most households modify or adapt regular activities to address seasonal fluctuations. In addition, most households resort to a variety of supplemental activities to help smooth out seasonal peaks and troughs, including collection of cleared fodder or fuel material; collection of rough fodder from fields; discriminating grazing and feeding; and collecting and converting every piece of dung (Jodha 1975). During 1987 in Maatisar, households attempted to diversify and modify their activities but found that it was increasingly difficult to do so as the severe shortfall in monsoon rains resulted in not only reduced local production but also increased competition for free goods.

The ways in which different occupation groups diversified their regular activities in response to the drought can be summarised as follows:

Cultivators:
— repeat plantation of monsoon crops
— substitute plantation of sorghum for paddy
— investment in new or improved ground-water resources:
    six new pump sets
    26 new bore pipes
— intensified or diversified plantation of winter crops, particularly lucerne for fodder

Shepherds:
— selective feeding and grazing between
    dry versus lactating animals
    poor versus good quality animals
— increased stall-feeding using purchased fodder
— migration with selected animals

Labourers:
— participation in government relief works
— search for alternative migration opportunities

Weavers:
— search for alternative markets
— interim closure of weaving operations
— participation in relief works
— alternative production: e.g., rope-making
— search for alternative migrant labour opportunities

Potters:
— participation in relief works
— interim closure of pottery production

Service castes:
— participation in relief works
— search for migrant labour opportunities

2. Reducing or Modifying Consumption

In his review of the empirical literature on recent droughts in India, Dreze (1988a: 79) summarises three repeatedly-observed patterns in consumption behaviour during drought conditions. First, that 'reducing food intake (*including* cereal consumption) seems to be an integral part of typical "responses to drought" in India not only on the part of landless labourers and poor artisans but *also* on the part of cultivators over a very wide range of landholding size groups.' Second, that during at least two droughts when landless labourers were able to maximise the employment offered by government relief works, in Gujarat during 1974–75 and in Maharashtra during 1972–73, 'the proportion of households who experienced a reduction in cereal intake during the drought was significantly *lower* for labourers and artisans than for cultivators in any landholding size class.' And, third, that 'frugality in consumption set in largely *before* the process of asset depletion, mortgaging and migration.'[34]

Our data from Maatisar reflect, with some variation or specificity, each of these patterns:

Changes in Dietary Contents
 — shift to coarse grains
 — eating *dhal* (lentils) cooked with pieces of leftover *rotla* (unleavened bread)
 — eating only *rotla* with a garlic–chilli paste
 — eating only *kitchari* (rice and salt gruel)
 — turning to 'famine' or 'indicator' foods:
    kandh (a bitter root) boiled and mixed into *rotla* dough[35]
    bid (a wild water-chestnut) initially fed to animals and eventually eaten by humans
    jitela (a type of lotus flower)
Reduction of Total Intake
 — reduced consumption of 'luxury' or 'protective' foods, such as milk, oil, tea, sugar and vegetables[36]
 — eating leftovers for breakfast
 — having only tea for breakfast
 — eating only one meal, rather than two or three, per day

In Maatisar, most landholding and occupational groups reduced their consumption of foodgrains, milk and vegetables between early and mid-1987. Because the production and availability of milk and vegetables are highly seasonal, the analysis of the data focuses on foodgrain consumption. Table 24 depicts the pattern of foodgrain consumption by season and by household groups.

---

[34] Dreze (1988a) reviews the data from several empirical studies, including Jodha's study of the 1963–64 drought in Rajasthan; the Desai et al. study of the 1974–75 drought in Gujarat; Chowdhury and Bapat's study of the 1969–70 droughts in Gujarat and Rajasthan; and the Caldwell et al. study of the 1983 drought in Karnataka.

[35] Rangaswami (1985) reports that tribals in Gujarat eat *kandh* to kill the appetite.

[36] Meat and fruit are not regular items on the diet even in normal years.

Table 24
Foodgrain Consumption (Grams of Cereals Per Capita) by Season and Household Groups

Household groups	Number	Winter consumption baseline	Summer Consumption	Summer % Change	Monsoon Consumption	Monsoon % Change
1. Landholding						
Landless	11	594	470	−21	386	−35
Small	4	355	449	+26	469	+32
Medium	6	624	421	−33	423	−32
Large	8	835	528	−37	523	−37
Surplus	1	567	645	+14	490	−14
2. Occupation						
Cultivation	13	710	515	−27	491	−31
Livestock	2	778	476	−39	252	−68
Labour	4	417	396	−5	361	−13
Weaving	3	573	476	−17	409	−29
Trade	2	596	442	−26	464	−22
Others	7	646	436	−33	458	−29
All households:	**31**	**641**	**471**	**−27**	**437**	**−32**

Our data on household consumption was gathered from 31 households in six rounds (two rounds for each of the three seasons in 1987). The survey was designed to compare interhousehold and interseasonal levels of consumption across the study year, not to collect data on the intrahousehold distribution of available food. In order to confirm whether the pattern of consumption can be attributed to the drought conditions prevailing in 1987, the data should be compared with consumption data for the same region in normal years. To date, no such comparable data set has been identified.[37]

In terms of landholding groups, the data show that both the landless households and larger farm households reduced consumption of foodgrains between the winter and monsoon seasons in 1987: the landless by 35 per cent and the large farm households by 37 per cent. Interestingly, the small farm households increased their consumption of foodgrains, presumably because their consumption in winter (taken as a baseline) was so low and their participation in relief works (which began in summer) was so high. In terms of the main occupational groups, those engaged primarily in animal husbandry (Bharwad shepherds) reduced their consumption significantly, by nearly 70 per cent. Two factors which may have contributed to this marked reduction were that many of the Bharwads had migrated with a large percentage of the community herd of animals in August 1987 and that none of the Bharwads joined the relief works until December 1987. Cultivators and weavers each reduced their consumption of foodgrains by about 30 per cent. Interestingly, labourers reduced their consumption of foodgrains the least (by 13 per cent).

3. Reducing Commitments

If we can't eat, how can we celeberate?

Group of Villagers

[37] A National Institute of Nutrition survey conducted from October to December 1987 in several states of India indicates that in two districts of Gujarat (Kutch and Banaskantha) there was a slight rise in cereal and calories consumption relative to non-drought years: to a daily average of 494 grams of cereals and over 2,200 calories (National Institute of Nutrition 1988). The study concluded that this 'apparently better' situation seemed to reflect the efficient management strategy adopted: foodgrain distribution system, provision of relief works and implementation of feeding and other welfare programmes. In both districts studied, supplemental feeding programmes, in addition to relief works, were undertaken. The study also reports that not a single household in Gujarat subsisted on what is called a 'starvation diet' (less than 500 Kcal per caput per day).

In their study of the 1980–83 drought in Karnataka, Caldwell et al. report that 'most families still regard their ability to weather droughts as being based on savage cutbacks to their living standards, dominated by reducing food to the minimum. The next largest saving, which filled many with deep guilt, was that on festivals, clothing, and entertainment and visiting' (1986a: 688). Similarly, in Maatisar, religious ceremonies or festivals were celebrated with less expenditure and less fervour during 1987.

In normal years, Diwali is the main festival, when new clothes are purchased and most houses are white-washed. For Diwali in 1987, however, few households spent money on new clothes, special foods or white-washing homes. One labourer reported that he had been saving for two years to buy a new shirt at Diwali but, because of the drought, could not afford to buy one.

In Karnataka, the drought had a 'dramatic impact on marriages' so much so that 'few marriages took place' (Caldwell et al. 1986a: 683). In Maatisar, the drought had a somewhat different effect on marriages. Immediately after the monsoon rains failed in 1987, villagers predicted that marriages would be postponed as it would be difficult to raise the standard bride-price or dowry. In mid-August, for example, a Vaghri girl's engagement was postponed by the groom's family which was expected to pay a bride-price of Rs 8,000. The bride's father predicted that the marriage would be postponed until after the 1988 monsoon. As it turned out, the girl was married in December 1987 after the groom's family managed to raise the Rs 8,000.

Interestingly, in response to caste community pressure, the inter-village caste councils of at least two caste groups met during the year to lower the standard bride-price and marriage costs to reflect the prevailing drought conditions. The Vankar caste council was the first to make such a decision. In early 1988, the Koli Patel intervillage council, covering some 25 to 30 villages, met and decided to reduce the standard bride-price for the Koli Patel community. Previously, the groom's family was expected to pay Rs 5,000–6,000 in bride-price and the bride's family was expected to spend three-quarters of that amount on wedding expenses. The council ruled that for the duration of the drought the bride-price should not exceed Rs 1,500 and expenses by the bride's family be reduced proportionately.[38] The Koli Patel caste

---

[38] The council adopted the following standards:

council also ruled that households which did not follow these norms would be socially boycotted until a fine of Rs 6,000 was paid. Soon after these decisions were taken, the *sarpanch* in a neighbouring village spent more than these amounts on a wedding and was, as the ruling demanded, socially boycotted until he paid the fine of Rs 6,000.

What is of particular interest is that by reducing the costs of marriages, the actual number of marriages in the village increased dramatically. Over 25 marriages took place in the first half of 1988.

4. Participating in Relief Works

In their study of the 1974–75 drought in neighbouring Dhanduka *taluka*, Desai et al. (1979) reported that participation in relief works is strongly and inversely correlated with landholding size.[39] By contrast, during 1987 in Maatisar, over half of the households in the medium, large and surplus land strata participated whereas less than half of the landless households did. The highest participation rate was among small farm households, nearly 70 per cent of which participated in relief works. In terms of occupational groups, over 85 per cent of Vankar weaver households and over half the cultivator and labour households participated. Table 25 presents the distribution of relief works participants at different times in the year, and average participation rates by landholding, occupation and caste groups.

During the 1985–87 drought in Maatisar, in contrast to what was observed during the 1974–75 drought in Dhanduka *taluka*, participation in relief works was strongly and inversely correlated with caste ranking, not with landholding. The lowest caste, Bhangis, had the

---

Bride-price	—	Rs 1,500 only
Groom's party	—	35 people only
Drummer	—	Rs 7 only
Priest	—	Rs 31 only

Previously, the groom's side was expected to spend a minimum of Rs 8,000 in bride-price and the bride's side a minimum of Rs 6,000 in marriage expenses. It should be noted that these new standards reduced not just the marriage costs of the Koli Patels but also the income of two service caste groups, the Bhangi or Rawal drummers and the Gosai priests.

[39] Dhanduka *taluka*, also in Ahmedabad District, lies to the south and west of Dholka *taluka* (see map of Ahmedabad District). Because most cultivators experienced crop losses yet chose not to join in relief works, Desai et al. (1979) observed an impressive 'reversal' of the normal income scale during that drought year.

Table 25
Relief Works Participation by Season and Household Groups

Household groups	Total No. of HHs	July 1987	October 1987	January 1988	Average No	Average Rate
1. Landholding						
Landless	118	47	49	51	49	42
Small	34	22	24	24	23	68
Medium	62	31	33	35	33	53
Large	61	32	34	35	34	56
Surplus	10	5	6	7	6	60
2. Occupation						
Cultivation	130	71	78	82	77	59
Livestock	11	0	0	3	1	1
Labour	68	37	39	38	38	56
Weaving	22	18	19	19	19	86
Trade	10	1	1	1	1	10
Others	44	10	9	12	10	23
3. Caste						
Koli Patel	142	78	86	91	85	60
Vaghri	51	30	31	31	31	61
Vankar	28	19	20	20	20	71
Bharwad	19	0	0	4	1	21
Prajapati	7	5	4	5	4	57
Brahmin	6	0	0	0	0	0
Thakkar	6	0	0	0	0	0
Bhangi	6	5	5	5	5	83
Barot	5	0	0	0	0	0
Rawal	4	0	0	0	0	0
Others	11	0	0	0	0	0
All households:	**285**	**137**	**146**	**152**	**145**	**51**

highest participation rate (over 80 per cent), whereas no household
from the two highest castes, Brahmins and Thakkars, participated.
The caste aspect of this finding reflects the caste-occupation profile of
the village in normal years with one exception: a few Bharwads joined
the relief works in late January 1988. Normally, Brahmins, Thakkars
and Bharwads never engage in wage labour, whereas landless and
land-poor households from all other major caste groups do. What
changed during the drought was that a large number of land-rich
households from these other major castes, not just landless and land-
poor households, joined the relief works.

The pattern of participation in relief works in Maatisar illustrates an important difference between *prolonged* droughts, when droughts recur for several years in succession, and *single-year* droughts, when a single year of drought follows several normal years. As Dreze observed in his study of the Maharashtra drought of 1970–73, 'when droughts recur for several years in succession, cultivators gradually lose their resilience and start flocking to the relief works in increasing numbers' (1988: 85). This difference could help explain why in the 1974–75 drought, which followed a good year, participation in relief works in a neighbouring *taluka* was positively and inversely correlated with landholding, whereas in the 1987–88 drought in Maatisar, which followed two bad years, participation was higher among landed than landless households.

In terms of gender, it is important to note that more women than men participated in relief works, despite the fact that there are fewer women than men in participating households. Table 26 presents the distribution of relief works participants by gender and by landholding, occupation and caste. Among the various landholding groups, the male rate of participation was higher only in the small farm group. Among occupational groups, the female rate of participation was higher throughout. And, among the various caste groups, the male rate was higher only among the Vaghris, Prajapatis and Bhangis. The female participation rate, relative to the male rate, was particularly high among the Vankar weavers.

Finally, the effective presence of relief works should not be allowed to obscure the specific vulnerability of landless labourers. If relief works had not been available landless labourers in Maatisar would have suffered severely. The study data indicate that labour households averaged 119 days of employment per adult worker (10 years or older) during all of 1987: 55 days in relief works, 44 days as migrant workers, and only 20 days on the local labour market. Table 27 presents the number of person days adult workers were hired in the migrant labour market, local labour market, and relief works during 1987.

5. Borrowing

A high demand for credit, particularly for consumption loans, is assumed in many discussions of drought and famine (Longhurst 1986; Corbett 1988). Our data from Maatisar indicate, however, that while the number of loan transactions was high during the drought, the total

Table 26
Relief Works Participation by Gender and Household Groups

Household groups	Adult men			Adult women		
	Baseline	Participation No.	%	Baseline	Participation No.	%
1. Landholding						
Landless	210	54	26	202	58	29
Small	71	25	35	63	21	33
Medium	146	31	21	128	34	27
Large	171	39	23	159	46	29
Surplus	39	8	21	34	8	24
2. Occupation						
Cultivation	314	82	26	288	90	31
Livestock	39	0	0	31	0	0
Labour	131	41	31	115	36	31
Weaving	51	24	47	54	29	54
Trade	21	0	0	20	1	5
Others	81	10	12	78	11	14
3. Caste						
Koli Patel	308	83	27	287	94	33
Vaghri	103	37	36	104	32	31
Vankar	58	25	43	62	30	48
Bharwad	52	0	0	43	0	0
Prajapati	20	6	30	15	4	27
Brahmin	22	0	0	17	0	0
Thakkar	19	0	0	13	0	0
Bhangi	9	6	67	12	7	58
Rawal	9	0	0	3	0	0
Others	30	0	0	23	0	0
All households:	637	157	25	586	167	28

volume of moneylending was probably not as high as in normal years.[40] The demand for production loans was significant. About 90 loans, averaging Rs 650 each and totalling Rs 57,420, were taken during the study year.[41] Of these, nearly three-quarters of the loans taken and just

[40] Our data suggest that the total volume of moneylending was lower than in normal years for both supply and demand reasons: earnings from relief works lowered the demand for consumption loans and, because of the perceived risk of lending during shortages, moneylenders reduced their lending.

[41] Our data on moneylending are from two sources: the economic survey of sample households (59) and a focused survey of credit operations, which involved intensive interviewing of multiple informants. The figures in Table 28 were derived from extrapolating the consolidated figures (from both surveys) for the total number of households (285).

Number of Days Wage Laborers Received Work During 1987

Household groups	Total		Person days				Av. days/worker	
	HHs*	Workers**	Relief	Local	Migrant	Total	Relief	Total
1. Landholding								
Landless	22	74	2073	326	1859	4258	28	58
Small	6	28	1570	280	0	1850	56	66
Medium	17	66	1131	524	24	1679	17	25
Large	12	71	1015	350	46	1411	14	20
Surplus	2	20	495	0	0	495	25	25
Total:	**59**	**259**	**6284**	**1480**	**1929**	**9693**	**24**	**37**
2. Occupation								
Cultivation	26	124	2775	503	200	3478	22	28
Livestock	3	17	60	0	0	60	4	4
Labour	10	35	1918	716	1546	4180	55	119
Weaving	5	25	1175	105	20	1300	47	52
Trade	3	17	35	0	0	35	2	2
Others	12	41	321	156	163	640	8	16
Total:	**59**	**259**	**6284**	**1480**	**1929**	**9693**	**24**	**37**
3. Caste								
Koli Patel	30	126	3359	1095	1069	5523	27	44
Vaghri	8	36	1280	220	840	2340	36	65
Vankar	8	34	1460	165	20	1645	43	48
Bharwad	4	19	60	0	0	60	3	3
Prajapati	1	6	0	0	0	0	0	0
Brahmin	1	7	0	0	0	0	0	0
Thakkar	2	14	0	0	0	0	0	0
Barot	2	6	55	0	0	55	9	9
Rawal	1	3	0	0	0	0	0	0
Others	2	8	70	0	0	70	9	9
Total:	**59**	**259**	**6284**	**1480**	**1929**	**9693**	**24**	**37**

Source: Agro–economic survey of 59 households.

* Households = households which sold wage labour.

** Worker = all men and women, 10 years of age or above.

under 40 per cent of the amount borrowed were from relatives or caste neighbours, including some from in-laws outside the village.[42] Only 10 loans each, totalling about 20 per cent of the total amount borrowed, were from the primary moneylenders of the village (traders and landlords). Fifteen were from unidentified 'other' sources: moneylenders, shopkeepers and relatives from outside the village. Only five bank loans were reported, all of which were taken by the Vankar weavers whose leader arranges loans each year for favoured relatives or clients.[43] Table 28 presents the distribution of loans by source and purpose.

Perhaps because of the active relief works which helped some 150 households meet day-to-day consumption needs, two-thirds of the loans taken, but only 40 per cent of the total amount taken, were for consumption needs, including social obligations (marriage and funeral costs). One-third of the loans, representing 60 per cent of the amount borrowed, were for productive purposes, both farm and non-farm. Farm loans were used to purchase seeds and irrigation equipment, and non-farm loans were used to transport animals (by the Bharwad shepherds when they migrated to south Gujarat), to invest in utensil trade (by a few Vaghri households), and as working capital (by the Vankar weavers).

Because they were wary of extending loans during a period of high risk, the village moneylenders introduced several changes in the normal terms and conditions of loans. First, some shopkeepers reduced their credit line on credit sales from several months to one month. Second, some moneylenders reduced the amount of credit they would extend against a given amount of pawned jewellery or utensils. And, third, some moneylenders requested a personal guarantee by a third party against even small loans. On the other hand, out of sympathy, two or three moneylenders extended interest-free, so-called 'charity' loans to poor households.

[42] During the 1985–87 drought, as mentioned earlier, some households were able to take help from the wife's parental family, in the form either of loans or employment. For example, several households obtained wage labour, either seasonal or more permanent, in the wife's natal village. Whether the wife's parental family was able to assist appeared to depend on whether their village was badly affected as Maatisar by the drought (some of the villages fell within the irrigated belt of Dholka *taluka* where guava and other cash crops are grown) and whether their overall economic position was better or worse than that of the daughter (or sister) requesting assistance.

[43] During the drought period, no government or bank loans were reported other than the loans for Vankar weavers.

Table 28
Loans Taken During 1987 by Source and Purpose

Loan source	Consumption		Farm production		Non-farm production		Total	
	No.	Average (Rs.)	No.	Average (Rs.)	No.	Average (Rs.)	No.	Average (Rs.)
1. Kin	19	439	5	773	—	—	24	509
2. Caste	19	117	—	—	—	—	19	117
3. In-laws	5	1,353	—	—	—	—	5	1,353
4. Landlord/employer	5	193	5	676	—	—	10	435
5. Trader/moneylender	5	676	5	773	—	—	10	725
6. Banks	—	—	—	—	5	966	5	966
7. Others	5	97	5	1,932	5	1,932	15	1,320
Total:	58	22,159	20	20,770	10	14,490	88	57,419

6. Migrating

In many studies on famine, large numbers of people on the move are interpreted as a major indicator that a famine is occurring. The types of movement reported range from intensification of normal migration for economic returns (Longhurst 1986), to moving to places where free food is being distributed, to aimless wandering as reported for nineteenth century famines in Western India (McAlpin 1983). The two major benefits from migration, other than of the latter type, are the income earned or the food received at the point of destination and the decreased claims on available food in the home area (Caldwell and Caldwell 1987). However, 'the effectiveness of migration as a famine strategy depends on the spread and extent of famine . . . and the effectiveness of relief efforts' (Longhurst 1986: 33).

In Maatisar, drought-induced migration took two broad forms: diversification, rather than intensification, of normal migration for employment and migration with animals in search of fodder.

Migrant Labour

> *If the relief works are not resumed soon, half the village will migrate.*
>
> Vankar Postmaster

In normal years, labourers from an estimated 50 households in Maatisar migrate for outside employment.[44] In 1987, by late November (the normal migration time), only 32 households had migrated. The primary reason for this decline in the migration rate was the prolonged and widespread nature of the 1985–87 drought which precipitated a drop in the demand for migrant labour.

It could be argued that another reason for the decline was the presence of relief works in and around Maatisar, which provided people with an alternative source of livelihood. However, by November, when migrants normally depart, relief works had been suspended for over a month and, despite repeated appeals to the state government, had not been resumed. Given the number of households which participated in relief works (150 households in October), it was predicted that more households would migrate than usual.

As the situation developed, neither event took place. The relief

---

[44] During the 1986–87 winter season, 42 households migrated. This number was said to be lower than for normal years because of the drought.

works were not resumed until early December, and the demand for migrant labour dropped. In normal years, sugar-cane factories in Saurashtra recruit labour for five months, beginning in November. In 1986, they recruited labour for only two months. In 1987, word was sent that the factories had closed down. Most of the sugar-cane crop in Gujarat had been sold green as fodder, according to directives issued by the state government in mid-1987. In the case of groundnut, another major source of demand for migrant labour, the crop had widely failed. A few households migrated for paddy harvesting instead, which turned out to be a poor substitute as they were able to get work for only two to three weeks.

In addition, the demand for non-farm migrant labour, notably in brickfields and rice mills, had dropped. The volume of rice mill operation was greatly reduced due to the partial and near-total failure of the paddy crop in 1986 and 1987 respectively. As of early November 1987, 24 households which had migrated either for rice mill or brick-field work in 1986 were still waiting for recruitment messages from their previous employers.

Among the households which did migrate in November 1987, half were landless, one-quarter were small landowners, and the remaining quarter owned medium or large farms.[45] Table 29 presents the distribution of migrant households by landholding. Of the total number of households, 20 had migrated in 1986 but 10 had not. Of those households which had not migrated in 1986, five (all Vankars) went for paddy harvesting, three sought wage work in agriculture, and two went to Ahmedabad city.

Migrant Shepherds

> *The Bharwads can migrate with their animals, but what about those who own only one or two animals?*
>
> Vaghri Labourer

---

[45] The pattern of recruitment during the drought was more or less the same as during normal years, as I described in Part II. McAlpin (1983) reports that, whereas in the nineteenth century famine migration took the form of aimless wandering, in the twentieth century a few men were typically sent out from each village to scout for work as soon as the failure of early rains made harvest losses inevitable. Accounts of later famines, McAlpin adds, do not suggest such communal cooperation. However, our data from Maatisar suggests that, as in normal years, scouts were sent by caste-related groups of labourers to search for work or contacts were made through caste-based networks.

Table 29
Migration During Winter 1987–88 by Landholding*

Landholding	No. of HHs	No. of Migrant HHs	Migration rate [%]
Landless	118	16	14
Small	34	8	24
Medium	62	5	8
Large	61	3	5
Surplus	10	0	0
Total:	**285**	**32**	**11**

* Excluding Bharwad shepherds.

For the first time in living memory, due to the acute shortage of fodder, local shepherd families migrated with their animals in search, literally, of greener pastures. During August, about 40 people from 10 shepherd households migrated with roughly 300 animals to a single village (Umarpara) in south Gujarat, where close relatives of the Maatisar Bharwads live.[46]

In July 1987, when the fodder shortage was already acute, one of the Umarpara relatives sent word that the local Bharwads should consider migrating to Umarpara. By late July, four or five Bharwad men set off on foot with 70 animals for Umarpara. The roughly 375 kilometre journey took 20 days, during which some 15 animals were reported to have died. After reaching Umarpara, which lies to edge of a tribal forest belt, the first migrants sent word back to Maatisar that all was well and that fodder was, indeed, available. In early August, men, women and children from another four or five Bharwad households left Maatisar. This time, the milch animals were transported by truck.[47]

[46] The Bharwad shepherds own a total of 521 animals of which 306 were taken to Umarpara, either by truck or on foot. According to local Bharwad lore, ancestors of the Maatisar shepherds migrated first to Dhanduka *taluka* and then to Umarpara some four to five generations ago. The Maatisar shepherds intermarry with their distant relations in Umarpara, whom they refer to as their own clan or *kutumb*, and maintain regular contact with these relatives, some of whom make annual pilgrimages to Maatisar to worship at the ancestral shrine. Recently, after a conflict with the titular head of the local Bharwads, four to five Bharwad cousins migrated from Maatisar to Umarpara. Umarpara is in the Rajpipla area of Baruch district in south Gujarat (see map of Gujarat State).

[47] One informant stated that the one-way cost from Maatisar to Umarpara by truck, each truck carrying 10 to 12 animals, was Rs 1,200. Another informant reported that the Maatisar Bharwads spent a total of Rs 18,000 transporting animals in nine or 10 trucks.

In Umarpara, the Bharwad migrants found 150 Bharwad house-holds living in several neighbourhoods or residential clusters bordering on tribal farms. The Maatisar migrants were accommodated in *kuccha* (bamboo and thatch) cowsheds in several of the Bharwad neighbour-hoods. Other than their accommodation, the Maatisar migrants found the situation in Umarpara better than they had anticipated. From July to November, monsoon grasses were readily available for cutting and grazing.[48] Moreover, animals could be grazed not only in the forest but also on fallow private fields (for a fee of Rs 7 per *bigha*).[49] As needed, they could buy cattle feed from the local dairy depot. Also, they were able to sell milk, both to the local dairy (at higher prices than they were paid in Maatisar) and locally (on a rotation basis at Rs 5 per kg).[50]

By November 1987, when the research team visited Umarpara, the Maatisar migrants seemed reasonably well-settled although fodder had by then become less readily available and a number of animals had died from an outbreak of cattle pox. By that time, the monson grasses had dried up so that the shepherds had to graze their animals deeper into the forest. Some had migrated with their dry animals to another tract of dense forest in Bilimora (see map of Gujarat State). However, the initial anxiety and uncertainty of the Maatisar migrants had eased, given the welcome afforded them by their distant kin and the avail-ability of fodder.

The Maatisar migrants represented only a small part of a mass movement of people and animals to south Gujarat from other parts of the state. As might be expected, this mass movement met with some

---

[48] In normal years in Umarpara, the price of grass is Rs 6 per 100 bundles, but in 1987 the price rose to Rs 40. Similarly, sorghum normally sells for Rs 25 per 100 bundles but in 1987 it sold for Rs 70. The sale of grass increased significantly. Every day four to five truckfulls of grass were sold from the Umarpara area. Despite its commercial value, grass was readily available for cutting and grazing from July to November.

[49] In Maatisar, no grazing fee is levied for grazing private fields. It is not known whether the grazing fee charged in Umarpara was a regular feature of normal-year grazing or a new feature introduced because the demand for grass and fodder had increased dramatically with the arrival of so many outside animals.

[50] A wealthy Bharwad reported he averaged Rs 100 per month per buffalo from the sale of milk, whereas in Maatisar he averages only Rs 80 per month. Others reported earning Rs 100–120 per month per buffalo and Rs 60–80 per month per cow in Umarpara. The following prices for milk were cited:

Buffalo	—	Rs 120 per *maund*
Cow	—	Rs 90 per *maund*
Goat	—	Rs 60 per *maund*

resistance from local residents.[51] In Umarpara, the local Bhil tribals initially tried to stop some of the trucks carrying animals to the area. But once the son of a Bharwad politician, an ex-Member of the Legislative Assembly, arrived with his animals, the resistance stopped. An underlying tension between the migrants and the Bhils and between the various neighbourhoods of Bharwads persisted but did not erupt into open conflict.

Not all the Bharwads who were forced to migrate with their animals incurred losses. One Bharwad migrated to Umarpara in early August, where he share-cropped out his animals to his son (who had migrated to Umarpara about five years earlier). He then set off for Maatisar, taking one buffalo with him. En route, he sold the buffalo for Rs 5,000 in Kheda District. From there, he went to Surendranagar District and bought two cows for Rs 800 each from a cattle camp (*punjrapole*). When he reached Dholka *taluka*, he sold these cows for Rs 1,500 each and returned to the Surendranagar cattle camp and bought two more cows for Rs 800 each. After this second purchase, the cattle camp administrators realised he was buying and selling cattle as a business and banned him from purchasing any more animals. By then, however, he had already made a profit trading cattle.

When they left in August 1987, the migrant shepherds planned to return to Maatisar when the monsoon rains arrived in June 1988. In actual fact, all but two Bharwads returned before Holi (March 1988). Only two young men with about 25 to 30 animals stayed behind. Three reasons were cited for returning before the monsoon rains, each relating to fodder supply. The first was that grass was no longer available in the Umarpara area. Second, some fodder was available in Maatisar: SEWA continued to distribute sugar-cane as fodder until June 1988 and wheat straw became available after the winter harvest. Third, many of the Bharwads planned to cultivate sorghum as fodder during the summer months.

7. Mortgaging or Selling Assets

I have never seen so many trees cut before.

Thakkar ex-Sarpanch

[51] According to one informant who visited Umarpara in late 1987, a total of 500 Bharwad households from all over Gujarat were living in and around Umarpara, of whom only 150 were permanent residents.

*We won't find any shade in summer. When people cut
their own trees, it is very bad year. When property is
divided, people fight over trees—now they're selling
these same trees.*

Bharwad Shepherd

According to conventional wisdom, drought (and more so famine)
victims are often forced into distress sale of assets. The growing body
of literature on seasonal and crisis coping mechanisms indicates,
however, that assets are managed in different ways depending on the
asset and the circumstances. For instance, there are preference hierarchies not only for the assets themselves but also for the modes for
drawing down or disposing of assets (Jodha 1975; Agarwal 1988;
Corbett 1988). In Maatisar, no assets, other than trees, were mortgaged
or sold during 1987. In discussing options and strategies with regard
to assets with a cross-section of village households, a common pattern
of asset management emerged.

The villagers differentiate between inventories of *free goods* (either
home-produced or collected) and *purchased goods* which are stocked
for planned use (notably for seasonal lean periods); *non-productive
assets* such as household utensils and jewellery, and *productive assets*
such as land, livestock, agricultural implements and trees. In a study of
Rajasthan villages, Jodha (1975) lists a range of goods which were
stocked for some planned use, such as marriage or seasonal lean
periods: fuelwood, dung-cakes, timbers, ropes and mats, spun wool,
wild flowers, pickles, dried vegetables, provisions and clothing. All of
these goods are stocked in Maatisar as well.

Running down or drawing upon stocked inventories is a recognised
seasonal phenomenon.[52] In fact, these inventories are often built up
specifically to fill in for seasonal troughs: for example, fuelwood and
cow-dung cakes are routinely stored during dry winter months for use
during the monsoon rains, when these goods are more difficult to
collect and store. Because they are routinely drawn upon, these inventories generally do not last long into more crisis conditions, such as
drought.

The investment in jewellery, particularly gold and silver jewellery,

---

[52] Several studies list body fat as one of the items stored up for lean seasons
(Longhurst 1986). As I discussed in the section on Consumption, households generally
prefer to reduce food intake and lose body weight before they deplete other stocks or
assets.

both as a sign of wealth and as a store of value to draw upon in times of shortage has a long and widespread tradition in India (Agarwal 1989). Household utensils, particularly metal ones, are also invested in as a sign of wealth and as a store of value. Both jewellery and utensils are regularly pawned as collateral for loans. During crisis periods, the leverage value of such pawned items may be reduced or their owners may be forced into selling these assets. Given the choice, households generally prefer to pawn rather than to sell assets. If forced to sell, households generally prefer to sell jewellery or utensils before they sell productive assets, such as livestock and land, or even agricultural implements and trees.

As I discussed in Part II, jewellery and utensils are often the only assets directly controlled by women and their loss, therefore, has a specific impact on them.

> Once these are disposed of, even if the household is able to protect its productive assets during the calamity, women would be left with nothing to fall back on if abandoned or in case of a drought recurrence—since in the cycle of mortgage–indebtedness–sale, jewellery once sold is unlikely to be easily redeemed .... This leaves women especially vulnerable during a severe calamity such as famine, when families may themselves begin to fragment and disintegrate. (Agarwal 1989: 55–56)

Another store of value are trees, which provide a variety of products for subsistence or sale but are generally overlooked by researchers.[53] These products are stored, pawned, mortgaged or sold to deal with contingencies. During the drought in Maatisar, some households sold trees to raise capital to purchase seeds and other inputs or to meet contingencies. Between 150 and 250 trees were sold. To handle the sales and transport of the trees, four Maatisar residents assumed the role of middle men between the households which sold the trees and the lumber yards in Bavla, the nearest market town, which purchased them.

In disposing of stock or assets, households implicitly, if not explicitly, address one central question: whether the action taken can be reversed. Households will typically start with responses which involve the smallest commitment of domestic resources and the greatest degree of

[53] Chambers has popularised the concept of trees as 'savings banks' and insurance for poor rural people (Chambers and Longhurst 1986). Refer to Table 17 for a list of the trees (and their uses or products) found in Maatisar.

reversibility (Corbett 1988). The common perception is that freely-collected and home-produced inventories can eventually be built up again, and pawned jewellery or utensils can eventually be redeemed. Even if jewellery and utensils have to be sold, that loss is not seen to impinge directly on the livelihood of the household. But if land or cattle are sold the productive base for livelihoods is depleted. Further, the chance of redeeming productive assets in full in the post-drought period are often slim, especially for small farmers and landless agricultural labourers.[54]

8. Drastic Measures

When drought conditions reach extreme or famine proportions, households are sometimes forced to take drastic measures. Several studies suggest that two common responses to extreme food crises are distress migration of the whole household in search of relief (Corbett 1988) and the striking fragmentation or disintegration of families (Greenough 1982). In many contexts, 'the sight of large numbers of people on the move is the major indicator that a famine is occurring' (Longhurst 1986). But, as mentioned in the discussion on migration, it is important to distinguish between different types of migration, all of which might be associated with drought, or more likely with famine conditions: the intensification of normal migration in search of employment opportunities; migration to places where free food or other relief measures might be available; and aimless wandering in search of food. In Maatisar in 1987, some labourers migrated for employment opportunities and some shepherds migrated with animals in search of fodder. However, largely due to the effective presence of relief works, neither form of migration assumed the aspects of distress migration associated with famine conditions.

Several studies have presented evidence on the disintegration of families and abandonment of women and children under severe famine conditions, such as Greenough's (1982) study of the 1943 Bengal famine; Alamgir's (1980) study of the 1974 Bangladesh famine; and Vaughan's (1987) study of the 1949 Malawi famine. In our study of 300 women participating in relief works during the 1974–75 Bangladesh famine, a colleague and I found that most of the women had been

[54] Jodha's (1978) comparison of the asset position of farmers in the pre-drought, drought and post-drought years in three states shows 'only a partial recovery in productive assets, and a further depletion in non-productive assets in virtually all cases in the post-drought years, suggesting lagged effects of the calamity' (Agarwal 1989: 52).

affected by one or another form of family disintegration: married women abandoned by their husbands; widows no longer supported by their sons; mothers no longer able to feed their children and forced to hand them over to orphanages or to relatives; and women, without adult males to support them, who were forced into begging or prostitution before they joined the relief works (Chen and Ghuznavi 1979).[55]

During the 1985–87 drought in Maatisar, there was little evidence of family disintegration. Although some of the reciprocal arrangements between kin broke down (more on this below), the sharing of work and responsibilities within the family did not appear to be unduly strained.[56] When asked whether anyone would consider abandoning their spouse or children, the response was uniformly negative. One outside visitor reported the case of a young widow forced to abandon her children but, as he noted, that incident took place in Saurashtra, where the drought had been longer and more severe and, as he further noted, that type of incident is very rare.

One sort of a typical social behaviour surfaced in Maatisar by late 1987: three reported cases of prostitution. One was that of a young widow forced into prostitution in order to maintain her family and the other two were the wives of labourers who, at the time the cases were reported, were waiting to be recruited as migrant labourers. By early 1988, three households were forced to beg for food: one Vaghri household in which the husband is lame, one young Bhangi household not supported by the extended family, and one elderly Vaghri couple.

Impact of Drought on Traditional Forms of Social Security

Several forms of traditional social security were discussed in Part II: patron–client relations; *jajmani* relations; family, kinship, and caste

[55] In Bangladesh, prior to 1974, very few women, no matter how poor, engaged in field work or construction work either as family labour or wage labour. The famine conditions forced countless women, both married women and women without adult males to support them, to join the relief works.

[56] This is not to say that age and/or gender biases did not operate within families in response to the drought. In deploying family labour to relief works sites, for example, large joint households sent married sons and their wives before men and women of the older generation. When asked why he sent his daughters-in-laws to the relief works before he sent some of his sons, one household patriarch (a rich landlord and caste leader) replied: 'They are not of our blood. And they are expected to work.'

support systems; and village or community rights.[57] Our findings
indicate a gradual erosion of these systems or relationships over time,
attributable in large measure to several trends, including demographic
pressures on land, natural resources and traditional occupations; and
the commercialisation of labour, tenancy, and product markets.[58] Our
findings also indicate differences in the operation of these systems
between peak and slack seasons in any given year and between normal,
unseasonal and bad years. Further, that the drought had varying
impacts on these different forms of traditional social security, as I will
discuss below.

1. Communal Resources: Intensified Use and Conflicts

During food shortages, dependence on common property resources
often increases significantly: people shift to 'famine' foods which are
collected from CPRs, cattle are grazed more intensively and extensively in search of fodder, and people turn to common water resources
when private water resources dry up. However, common property
resources, which are 'already strained in their ability to cushion
seasonal fluctuations' (Agarwal 1989: 38), are often strained to their
limits or simply dry up during droughts. During the 1987 drought
year, for instance, the grasses which normally grow from July to
November in years of good monsoon rains simply did not sprout. As a
result, the pressure for grazing shifted from the common pasture land
to private fields, both fallow (which in normal times are treated as
CPRs) and those with standing crops (which are never open to the
public).

Because of the strain placed on common property resources during
droughts or other crises, areas of traditional *reciprocity* or cooperation
often become areas of *conflict*. A variety of conflicts were reported in
Maatisar, of which the most common related to grazing. The conflicts
over grazing became, predictably, most violent when cattle were
grazed on standing fields. But conflicts also broke out when animals

[57] To name a few, Wiser (1936), Epstein (1967), Breman (1985), and Dasgupta (1987)
on patron–client and *jajmani* relationships; Dasgupta (1987) and Caldwell et al. (1986)
on kinship support mechanisms; and Jodha (1978, 1985) on common property resources.

[58] For example, the competition between migrant labour and local labour for limited
wage employment and the sale of goods which were earlier distributed free to labourers
or clients.

were grazed on fallow fields, which in normal years are open to all. Conflicts over the right to collect weeds, grass or leaves from fields and field boundaries were also reported. In one case, a widow was denied by her brother-in-law the right to collect fodder from the boundaries of his fields. Conflicts over the rights to collect cow-dung also broke out. Normally, cow-dung dropped on public spaces can be collected freely by anyone. During 1987, however, women began claiming exclusive rights to cow-dung dropped by their own animals, by marking the fresh droppings with a small twig until the dung dried and could be collected. However, there were no conflicts over water because the ground-water table did not drop too sharply and several water sources remained usable: private wells for irrigation and two public wells (the *gram panchayat* and the SEWA wells) for drinking water.

2. Social Obligations: Decreasing Reliability

As I discussed in Part II, caste-based support systems operate only in peak seasons in normal years leaving kin-based support systems to cushion shortfalls in slack seasons. However, kinship support systems have also eroded over time and are often strained beyond their capacity to respond during droughts. During the current drought, for example, small gifts or loans of food, fuel and fodder between kin virtually dried up. The impact of drought on these kin-based support systems appears to have gone through four phases: below-normal levels of reciprocity or support; occasional evasions of reciprocity or support; denial of reciprocity and support; and, finally, outright competition over resources. The villagers assumed that, once the lagged effects of the drought had played themselves out, kin-based support systems would revert to the level and conditions under which they operated before the drought.

Under the *jajmani* system, as mentioned earlier, certain caste groups render specified services to a fixed group of patrons throughout the year in return for a fixed payment in kind at harvest and other concessions. During the 1985–87 drought, none of these regular caste-defined relationships were broken. However, the priests reported a drop in the volume of grain payments, both those given every day and those given at harvest, and the genealogists reported a reduced demand for their services, so much so that some decided not to embark on their annual round of patron villages. One genealogist, albeit not a particularly industrious one, resorted to two rather drastic measures involving the women of his household. First, he sent his young, second wife for a tubectomy in order to collect the Rs 290 incentive payment from the government: he already had three children from the first wife. Second, he delayed sending his newly-wed daughter to her husband's home as she was earning a stipend working for SEWA in Maatisar.

In the past, the potters provided a regular, specified number of pots to designated groups of customers throughout the year in return for a fixed payment in kind at harvest. Over the past 15 to 20 years, all but one of the seven potter households have transferred from kind to cash payments. During the drought, the potter households were affected by a drop in demand for pots and a shortage and subsequent rise in price of fuel and raw materials (clay).

Again the villagers assumed that the drop in demand or payments during the drought did not signal an irreversible break in the *jajmani* system, but reflected only a temporary setback. The failure of patrons to meet their obligations to clients was attributed by the clients to the patrons' inability to do so in a period of overall shortage, not to a permanent breakdown in the *jajmani* relationships.

Impact of Drought on Different Livelihood Systems

In his important analysis of poverty and famines, Sen (1981) argues that one cannot predict, without careful analysis of the specifics of each drought or famine, which particular groups within the population will suffer most or least. To carry out such an analysis, Sen recommends that four parameters of each group be measured. The first is the bundle of commodities owned by each unit of analysis, what Sen refers to as *endowment*. The second is the set of alternative commodity bundles each unit can command in exchange for its endowment bundle, what Sen refers to as *exchange entitlement mapping*. These basic parameters enable each group to generate varying degrees of *direct entitlements* (i.e., production for own consumption) and *trade entitlements* (i.e., exchange of commodity bundles for food). Conversely, unfavourable shifts in either basic parameter, due to drought or other factors, can lead to varying degrees of direct and/or trade entitlement failures.

The entitlement approach, which focuses on both ownership and exchange, offers a useful framwork for summarising the impact of the drought on different livelihood groups in Maatisar. Using the Sen framework, I will discuss below the impact of the drought on the endowments, entitlements and ability to command food of different household groups. In this analysis, I use levels of consumption across the three seasons of 1987 as a proxy for the ability to 'command food'.[59] A drop in the ability to command food is seen as occurring because of either a reduction in a household's endowment bundle or an unfavourable shift in a household's entitlements.

Given the employment offered by the government relief system, those households whose major endowment is their human capital did not suffer significant trade entitlement failure despite the fact that both the local and migrant labour markets collapsed after the 1986–87 winter harvest. In fact, labour households were able to exchange their labour for more days and for higher wages in 1987 than they are able to in normal years.

Interestingly, a smaller percentage of labour households than cultivator households participated in relief works. However, relative to cultivator households, labour households engaged in significantly more days of relief works and other wage labour: 55 days of relief works out of a total of 119 days of wage employment per adult worker in labour households compared to 22 days of relief works out of a total of 28 days of wage employment per adult worker in cultivator households.

However, landless labour households did experience moderate direct entitlement failure. They reduced their volume of tenant cultivation (after experiencing some loss during the 1986–87 winter season) and had to compete for a reduced supply of free goods (which they normally collect, process and store to a greater degree than other household groups). But, if one takes consumption of foodgrains as a proxy for command over food, the labour households' command over food was reduced by less than 15 per cent between early and late 1987.

Given the prolonged nature of the drought, peasant cultivators and tenant farm households suffered both direct entitlement and trade entitlement failures. During three years of decreased crop yields, farm households produced fewer commodities both for their own consumption (direct entitlement) and for sale (trade entitlement). In

---

[59] As no comparable data have been identified, the seasonal variation in consumption in 1987 has not been compared to seasonal variation in normal years. However, the study data have been used to compare relative reductions in consumption between different groups across seasons.

addition, many cultivators rear animals and/or engage in wage labour and they suffered moderate trade entitlement failures in both these sectors. Although they were not forced to dispose of their productive assets, these households did have significant endowment losses in that they had to deplete their stocks (notably their seed stocks) and either deplete their capital reserves (if any) or go into debt in order to cultivate. Over the three years, crop yields were uniformly below normal although winter crops, under irrigated conditions, generally fared better than rain-fed monsoon crops. Because of the accumulated toll of the prolonged drought on their direct and indirect entitlements, many cultivator households were in debt by 1987.

According to some farmers, indebtedness forced them to participate in relief works: almost 60 per cent of cultivator households engaged in relief works.[60] However, during 1987, farm households averaged only 22 days of relief works and six days of other wage employment per adult worker. Therefore, wage earnings did not compensate for the accumulated toll of the drought on farm households. This fact is reflected in their relative command over food: the cultivators reduced their consumption of foodgrains by 30 per cent between early and late 1987.

Given the acute shortage of fodder throughout the drought, households which rear milch cattle, particularly the shepherds, suffered both direct entitlement and trade entitlement failures in that they produced less milk both for consumption and sale. The fodder shortage forced half the Bharwad shepherd households to migrate with more than half of the total Bharwad herd to south Gujarat for 10 months from August 1987 to May 1988. During their forced migration, they lost some animals which represent their major endowment.[61] Most of the shepherds who did not migrate stayed home to cultivate their fields and, like other cultivators, suffered near-total crop losses in the monsoon season. However, unlike other cultivators, the Bharwads did not join the relief works since, because of caste norms and tradition, they do not engage in wage labour.[62] With no earnings from relief works to cushion them, the accumulated toll of forced migration,

---

[60] When asked why members of his household participated in relief works, one surplus farmer explained that he had taken a sizeable loan in 1986 to extend his irrigation channels, that his crops had totally failed in both 1986 and 1987, so that there was no point in sitting idle when employment was available.

[61] It is difficult to estimate how many animals died when the Bharwads migrated because, in describing their predicament, they tended to exaggerate animal deaths.

[62] Two relatively poor Bharwad households eventually joined the relief works, but not until late January 1988.

animal deaths and reduced milk and crop yields forced the Bharwads to reduce consumption dramatically by over 65 per cent between early and late 1987.

Given that the fodder crisis affected shepherding communities in many parts of Gujarat and that these communities provide the main market for the wool shawls woven by Vankar weavers in the village, the weavers suffered a dramatic trade entitlement failure. Perhaps as unprecedented as the forced migration of Bharwads was the forced closure of weaving operations by the Vankars for about six months from May to December 1987. However, this closure was not accompanied by any endowment loss. Moreover, unlike the Bharwads, the Vankars have a long tradition of engaging in wage labour and were able to partially compensate for trade entitlement failures in two markets (wool weaving and labour) by participating in relief works. Indeed, 19 of the 22 Vankar households which declared weaving as their primary occupation participated in relief works, the highest participation rate for any occupational group. As a result, they suffered a reduction in consumption (29 per cent) that was greater than the labour households but less than the cultivator and shepherd households.

Given that the drought was prolonged and affected most sections of the population, the demand and payments for caste services and artisan goods dropped. However, in that they had few endowments to protect other than their own skills and labour, the service castes got by on whatever payments or charity they received. None of the service castes joined the relief works.* In contrast, four of the seven potter households, some of which are cultivators as well, joined the relief works. As a result, the service castes reduced their consumption by 16 per cent whereas the potters increased their consumption by six per cent between early and late 1987.

As cultivators, the Brahmins suffered significant entitlement failures, particularly in 1987, and probably some endowment loss in stocks and capital as well. As traders and moneylenders, the Thakkars did not suffer significant failure or loss. However, they did not, as might have been expected, enjoy trade entitlement gains: their volume of trade and moneylending was reduced, prices did not escalate, and their capital remained tied up in outstanding loans. In fact, even the Thakkars reduced their consumption of foodgrains (by 22 per cent) between early and late 1987.

* The Bhangis have not been classified as a service caste as they have given up their caste service, scavenging, for cultivation.

Analysis of Droughts

Our study of Maatisar suggests that, in the analysis of droughts, three important spatial or temporal dimensions need to be considered. The first is that the pattern of entitlement failures depends in part on whether the drought is a *single-year* or *prolonged* phenomenon. If the drought in Maatisar had not persisted for three years, the accumulated toll on the capital, stock and credit-worthiness of farmers would not have been so great. As it was, the prolonged nature of the drought forced some surplus farm households not only to take loans after crop failures in order to reinvest in farming assets and inputs but also to deploy some household labour to the relief works. Second, the pattern of entitlement failures also depends in part on whether the drought is a *localised* or *widespread* phenomenon. If the drought had been localised in and around Maatisar, the households that normally migrate each year would have been able to migrate as usual. Because the drought was so widespread, the migrant labour markets collapsed to a significant degree, forcing many migrant households either to explore new migration routes or to remain at home.

The third dimension relates to the *short-term, medium-term* and *long-term* impact of droughts and has direct implications for government relief policies. The Maatisar data suggest that it is important to calculate the impact of the drought not only on the day-to-day consumption needs of different groups, but also on the season-to-season and medium-term needs for fixed assets and working capital: that is, to analyse the impact of the drought on both *entitlements to food* and *entitlements to produce food.* Many households in Maatisar were forced to go into debt in order to replant in the monsoon season after their seed stock had been exhausted with the first planting and to plant in the winter season after suffering monsoon crop losses. These households required not only fixed capital to invest in more or improved irrigation resources but also working capital to invest in seeds and other inputs. The Maatisar data also suggest significant long-term or lagged effects of droughts which affect the ability of indiviudal households and traditional social security systems to recover after the drought.

Analysis of Household Responses to Droughts

Our study also suggests that, in the analysis of household responses to drought, four important dimensions need to be considered: the *types* of strategies adopted, the *level* at which each strategy is negotiated, the *sequencing* of the strategies and the *reversibility* of each strategy. Each type of strategy involves different kinds of adjustments: those associated with production or work, those associated with household inventories or assets, those which involve consumption adjustments and those which involve social adjustments. Further, each type of strategy is negotiated or mediated at the following levels of adjustment: intrahousehold (by gender and age), interhousehold (through kinship, caste or patronage relationships), communal (drawing on CPRs or other village rights) and public (through either relief or general development services). In analysing household strategies, therefore, it is important to understand both the *type* of adjustment being made and the *level* at which adjustment is being made. To illustrate, the range of drought-induced strategies adopted in Maatisar have been grouped by type and level in Table 30.

As our study illustrates, the strategies adopted in response to drought conditions appear similar to, but differ in significant ways, from those adopted in response to seasonal fluctuations. The first difference is that certain options open to households under seasonal conditions are limited or closed under drought conditions: the ability to generate surplus and build up stocks is greatly reduced and inventories or stocks are, therefore, quickly depleted; local employment opportunities are reduced and options within agriculture (e.g., sharecropping) become too risky. Second, drought conditions limit the scope for reciprocity, charity or patronage and increase the competition for common property resources. During droughts, common pastures and water resources either wither and dry up or are overused, often leading to conflicts over rights of access. And traditional social security systems, which require the presence of real resources and the absence of collective risk, are often strained beyond their capacity to respond. Third, whereas the government generally does not respond to seasonal requirements, it often responds effectively—by providing employment at relief works—during droughts.

Finally, because of these other differences, the sequencing or staging of households strategies varies according to the prevailing conditions. Table 31 represents a staged model of household responses, which compares the sequencing of coping strategies under normal seasonal conditions and under the 1987 drought conditions.[63]

---

[63] For other staged models of household responses, refer to Dirks (1980) and Corbett (1988).

Table 30
Types and Levels of Household Strategies

Strategy	Intra-HH	Inter-HH	Communal	Public
Adapting or diversifying activities	P			
Drawing down inventories	I			
Seeking employment		P		
Share-cropping		P		
Drawing upon common property resources			P, I, C	
Drawing upon social relationships		P, A, C		
Reducing or modifying consumption	C	S		
Borrowing		P, A, C		
Disposing non-productive assets	A			
Migrating	P			
Disposing productive assets	A			
Drastic measures	S			
Participating in relief works				P

Key: Adjustments associated with
P = Production or work
I = Inventories
A = Assets
C = Consumption
S = Social relationships

As I have described, certain seasonal options were either limited or closed during the drought, notably those of drawing down inventories, seeking local employment, share-cropping and drawing upon common property resources or social networks. And certain strategies were resorted to sooner under drought conditions than they were under normal seasonal conditions, notably reducing consumption and borrowing. If the drought conditions had not been mitigated by the effective presence of relief works in 1987, households in Maatisar might have been forced to dispose of their productive assets or resort to more drastic measures.

Strategies can also be grouped according to their relative degrees of reversibility. Chambers (1981a) has popularised two concepts to measure the degree of reversibility: 'rachets' and 'screws'. As defined by Chambers, *screws* refer to pressures which are created in certain seasons or under certain conditions from which the household can recover in other seasons or after the condition has passed. *Rachets* refer to seasonal troughs or crisis conditions which leave poor household worse off than before to the extent that they are unable to replenish the assets or repay the loans incurred by the end of the lean

Table 31
Sequencing of Household Strategies

Strategy	Seasonal	Drought
Adapting or diversifying activities	1	1
Drawing down inventories	2	–
Seeking employment	3	–
Share-cropping	4	–
Drawing upon common property resources	5	–
Drawing upon social relationships	6	–
Reducing or modifying consumption	7	2
Borrowing	8	4
Disposing non-productive assets	9	5
Migrating	10	6
Disposing productive assets	–	–
Participating in relief works	–	3
Drastic measures	–	–

period or crisis. Correspondingly, as used here, *reversible* strategies are those from which households can recover in another season or after the drought is over. *Less reversible* strategies are those which leave households worse off than before to the extent that they are unable to replenish their assets or repay their loans. Tables 30 and 31 list strategies in the order of reversibility: those at the top of the list are generally most easily reversed, those at the bottom are generally least easily reversed. And, generally, the more severe the conditions the sooner households resort to the less reversible strategies.

Drought as a Developmental Issue

In the design of this study, seasonality was hypothesised to be a critical dimension of household livelihood systems. Rural households were seen to have developed a range of strategies with which to cope with seasonal fluctuations. In carrying out the study, which was modified mid-year to incorporate a focus on the drought, it became clear that rural households have developed a range of strategies to deal not only with seasonality but also with drought. Further, that drought is endemic to life in Maatisar and that the strategies to prepare for, react to, and adapt to drought are as deeply engrained in local livelihood systems as seasonal adjustment strategies.

For those in arid or semi-arid climates, such as Maatisar, the timing and predictability of rainfall is often the most important constraint, and the factor which sets the rhythm of annual activities (Huss-Ashmore 1988). Rainfall follows three predictable patterns: annual, seasonal and sub-seasonal. A change in any of these patterns can increase vulnerability. Within seasons, there are hidden periodicites in the rainfall distribution pattern (Rao et al. 1988). Changes in these periodicities, measured by farmers in intervals of 10 days or less, affect cultivation directly. Farm households must be prepared to make mid-season adjustments to delayed or untimely rainfall. Across seasons, rainfall distribution can also differ affecting, most directly, the variety and mix of crops grown and the sources of fodder in any given year. Normal rainfall patterns can also be disturbed for more than one season or year, resulting in various degrees of drought conditions.

Over the past three decades, Gujarat has experienced four major droughts (affecting more than half of its villages), five widespread droughts (affecting more than 20 per cent of its villages), and localised droughts in one or more areas every year. Maatisar was badly affected by the four major droughts and somewhat affected by several of the minor droughts. That is, Maatisar residents have had to adjust to drought conditions every fifth year over the past three decades. There-fore, even in normal years, the possibility of drought remains in the consciousness of the villagers and influences both their options and their strategies.

Increased irrigation facilities have provided some control over climatic factors in Maatisar. However, local irrigation facilities are used only in winter and summer. All monsoon crops are grown under rain-fed conditions and are, therefore, highly vulnerable to changes in rainfall, including increasing amounts of paddy, which requires more water than the traditional coarse grain which it has displaced. Further, increased use of high-yielding crop varieties (HYVs) demands increased use of fertilisers which, in turn, means increased dependence on water. Intensified agriculture in Maatisar has, therefore, probably led to higher yields but also higher vulnerability to fluctuations in rainfall.[64]

In addition to agriculture, other occupations and resources in the village are sensitive to variations in rainfall. Opportunities for wage

[64] As a whole, Gujarat has experienced a sharp rise in the instability in its foodgrains output since 1961, one of the highest instability rates in the country, 'which may be attributed to rise in the variability of rainfall itself' during that period (Rao et al. 1988: 24) but also to increased dependence on rainfall, in that high-yielding crop varieties demand greater use of fertilisers which, in turn, demand greater use of water.

employment expand or contract in response to levels of agricultural activity. Rainfall obviously affects supplies 'of water, fodder, fuel and raw materials which, in turn, affect the viability of animal husbandry, artisan production and subsistence generally. Widespread or extreme shortfalls in rainfall can lead to significant or total losses in agriculture; shortages of water, fodder and fuel; decreased demands for local and migrant labour; and a breakdown of local social security system. Understandably, therefore, both seasonality and drought are critical factors in household livelihood systems. That is, rural households—peasant, pastoral, artisan or labourer—do not manage drought in isolation from, but as an integral dimension of, their overall livelihood systems, which are designed to handle normal, unseasonal and drought years.

Whereas rural households routinely adjust to both seasonality and drought, policy-makers and administrators often respond only to drought situations and only with short-term relief measures. That is, unlike private drought management by individual households, public drought management by government is generally isolated from regular development strategies (Jodha 1989). Given that drought, and even seasonality, can threaten the viability of different livelihood systems, they represent important constraints to be addressed by future programmes and action. In other words, both seasonality and drought should be considered key variables in development policy and research. Further, an integrated and long-term approach to seasonality and drought should be developed to replace the current short-term crisis management approach.

Conclusion

Maatisar has experienced substantial change over the past 40 years. Although it does not fall within the command area of any major irrigation scheme, a large number of pump sets have been purchased, increasing amounts of non-traditional crops (paddy and wheat) are grown, and agriculture production has increased overall. Given both increased yields and improved transportation, farm households now purchase inputs and sell produce at the nearest market town. Although there are no tractors and only one mechanised thresher in the village, all wheat is threshed mechanically (by hired threshers) and all irrigation is mechanised. And while the local labour market has not expanded significantly, opportunities for wage employment outside the village have increased dramatically, in part because of improved transportation and in part because of regional growth in agriculture and industry.

Several government programmes have reached the village with varying coverage and impact, including subsidised credit, agricultural extension and the national dairy programme. In terms of infrastructure and ongoing programmes, the village has a functioning primary school, electricity, a fair price shop, a public well and pump, and two child care centres. Further, due to the efforts of SEWA, two local cooperatives for women (dairy and weaving) have been established, IRDP loans for milch animals have been channelled to women, and several employment schemes (in cotton spinning, roof tile manufacturing, and bamboo crafts) have been introduced.

These developments notwithstanding, several opposing trends within the economy, together with increasing population density, appear to have negated, at least for some sections of the population, many of the gains from an expanded economy. Over the past 40 years, the population of the village has nearly doubled, leading to over-crowding of land, other resources and hereditary occupations. As a result, many households are forced to supplement their primary occupation with increasing amounts of wage labour; thereby over-crowding the labour market. The introduction of high-yielding crop varieties, and the intensified use of fertilisers and water associated with HYVs, increased crop yields but also increased crop instability.[1]

In addition, the local economy remains a 'gamble on the monsoon'. Over the past three decades, Gujarat experienced widespread drought every eight years and localised droughts every year. Maatisar lies in a relatively drought-prone region and has been severely affected by droughts every fifth year. Monsoon crops are still grown under rain-fed conditions and remain, therefore, highly sensitive to variations in rainfall. Although the area under irrigation for winter cultivation has expanded, ground-water aquifers need to be regularly recharged and are, therefore, sensitive to shortfalls in rainfall. The other major sectors of the economy—animal husbandry and wage labour—expand and contract in response to performance in the agricultural sector. Because of these and other factors, the local economy remains highly vulner-able to the vagaries of the weather.

As it expanded, the local economy was also commercialised, leading to the introduction of market forces in several sectors. In the past, several forms of local institutions operated on the principle of a guaranteed subsistence for all, including patron–client and *jajmani* relationships. Patronage relationships have given way to competitive market relationships in both the labour and tenancy markets. For labourers, this has meant that they are now free to work for one or more employers but are no longer entitled to wage advances or to slack season subsistence loans from their employers. For tenants, this has meant that they are now free to share-crop land from one or more landlords and to sell their produce directly but are less likely to receive production or consumption loans from landlords. Market forces have

---

[1] In their cross-classification of states according to levels of instability and rates of growth in foodgrain production, Rao et al. (1988: 21) note that Gujarat experienced a medium growth rate but a high instability rate between 1971 and 1985. Rao et al. attribute these trends to both an increased instability in rainfall itself and an increased sensitivity to rainfall, in that intensified fertiliser use, associated with HYV crops, requires intensified water use.

also eroded the economic base of many *jajmani* relations. Because their *jajman* patrons can now purchase alternative goods or services in the open market, several carpenters and potters have had to abandon their hereditary occupation. Because their *jajman* patrons place decreasing value on genealogies, the younger generation of genealogists are leaving their hereditary occupation and the village for other occupations in Ahmedabad city.

In brief, the study data suggest that Maatisar village has experienced moderate rates of growth and development but moderate-to-high rates of vulnerability since the early 1950s. That is, despite overall growth and development, the local economy remains vulnerable to the vagaries of both the weather and the wider economy. In this concluding discussion, I summarise our findings on vulnerability in Maatisar and examine the role of individual households, local institutions and the state in reducing this vulnerability.

Our findings suggest that labourers probably face the highest vulnerability across and within seasons in normal years, given the marked periodicities of the labour markets and the relative inability of labour households to generate and store surplus. However, in drought years the vulnerability of labourers often decreases if the government responds by offering regular employment at relief works. In drought years and even in some unseasonal years, the vulnerability of peasant and shepherd households often increases, given decreased crop yields and depleted fodder sources. During 1987 in Maatisar, when the employment needs of labourers were addressed while the production needs of peasants were not, the vulnerability of peasant households (measured in terms of relative decreases in command over food) exceeded that of labour households. In normal years, the vulnerability of weavers, traders and shepherds is low, in that weavers supplement weaving with wage labour, traders profit from daily transactions in their shops, and shepherds sell raw milk daily (albeit in varying amounts according to the season) to the state dairy and supplement animal husbandry with crop husbandry.

In terms of trends over time, certain occupation or caste groups have done better than others. Of the two higher castes, the Thakkar traders have done relatively well and the Brahmin farmers have remained stable. The Bharwad shepherds have assumed a leading role as both moneylenders and farmers, in addition to animal husbandry. However, these three caste groups account for only 12 per cent of the total population. Certain households from other caste groups have taken advantage of opportunities for occupational or spatial mobility. A significant percentage of Vaghri and Bhangi households have entered agriculture, and a large number of households from several caste groups engage in moneylending.

The largest caste groups—the Koli Patels, Vaghris and Vankars—have a mixed record in terms of economic development. Nearly 50 per cent of them have suffered downward mobility, supplementing their hereditary occupations with increasing amounts of wage labour. One-fourth have enjoyed upward mobility, acquiring land to cultivate or generating surplus to invest in moneylending. The balance have remained stable, supplementing their hereditary occupation with wage labour as needed. At present, just under half of all households in the village engage in wage labour for some portion of the year.

In terms of chronic vulnerability, certain sub-groups of the population are at a particular disadvantage. Within the cultivation, livestock and labour groups, the degree of household vulnerability is inversely correlated with the amount of land owned. Within all occupation groups, except the Thakkar traders who do not engage in wage labour, the degree of household vulnerability is positively correlated with their degree of dependence on wage labour. As a general rule, given the overcrowding and periodicities of the labour market, the more a household relies on wage labour for its subsistence, the more vulnerable it remains. Across all occupation groups, those households with no able adult males are highly vulnerable: households headed by elderly men, disabled men or by widows without grown sons to assist them. As a general rule, given the problems of managing cultivation single-handed, of gaining access to joint family resources, and of meeting subsistence needs, widows without grown sons face particularly high vulnerability.

Whatever their degree of chronic vulnerability, most households face heightened vulnerability during drought. Even households which have enjoyed upward mobility are often forced to adopt protective strategies in response to unseasonal and drought-induced fluctuations. For instance, during the 1987 drought, Bharwads, who otherwise had been gaining economic power, were forced to migrate with their cattle in search of fodder.

In coping with seasonality, most households attempt to protect themselves from short-term reverses in income and subsistence flows. Adapting or diversifying normal activities, building up or drawing down inventories, seeking employment, share-cropping land, borrowing for consumption or production and migrating for employment are all common ways of dealing with the risks and uncertainties associated with seasonality. For additional support, households turn to family, kin and caste neighbours or draw upon common property resources. When all else fails, households are forced to mortgage or sell assets.

In coping with drought, most households guard against long-term reverses in asset-holding and production potential. To do so, they resort to many of the seasonal strategies listed above and to the same local institutions. However, drought conditions limit the scope for reciprocity, charity or patronage under the traditional social security system and increase the competition for common property resources.

In the past, four types of local institutions provided social security across seasonal fluctuations: patron–client relations; *jajmani* relations; communal or village rights; and caste, kinship and family support mechanisms. Earlier, all four types operated on the principle of a guaranteed subsistence to all households in the village; or in, what some scholars term, a moral economy (Appadurai 1984). Over time, these institutions have, to varying degrees, been eroded. As noted above, patronage relationships have given way in the labour and tenancy markets to competitive market relations, which do not guarantee subsistence during slack seasons. Traditional goods and services supplied to the village at large or to designated patrons under the *jajmani* system have given way to commercial goods and services, purchased in the open market. As a result, the younger generation of carpenters, potters and genealogists are leaving their hereditary occupations.

Market forces have not yet fully displaced caste, kinship or family relations or fully undermined village and communal rights. However, the traditional social security system can operate only from a real resource base. Given the overcrowding of village resources and hereditary occupations, the capacity of common property resources or social support mechanisms to cushion seasonal fluctuations has decreased over time. In peak seasons in normal years, caste neighbours frequently make small loans or gifts to one another. In slack seasons in normal years, however, the circle to which these reciprocal or charitable transactions are extended often narrows from caste neighbours to kinship networks. Further, over the past few decades, the demand and competition for common property resources have increased while the quantity and quality of these resources have decreased.

In brief, the capacity of individual households to withstand, and the traditional social security system to cushion, seasonal fluctuations has declined over time. In the past, as well as in the present, the traditional social security system required a real resource base and tended to break down under conditions of widespread or collective shortages. In times of collective shortages and risk, as during the 1985–87 drought, mutual kinship obligations are often undermined. And, under famine conditions, even family structures can break down (as during the 1943 Bengal famine and the 1974 Bangladesh famine).

Fortunately, the government generally activates a public social security system in the event of a severe drought or other crises in India. During the early stages of a crisis, newspaper reports often serve to trigger the government's response (Sen 1981). Indeed, as Sen and Dreze (1988) argue, the presence of both a free press (to activate the public system) and an effective relief system (notably public works) has dramatically reduced famine mortality in India since Independence.

Ever since the Famine Codes were promulgated by the British Administration towards the end of the nineteenth century, India's famine relief system, particularly the relief or scarcity works schemes, have played 'an undeniable and crucial role in averting large-scale starvation' (Dreze 1988: 73–74). As a case in point, during the 1985–87 drought, relief works played an undeniable role in generating employment and, thereby, helping to avert widespread hunger in Maatisar. In the arid and semi-arid parts of India, like the region around Maatisar, where the likelihood of drought is as great or greater than in the past, the need persists for an extensive and responsive government relief system.

However, the effective presence of relief works in certain areas at certain times should not obscure several weaknesses in the government relief system. The first is that the coverage of relief works and the extent of employment generated do not often meet the demand, especially during severe droughts. Rao et al. (1988) estimate that the national public works programmes provide only one-third of the employment needed to protect the incomes of the poor. Second, more attention needs to be paid to the productive components of relief works, including the building of public infrastructure or private assets.[2]

Thirdly, other components of the relief system are often not as

---

[2] During the 1987 drought, the Rajasthan state government engaged relief works labour to create private assets (irrigation wells, houses, etc.). Except for wages, other costs were borne by the private beneficiaries (Jodha 1989).

effecively, or even as widely offered, as relief works. In his analysis of the 1970–73 drought in Maharashtra, Dreze (1988: 104) concludes that the role of 'free feeding or other forms of gratuitous relief, the remission of land revenue, or even the vast network of ration shops . . . is much overrated.' The data from the 1985–87 drought in Maatisar confirm Dreze's findings. In the first half of 1987, when payments for relief works were in kind, the local fair price or ration shop was taxed beyond capacity in handling these payments. By the second half of 1987, when the payments were in cash, the ration shop could not meet the demand for fair price grains. Moreover, other components of the relief system were simply not offered in Maatisar. Despite the fact that some households were not able to participate in relief works and despite the demand for emergency credit, other than a cash dole of Rs 4 per day to 12 households for roughly eight months, no free feeding and no *taccavi* or other low-interest emergency loans were offered.

The fourth weakness is that the need for relief assistance, particularly public works, persists beyond the crisis period into chronic lean seasons. In Maatisar, just under half the households engage in wage labour: 70 households as their primary occupation and 60 as a secondary occupation. However, the demand for hired farm labour in and around Maatisar is limited. About 50 households migrate each year from early November to mid-March in search of work, and about 15 households migrate during other slack periods. There is clearly a latent demand for seasonal public works on a regular basis.

In areas officially classified as drought-prone, the government offers seasonal employment schemes in normal years. Experience suggests that such employment programmes, notably the Employment Guarantee Scheme in Maharashtra, perform an important role in stabilising incomes and employment across seasons (Rao et al. 1988). In other arid or semi-arid areas, such as Maatisar, villagers must cope with seasonal employment shortfalls either by migrating for wage employment, pursuing whatever non-labour options are locally available, or resorting to the traditional social security system.

Although various government programmes are designed to address the chronic shortages of the poor by providing subsidies or credit, they are seldom targeted or timed to address seasonal requirements. The majority of government loans are targeted to finance fixed capital requirements. Far fewer loans are targeted to working capital requirements. Moreover, bank formalities often preclude effective timing or fine-tuning in the delivery of loans, so that time-bound seasonal requirements are often missed.

Finally, drought management has been emphasised over drought proofing. Although increasing attention has been paid in the recent past to dryland farming, agricultural planning and development have focused to date on high-value crops in irrigated areas. During the 1950s and 1960s, rural development programmes paid little attention to the resource specificities of arid or semi-arid areas and agricultural research and extension focused on high potential, well-irrigated areas to the neglect of dry areas (Jodha 1989). During the 1970s, research on crop, soil, water management and biomass technologies for dry areas was undertaken but was largely confined to demonstration sites or pilot areas (*ibid*). During the 1980s, some efforts have been made to extend these technologies to dry areas but the coverage has been low.

Given the gradual erosion of the traditional social security system, the increasing pressures on common property resources and the absence of season-specific or dryland-specific government programmes, residents of Maatisar have to rely increasingly on their own initiatives in adjusting to seasonal shortages. Although improved irrigation and transportation have increased the options for agriculture and wage employment, many households remain highly vulnerable to shortages in food supply, wage employment and other livelihood flows.

Unlike private drought management by individual households, public drought management has been developed in isolation from ongoing development strategies or chronic subsistence needs. By focusing on the short term, public drought management does not address the need to develop appropriate dryland technologies (crop, soil, water management), to regenerate and conserve the bio-mass, to provide employment on a regular basis and to provide seasonal loans and inputs in normal years.

In conclusion, the rural economy of Maatisar, like countless other villages in semi-arid regions of India, is characterised by modest progress yet persistent vulnerability to the vagaries of both the weather and the wider economy. Rural households, both rich and poor, have adopted strategies to cushion themselves against these uncertainties. The tendencies of some to view villages as static isolates and of others to view villages in terms of aggregate output or market behaviour have failed to illuminate this dynamism.

This study explored the specific vulnerabilities and responses of various household groups in a single village. The changes over time described in Part I indicate that the village economy remains vulnerable despite moderate growth and development. As shown in Part II, seasonal fluctuations can heighten this vulnerability. And, as discussed in Part III, drought conditions further heighten and often draw attention to this vulnerability. The study argues that droughts need to be analysed not only as short-term isolated phenomena but also as longer-term repeated phenomena which, together with seasonal fluctuations, help determine rural livelihood options and patterns. By describing and analysing how households cope with seasonality and drought in a single villlage, this study is intended to contribute to the understanding of the dynamics of rural poverty in India, if not more broadly.

Glossary

Agewan	scout or leader for team of labourers
Ambar-charka	type of spinning wheel
Ardhu bhaje	one-half share
Avedo	cattle trough
Babul	type of tree
Banyan	a sacred tree
Barot	genealogist caste; a local Scheduled Caste
Bel	type of tree; also called *billi*
Ber	type of tree
Bhadarvo	month in Hindu calendar
Bhangi	scavenger caste; a Scheduled Caste
Bhare	system of mortgaging land whereby owner retains use rights; also referred to as *giro haath*
Bharwad	shepherd caste; a local Backward Caste
Bhata	brick kiln
Bhatha	a variety of shrub grass
Bhelan	system of patrolling private fields
Bid	a kind of water chestnut
Bidi	hand-rolled cigarettes
Bigha	unit of land equal to 0.57 acre
Billi	type of tree; also called *bel*
Bua	spirit possessor
Bunti	a coarse reddish grain; also called *kodara*
Byaj	interest-bearing loans without collateral
Chaas	buttermilk
Chaitra	month in Hindu calendar
Chamar	tanner caste; a Scheduled Caste
Chappals	sandals
Chappanu	literally, 'fifty-six'; local name for drought of 1899 (or the year Samvat 1856 of the Hindu calendar)
Danda	means of earning or livelihood

Darbar	local Rajput caste
Dari	daily wage system
Dattan	reeds for brushing teeth
Desi	traditional; local
Desi babul	type of tree
Dhabla	thick, woollen shawl woven by local Vankar caste
Dhal	lentils
Dholi	drum
Diwali	Hindu festival of lights
Ekatrij	Farmer's New Year; third day of Vaisakh month in Hindu calendar
Garas	designated set of customer–patrons
Gauchar	permanent pasture land
Ghee	clarified butter
Giro	mortgaging property
Giro haath	system of mortgaging land whereby owner retains use rights
Gokharu	medicinal herb
Gol	designated circle of villagers for each caste group within which marriages are transacted
Goradu	medium brown soil
Gram panchayat	village council
Guar	a variety of bean
Gundi	gifts or concessions for providing caste-services
Holi	Hindu festival of colors
Hookah	water bowl tobacco pipe
Inams	concessions for providing caste-services
Jajman	patrons under *jajmani* system
Jajmani	caste-based system whereby castes render specified services to other castes
Jinjua	type of plant
Jitela	type of lotus flower
Jividar	peon
Juwar	sorghum
Kahavat	saying
Kamins	clients under *jajmani* system, such as barbers or carpenters
Kandh	a bitter root
Kharif	monsoon season (June–September)
Kitchari	rice and lentil gruel; also a rice and salt gruel eaten in droughts
kodara	coarse reddish grain; also called *bunti*
Koli Patel	peasant caste; a local Backward Caste
Kos	traditional system of lift irrigation which relied on bullock power
Kuccha	literally, 'raw' or unfinished; when used to describe housing, refers to simple huts made of thatch and bamboo
Kutumb	clan
Kyari	low-lying alluvial soil
Lakh	hundred thousand
Mahowra	type of tree
Mandi didu	loans against mortgaged property (houses or assets)
Maund	20 kilograms
Mehsal	revenue tax; also called *vighoti*

Mugh	local pulse variety
Mukadam	jobber or contractor for migrant labourers
Mukhi	local police chief
Muth	red gram
Naiks	barbers
Nama	credit sales
Neem	type of tree
Paan	mixture of betel nut with lime wrapped in betel leaf
Pachavi padu	foreclosure on mortgaged land
Panch	caste council
Panchayat	council
Panch patel	member of caste council
Pasayita	payments for caste-based services
Peepal	type of tree
Piloo	type of tree
Prajapati	potter caste; a local Backward Caste
Pujari	priest
Punjrapole	cattle camp
Rabi	winter season (November–March)
Rakhai	pawning
Rawal	camel carter caste; a local Backward Caste
Rayan	type of tree
Rojio	daily wage labour
Rotla	unleavened bread
Saathi	attached labour
Sari	six-yard length of cloth worn by women
Sarpanch	village headman
Shravan	month in Hindu calendar
Sutars	carpenter caste; a Backward Caste
Taccavi	emergency loans
Talati	village accountant
Talav/Talavdi	water tanks
Taluka	sub-district administrative area
Talukdar	feudal landlords; also spelt *taluqdar*
Talukdari	system of tenancy resembling independent princely states
Thakkar	trader caste; a local Vaishya caste
Thaliya	sandy loam soil
Tikka	coloured marking on forehead
Toli	team of labourers
Triju bhaje	one-third share
Tuar	local pulse
Uchina	short-term, interest-free loan
Udhad/Udhadu	piece-rate or contract system
Udhar	credit sales
Upadh	credit advances
Vaan	locally-made rope to string cots
Vaghri	vendor caste; a local Backward Caste
Vankar	weaver caste; a local Scheduled Caste

Varna	caste groups
Vas	neighbourhood
Vasvayas	Gujarati term for service castes under *jajmani* system
Veth	mandatory caste-based services to feudal landlord
Vighoti	revenue tax

Bibliography

ACHARYA, MEENA (1982) 'Time Use Data and the Living Standards Measurement Study', Living Standard Measurement Study Working Paper No. 18. Washington DC: The World Bank.

ACHARYA, MEENA and LYNN BENNETT (1983) 'Women and the Subsistence Sector: Economic Participation and Household Decision Making in Nepal', Staff Working Papers No. 526. Washington DC: The World Bank.

AGA KHAN RURAL SUPPORT PROGRAMME (1989) 'Common Property Land Resources (CPR-Land) in Gujarat and Problems of Their Development', Proceedings of the Workshop on CPR-Land. Ahmedabad, India: Gujarat Institute of Area Planning.

AGARWAL, BINA (1979) 'Work Participation of Women in Rural India: Some Data and Conceptual Biases', Sussex, UK: IDS. University of Sussex.

————— (1981) 'Agricultural Modernization and Third World Women: Pointers from the Literature and An Empirical Analysis', Rural Employment Policy Research Program, Geneva: ILO.

————— (1985) 'Women and Technological Change in Agriculture: Asian and African Experience', in Iftikar Ahmed (ed.) *Technology and Rural Women: Conceptual and Empirical Issues*, Geneva: ILO.

————— (1986) 'Women, Poverty, and Agricultural Growth in India', *The Journal of Peasant Studies*, Vol. 13, No. 4.

————— (1987) 'Under the Cooking Pot: The Political Economy of the Domestic Fuel Crisis in Rural South Asia', *IDS Bulletin*, Vol. 18, No. 1.

————— (1988) 'Who Sows? Who Reaps? Women and Land Rights in India', *The Journal of Peasant Studies*. Vol. 15, No. 4.

————— (1989) 'Social Security and the Family in Rural India', DEP No. 21, The Development Economics Research Programme, London: London School of Economics.

AHUJA, KANTA (1979) 'Measurement of Rural Labour Surpluses', *Contribution of Asian Studies*, 13.

————— (1979) *Women Workers in Rural Rajasthan*, Jaipur, India: The HCM Institute of Public Administration.

ALAMGIR, M. (1980) *Famine in South Asia: Political Economy of Mass Starvation.* Cambridge, Mass.: Oelgeschlager, Gunn and Hain, Publishers, Inc.

ALHUWALIA, MONTEK S. (1978) *Rural Poverty in India: 1956–57 to 1973–74.* Washington, DC: The World Bank.

ANKER, RICHARD (1980) 'Research on Women's Roles and Demographic Change: Survey Questionnaires for Households, Women, Men, and Communities with Background Explanations', Geneva: ILO.

——————— (1983) 'Female Labour Force Participation in Developing Countries: A Critique of Current Definitions and Data Collection Methods', *International Labour Review*, Vol. 122, No. 6.

APPADURAI, ARJUN (1984) 'How Moral is South Asia's Economy? A Review Article', *Journal of Asian Studies*, Vol. 43, No. 3.

ARIZPE, LOURDES (1982) 'Relay Migration and the Survival of the Peasant Household', in Helen I. Safa (ed.) *Towards a Political Economy of Urbanization in the Third World Countries*, Delhi: Oxford University Press.

ASAG (1982) 'Handloom Weavers of Dholka', Ahmedabad, India: ASAG.

ASIA SOCIETY (1978) 'Time Use Data: Policy Uses and Methods of Collection', Report of a Workshop on Time Use Data, New York: The Asia Society.

ATTWOOD, D.W. (1979) 'Why Some of the Poor Get Richer: Economic Change and Mobility in Rural Western India', *Current Anthropology*, Vol. 20, No. 3.

BANDYOPADHYAY, JAYANTA (1987) 'Political Ecology of Drought and Water Scarcity: Need for an Ecological Water Resources Policy', *Economic and Political Weekly*, Vol. XXII, No. 50.

BANERJEE, NARAYAN (1988) 'Women's Work and Family Strategies: A Case Study from Bankura, West Bengal', New Delhi: Centre for Women's Development Studies.

BANERJEE, NIRMALA (1982) 'Women in the Labor Force—The Bengal Experience', Paper prepared for a Technical Seminar on Women's Work and Employment, New Delhi.

——————— 1983. 'Women's Work', Paper presented at a Workshop on Women and Poverty, ICSSR, Eastern Regional Centre and CSSS, Calcutta.

BARDHAN, KALPANA (1985) 'Women's Work, Welfare and Status: Forces of Tradition and Change in India', *Economic and Political Weekly*, Vol. XX, Nos. 50–51.

BARDHAN, PRANAB K. (1976) 'Variations in Extent and Forms of Agricultural Tenancy: An Analysis of Indian Data Across Regions and Over Time', *Economic and Political Weekly*, Parts I & II, Vol. XI, Nos. 37 & 38.

——————— (1978a) 'Some Employment and Unemployment Characteristics of Rural Women: An Analysis of NSS Data for West Bengal 1972–73', *Economic and Political Weekly*, Vol. XIII, No. 12.

——————— (1978b) 'On Measuring Rural Unemployment', *Journal of Development Studies*, Vol. 14.

——————— (1979a) 'Work as a Medium of Earning and Social Differentiation: Rural Women of West Bengal', Prepared for the ADC-ICRISAT Conference on Adjustment Mechanisms of Rural Labour Markets in Developing Areas, Hyderabad: ICRISAT.

——————— (1979b) 'Labor Supply Functions in a Poor Agrarian Economy', *The American Economic Review*, 69, No. 1.

BARDHAN, PRANAB K. (1984a) *Land, Labour, and Rural Poverty: Essays in Development Economics*, Delhi: Oxford University Press.

———— (1984b) *The Political Economy of Development in India*, Oxford: Basil Blackwell Publisher Ltd.

BARDHAN, P.K. and A. RUDRA (1978) 'Inter-Linkage of Land, Labour and Credit Relations: An Analysis of Village Survey Data in East India', *Economic and Political Weekly*, Annual Number, Vol. 13.

BARDHAN, P.K. and T.N. SRINIVASAN (eds.) (1985) *Rural Poverty in South Asia*, New York: Columbia University Press.

BATES, ROBERT H. (1986) 'From Drought to Famine in Kenya', Program in International Political Economy, Working Paper No. 5. Durham, North Carolina: Duke University.

BATLIWALA, S. (1983) 'Women in Poverty: The Energy, Health, and Nutrition Syndrome', Paper presented at the Workshop on Women and Poverty, Calcutta: Centre for Studies in Social Sciences.

BEHRMAN, JERE R. (1988a). 'Nutrition, Health, Birth Order, and Seasonality: Intrahousehold Allocation Among Children in Rural India', *Journal of Development Economics*, 28.

———— (1988b) 'Intrahousehold Allocation of Nutrients in Rural India: Are Boys Favored? Do Parents Exhibit Inequality Aversion?', *Oxford Economic Papers*, 40.

BEHRMAN, JERE and A.B. DEOLALIKAR (1987) 'Will Developing Country Nutrition Improve with Income? A Case Study for Rural South India', *Journal of Political Economy*, Vol. 95, No. 3.

———— (1989a) 'Is Variety the Spice of Life? Implications for Calorie Intake', *Review of Economics and Statistics*, Vol. 71, No. 4.

———— (1989b) 'Seasonal Demands for Nutrient Intakes and Health Status in Rural South India', in D.E. Sahn (ed.) *Causes and Implications of Seasonal Variability in Household Food Security*, Baltimore: Johns Hopkins University Press.

———— (1990) 'The Intrahousehold Demand for Nutrients in Rural South India: Individual Estimates, Fixed Effects, and Permanent Income', *The Journal of Human Resources*, Vol. 25, No. 4.

BEHRMAN, JERE, A.B. DEOLALIKAR, and B.L. WOLFE (1988) 'Nutrients: Impacts and Determinants', *The World Bank Economic Review*, Vol. 2, No. 3.

BENERIA, LOURDES and G. SEN (1982) 'Class and Gender Inequalities and Women's Role in Economic Development—Theoretical and Practical Implications', *Feminist Studies*, 8, No. 1.

BETEILLE, A. and T.N. MADAN (eds.) (1975) *Encounter and Experience: Personal Accounts of Fieldwork*, Delhi: Vikas Publishing House.

BHADURI, A. (1973) 'Agricultural Backwardness Under Semi-Feudalism', *Economic Journal*, Vol. 83.

BHARADWAJ, KRISHNA (1974) *Production Conditions in Indian Agriculture*, Cambridge: Cambridge University Press.

BHARADWAJ, KRISHNA and P.K. DAS (1975) 'Tenurial Conditions and Mode of Exploitation: A Study of Some Villages in Orissa', *Economic and Political Weekly*, Vol. 10.

BHARARA, L.P. (1982) 'Notes on the Experience of Drought: Perception, Recollection, and Prediction' in B. Spooner and H.S. Manu (eds.) *Desertification and Development: Dryland Ecology in Social Perspective*, New York: Academic Press.

BINSWANGER, H.P., N.S. JODHA and B.C. BARAH (1979) 'The Nature and Significance of Risk in the Semi-Arid Tropics', Paper prepared for the Workshop on Socioeconomic Constraints to Development of Semi-Arid Tropical Agriculture, Hyderabad: ICRISAT.

BINSWANGER, HANS P., R.E. EVENSON, C.A FLORENCIO and B. WHITE (1980) *Rural Household Studies in Asia*, Singapore: Singapore University Press.

BINSWANGER, H.P. and M.R. ROSENZWEIG (eds.) (1981) *Contractual Arrangements, Employment and Wages in Rural Labor Markets: A Critical Review*, New York: ADC and Hyderabad: ICRISAT.

BIRDSALL, N. (1978) 'Rapporteur's Report', Workshop on Time Use Data, New York: The Asia Society.

————— (1980) 'Measuring Time Use and Non-Market Exchange', in W.P. McGreeny (ed.) *Third World Poverty*, Toronto: Lexington Books.

BLAIKIE, PIERS, J. HARRISS and A.N. PAIN (1985) 'The Management and Use of Common Property Resources in Tamil Nadu, India', Paper prepared for the Common Property Steering Committee, Board on Science and Technology for International Development (BOSTID), Washington, DC: National Research Council.

BLISS, C.J. and N.H. STERN (1982) *Palanpur: The Economy of an Indian Village*, Oxford: Oxford University Press.

BOLLES, A. LYNN (1981) 'Household Economic Strategies in Kingston Jamaica', in N. Black and A.B. Cottrell (eds.) *Women and Social Change: Equity Issues in Development*, Beverly Hills and London: Sage.

BOSE, A.B. and N.S. JODHA (1965) 'The *Jajmani* System in a Desert Village', *Man in India*, Vol. 45, No. 2.

BOULDING, E. (n.d.) 'Productivity and Poverty of Third World Women: Problems in Measurement', in M. Buvinic (ed.) *Poverty as a Women's Issue*, Washington, DC: International Center for Research on Women.

BOULIER, BRYAN L. (1977) 'An Evaluation of Time Budget Studies as Complements to Conventional Labor Force Surveys', Annual meeting of the Population Association of America, St. Louis, Missouri.

BREMAN, J. (1974) *Patronage and Exploitation: Changing Agrarian Relations in South Gujarat, India*, Berkeley: University of California Press.

————— (1985) *Of Peasants, Migrants and Paupers: Rural Labour Circulation and Capitalist Production in West India*, Delhi: Oxford University Press.

BUVINIC, MAYRA and NADYA YOUSSEF (1978) 'Women-Headed Households: The Ignored Factor in Development', Report prepared for USAID, Office of Women in Development, Washington, DC: International Center for Research on Women.

CAHILL, K.M. (ed.) (1982) *Famine*, Maryknoll, New York: Orbis Books.

CAIN, MEAD (1977) 'Household Time Budgets', Village Fertility Study Methodology Report No. 1, Dhaka, Bangladesh: BIDS.

————— (1983) 'Intensive Community Studies', Paper prepared for the seminar on

Collection and Analysis of Data on Community and International Factors, London: World Fertility Survey, International Statistical Institute.

CALDWELL, JOHN C. (1975) 'The Sahelian Drought and Its Demographic Implications', Washington, DC: Overseas Liaison Committee, American Council on Education.

———— n.d. 'Food Production and Crisis in the West African Savarnah', Occasional Paper No. 25, Canberra: Development Studies Centre, Australian National University.

———— (1984) 'Desertification: Demographic Evidence, 1973–83', A Report to the United Nations Environmental Programme Desertification Section, Canberra: Development Studies Centre, Australian National University.

———— (1986) 'Micro-Approaches: Similarities and Different Strengths and Weaknesses', in Hill, Caldwell, Hill (eds.) *The Mircro-Approach to Demographic Research*.

CALDWELL, JOHN C., P.H. REDDY and PAT CALDWELL (1984) 'Causes of Fertility Decline in South India', *Fertility Determinants Research Notes*, No. 3. New York: The Population Council.

———— (1986a) 'Periodic High Risk as a Cause of Fertility Decline in a Changing Rural Environment: Survival Strategies in the 1980–83 South Indian Drought', *Economic Development and Cultural Change*, Vol. 34, No. 4.

———— (1986b) 'Investigating the Nature of Population Change in South India: Experimenting with a Micro-Approach', in Hill, Caldwell, Hill (eds.) *The Micro-Approach to Demographic Research*.

———— (1986c) 'Experimental Research in South India', Paper presented at the XI World Congress of Sociology, New Delhi.

CALDWELL, JOHN and PAT CALDWELL (1986) 'Research on Policy Significance on Fertility and Its Control', Paper presented at the XI World Conference on Sociology, New Delhi.

———— (1987) 'Famine in Africa', Paper for presentation to IUSSP Seminar on Mortality, Society in Sub-Saharan Africa, Iford, Yaounde.

CAMPBELL, DAVID (1984) 'Response to Drought Among Farmers and Herders in Southern Kajiado District, Kenya', *Human Ecology*, Vol. 12, No. 1.

CENTRE FOR SCIENCE AND ENVIRONMENT (1982 and 1986) *The State of India's Environment: A Citizen's Report*, New Delhi: Centre for Science and Environment.

CENTRE FOR WOMEN'S DEVELOPMENT STUDIES (n.d.) *Women's Work and Family Strategies: The Indian National Study*, New Delhi: Centre for Women's Development Studies.

CHAMBERS, ROBERT (1981a) 'Introduction', in R. Chambers et al. (eds.) *Seasonal Dimensions of Rural Poverty*.

———— (1981b) 'Seasonality in Rural Experience', in R. Chambers et al. (eds.) *Seasonal Dimensions of Rural Poverty*.

———— (1986) 'Poverty in India: Concepts, Research and Reality', Sussex, UK: IDS, University of Sussex.

———— (1989) 'Editorial Introduction: Vulnerability, Coping and Policy', *IDS Bulletin*, Vol. 20, No. 2.

———— (1989) 'Vulnerability: How the Poor Cope', *IDS Bulletin*, Vol. 20, No. 2.

CHAMBERS, R. and R. LONGHURST (1986) 'Trees, Seasons, and the Poor', *IDS Bulletin*, Vol. 17, No. 3.

CHAMBERS, R., R. LONGHURST and A. PACEY (eds.) (1981) *Seasonal Dimensions of Rural Poverty*, UK: Frances Pinter.

CHEN, MARTY (1989) 'Women's Work in Indian Agriculture by Agro-Ecological Zones: Meeting the Needs of Landless and Landpoor Women', *Economic and Political Weekly*, Vol. XXI, No. 5.

CHEN, MARTY and R. GHUZNAVI (1979) *Women in Food for Work*, Rome: United Nations World Food Programme.

CHEN, MARTY et al. (1985) *Indian Women: A Study of their Role in the Dairy Movement*, New Delhi: Vikas Publishers.

CHOPRA, KUSUM (1977) 'Female Work Participation in the Three Crop Regions of India: An Inter-Temporal Study of Rural India Between 1951, 1961 and 1971', Programme of Women's Studies, New Delhi: ICSSR.

CHOPRA, R.N. (1981) *Evolution of Food Policy in India*, New Delhi: Macmillan India Ltd.

CHOWDHURY, K.M. and M.T. BAPAT (1975) 'A Study of Impact of Famine and Relief Measures in Gujarat and Rajasthan', Research Study No. 44. Ahmedabad: Agro–Economic Research Centre, Sardar Patel University.

CHUA, CATHY (1986) 'Development of Capitalism in Indian Agriculture: Gujarat, 1850–1900', *Economic and Political Weekly*, Vol. XXI, No. 48.

CONNELL, J., DASGUPTA, B., LAISHLEY, R. and M. LIPTON (1976) *Migration from Rural Areas: The Evidence from Village Studies*, Delhi: Oxford University Press.

CORBETT, J.E.M. (1988) 'Famine and Household Coping Strategies', *World Development*, Vol. 16, No. 9.

DANDEKAR, K. (1983) *Employment Guarantee Scheme: An Employment Opportunity for Women*, Pune: Gokhale Institute of Politics and Economics.

DANDEKAR, V.M. and NILAKANTHA RATH (1971) *Poverty in India*, Pune: Indian School of Political Economy.

DANTWALA, M.L. (1985) ' "Garibi Hatao": Strategy Options', *Economic and Political Weekly*, Vol. XX, No. 11.

DASGUPTA, MONICA (1986) 'The Use of Genealogies for Reconstructing Social History and Analysing Fertility Behaviour in a North Indian Village.' In *The Micro-Approach to Demographic Research*, (eds.) Hill, Caldwell, Hill.

————— (1987) 'Informal Security Systems and Population Retention in Rural India', *Economic Development and Cultural Change*, Vol. 35, No. 2.

DASGUPTA, S. and A.K. MAIT (1987) 'The Rural Energy Crisis, Poverty, and Women's Roles in Five Indian Villages', Technical Cooperation Report, World Employment Programme, Geneva: ILO.

DE JANVRY, ALAIN (1979) 'A Conceptual Framework for the Empirical Analysis of Peasants', *American Journal of Agricultural Economics*, Vol. 61, No. 4.

DESAI, G.M., SINGH G. and D.C. SAH (1979) 'Impact of Scarcity on Farm Economy and Significance of Relief Operations', CMA, Monograph No. 84. Ahmedabad: Indian Institute of Management.

DESAI, R.X. (1982) 'Migration Labour and Women: The Case of Ratnagiri', World Employment Programme, Research Working Paper No. 8, 28, Geneva: ILO.

DE TRAY, DENNIS N. (1977) 'Household Studies Workshop', Seminar Report, No. 13, New York: Agricultural Development Council.

————— (1980) 'On the Micro-Economics of Family Behavior in Developing Societies.' In *Rural Household Studies in Asia*, (eds.) Binswanger et al.

DIRKS, R. (1980) 'Social Responses During Severe Food Shortages and Famine', *Current Anthropology*, 21 (1).

DISHA (1988) 'Survey Report on the Working Conditions, Daily Wages, and the Problems of the Labourers Engaged on Drought Relief Works in Tribal Areas of Sabarkantha district, Gujarat', Ahmedabad: DISHA.

DREZE, JEAN (1988a) 'Famine Prevention in India', DEP No. 3, The Development Economics Research Programme, London: London School of Economics.

———— (1988b) 'Social Insecurity in India: A Case Study', Paper prepared for a STICERD/WIDER Workshop on Social Security in Developing Countries. London: London School of Economics.

DREZE, JEAN and A. MUKHERJEE (1987) 'Labour Contracts in Rural India: Theories and Evidence', Discussion Paper No. 7, Development Research Programme, London: London School of Economics.

DREZE, J. and A.K. SEN (1988) 'Public Action for Social Security: Foundation and Strategy', Paper prepared for STICERD/WIDER Workshop on Social Security in Developing Countries, London: London School of Economics.

DYSON, T. and M. MOORE (1983) 'Kinship Structure, Female Autonomy, and Demographic Behaviour in India', *Population and Development Review*, 9, 1.

EPSTEIN, S. (1967) 'Productive Efficiency and Customary Systems of Rewards in Rural South India', in Raymond Firth (ed.) *Themes in Economic Anthropology*, London: Tavistock Publications.

EVENSON, ROBERT E. (1976) 'On the New Household Economics', *Journal of Agricultural Economics and Development*, Vol. VI, No. 1.

———— (1978) 'Philippine Household Economics: An Introduction to the Symposium Papers', *Philippine Economic Journal*, No. 36, Vol. XVII, Nos. 1 & 2.

EVENSON, ROBERT E., B.M. POPKIN and E.K. QUIZON (1980) 'Nutrition, Work, and Demographic Behavior in Rural Philippine Households: A Synopsis of Several Laguna Household Studies', in Binswanger et al. (eds.) *Rural Household Studies in Asia*.

FAO (1983) 'Time Allocation Survey: A Tool for Antropologists, Economists, and Nutritionists', Rome: Food Policy and Nutrition Division, FAO.

FELDSTEIN, HILARY S. (1986) 'Intra-Household Dynamics and Farming Systems Research and Extension: Conceptual Framework and Worksheets', Paper prepared for the Conference on Gender Issues in Farming Systems Research and Extension, Gainesville, Florida: University of Florida.

FOLBRE, NANCY (1982) 'Exploitation Comes Home: A Critique of the Marxian Theory of Family Labor', *Cambridge Journal of Economics*, 6.

———— (1983) 'Household Production in the Philippines: A Neo-Classical Approach', WID Working Paper No. 26. Michigan: Michigan State University.

FRANKEL, FRANCINE R. (1978) *India's Political Economy, 1974–77: The Gradual Revolution*, Princeton, New Jersey: Princeton University Press.

GHOSH, B. and S.K. MUKHOPADHYAY (1984) 'Displacement of the Female in the Indian Labour Force', *Economic and Political Weekly*, Vol. XIX, No. 47.

GILL, TEENA (1989) 'Case of Famine Monitoring: A Gender Perspective', *Economic and Political Weekly*, Vol. XXIV, No. 43.

GOLDSCHMIDT-CLERMONT, LUISELLA (1983) 'Output-Related Evaluations of

Unpaid Household Work: A Challenge for Time Use Studies', *Home Economics Research Journal*, Vol. 12, No. 2.

GOVERNMENT OF GUJARAT (1966) 'Territorial Changes in Gujarat State', Gujarat: Government Central Press.

———— (1976) 'Evaluation Study of Impact of Land Reform Measures in Gujarat State', Gandhinagar: Directorate of Evaluation.

———— (1979) 'Report of the Gujarat State Land Commission.'

———— (1982) Statistical Atlas, Vols. I and II.

———— (1961, 1971, 1981) Gujarat Census: District Census Handbooks.

———— (1984) Gujarat State Gazetteers: Ahmedabad District.

———— (1987a) Taluka-Wise Figures on Rainfall (mimeo).

———— (1987b) District-Wise List of Scarcity Works (mimeo).

GOVERNMENT OF INDIA (1989) *Economic Survey 1988–89*, New Delhi: Ministry of Finance.

———— (1974 and 1975) *Rural Labor Enquiry*.

GREENOUGH, P.R. (1982) *Prosperity and Misery in Modern Bengal: The Famine of 1943–44*, New York: Oxford University Press.

GRONAU, REUBEN (1980) 'Leisure, Home Production, and Work: The Theory of the Allocation of Time Revisited', in Binswanger et al (eds.) *Rural Household Studies in Asia*, Singapore: Singapore University Press.

GROSVENOR-ALSOP, RUTH (1986) 'Viability and Method—The Possibilities for Farming Systems Research in Bihar, India', Paper prepared for the Conference on Gender Issues in Farming Systems Research and Extension, Gainesville, Florida: University of Florida.

GUHAN, S. (1981) 'Social Security: Lessons and Possibilities from the Tamil Nadu Experience', *Madras Institute of Development Studies Bulletin*, XI (1).

———— (1981) *A Primer on Poverty: India and Tamil Nadu*, Popular Series No. 2, Madras: Madras Institute of Development Studies.

GULATI, LEELA (1975) 'Occupational Distribution of Working Women: A Later State Comparison', *Economic and Political Weekly*, Vol. X, No. 43.

———— (1976) 'Unemployment Among Female Agricultural Laborers', *Economic and Political Weekly*, Vol. XI, No. 13, Review of Agriculture.

———— (1978) 'Profile of a Female Agricultural Labor', *Economic and Political Weekly*, Vol. XIII, No. 12.

———— (1982) *Profiles in Female Poverty: A Study of Five Working Women in Kerala*, New York: Pergamon Press and Delhi: Hindustan Publishers.

GUPTA, ANIL K. (1984) 'Socio-Ecology of Land Use Planning in Semi-Arid Regions', Working Paper No. 524, Ahmedabad: Indian Institute of Management.

———— (1985) 'Small Farmer Household Economy in Semi-Arid Regions: Socio-Ecological Perspective', CMA Project Report, Ahmedabad: Indian Institute of Management.

———— (1986a) 'Socio-Ecology of Grazing Land Management', in P.J. Ross, P.W. Lynch and O.B. Williams (eds.) *Rangelands: A Resource Under Siege*, Proceedings of the Second International Rangeland Congress.

———— (1986b) 'How Common is Commons: Political Economy of Wasteland Development', Paper prepared for a Seminar on Control of Drought, Desertification and Famine, New Delhi.

———— (1986c) 'Sociology of Stress: Why Do Common Property Resource

Management Projects Fail?', in Proceedings of the Conference on Common Property Resource Management, Washington, DC: National Research Council.

GUPTA, ANIL K. (1988a) 'Household Survival Strategies in Risky Ecological Context: Matching Individual, Institutional and State Responses', Paper presented at 7th World Congress of Rural Sociology, Bologna.

———— (1988b) 'Survival Under Stress: Socioecological Perspective on Farmers' Innovation and Risk Adjustments', Working Paper No. 738, Ahmedabad: Indian Institute of Management.

GUPTA, ANIL K., Y. MANDAVKAR, S. AMIN and R.N. SHAH (1987) 'Role of Women in Risk Adjustment in Drought Prone Regions', Working Paper No. 704, Ahmedabad: Indian Institute of Management.

GUYER, JANE I. (1980) 'Household Budgets and Women's Incomes', Working Paper No. 28, Boston: African Studies Center, Boston University.

———— (1981) 'The Raw, the Cooked and the Half-Baked: A Note on the Division of Labor by Sex', Working Paper No. 48, Boston: African Studies Center, Boston University.

———— (1984) *Family and Farm in Southern Cameroon*, African Studies No. 15, Boston: African Studies Center, Boston University.

———— (1985) 'On the Multiplication of Labor', Paper presented for the Construction of Natural Economy, Invited Session, American Anthropological Association Meetings.

———— (1986) 'Synchronising Seasonalities', Boston: African Studies Center, Boston University.

HARRIS, JOHN (1985) 'What Happened to the Green Revolution in South India: Economic Trends, Household Mobility and the Politics of an "Awkward Class" ', Discussion Paper No. 175, East Anglia, UK: School of Development Studies, University of East Anglia.

———— (n.d.) 'Making Out on Limited Resources: or What Happened to Semi-Feudalism in a Bengal District', *Transactions*, Vol. 2, Nos. 1 and 2.

HART, GILLIAN (1980) 'Patterns of Labor Allocation in a Javanese Village', in Binswanger et al. (eds.) *Rural Household Studies in Asia*, Singapore: Singapore University Press.

HAWRYLYSHYN, OLI (1976) 'The Value of Household Services: A Survey of Empirical Estimates', *The Review of Income and Wealth*, Vol. 22, No. 2.

———— (1977) 'Towards a Definition of Non-Market Activities', *The Review of Income and Wealth*, Vol. 23, No. 1.

HERRING, RONALD J. and R.M. EDWARDS (1983) 'Guaranteeing Employment for the Rural Poor: Social Functions and Class Interests in the Employment Guarantee Scheme in Western India', *World Development*, Vol. II, No. 7.

HEYER, JUDITH (1989) 'Landless Agricultural Labourers' Asset Strategies', *IDS Bulletin*, Vol. 20, No. 2.

HILL, POLLY (1982) *Dry Grain Farming Families: Hausaland (Nigeria) and Karnataka (India) Compared*, Cambridge: Cambridge University Press.

HILL, VALLERIE J., JOHN C. CALDWELL and ALLAN HILL (eds.) (1986) *The Micro-Approach to Demographic Research*, London: Kegan Paul International.

HUSS-ASHMORE, REBECCA (1988) 'Introduction: Why Study Seasons', in R. Huss-Ashmore, J.J. Cury, and R.K. Hitchcock (eds.) *Coping with Seasonal Constraints*.

HUSS-ASHMORE, REBECCA, J.J. CURRY and R.K. HITCHCOCK (eds.) (1988) *Coping with Seasonal Constraints*, MASCA Research Papers in *Science and Archaeology*, Vol. 15, Philadelphia: The University Museum, University of Pennsylvania.

INTERNATIONAL CENTER FOR RESEARCH ON WOMEN (1980) 'The Productivity of Women in Developing Countries: Measurement Issues and Recommendations', Washington, DC: International Center for Research on Women.

IYENGAR, SUDARSHAN (1988) 'Common Property Land Resources in Gujarat: Some Findings about their Size, Status and Use', Working Paper No. 18, Ahmedabad: Gujarat Institute of Area Planning.

JAIN, DEVAKI and MALINI CHAND (1980) 'An Investigation into the Time Allocation of Men, Women and Children in Selected Rural Households', Paper prepared for the Seminar on Women in the Indian Labour Force, Trivandrum: Center for Development Studies.

JAIN, DEVAKI and N. BANERJEE (1985) *Tyranny of the Household*, New Delhi: Shakti Books, Vikas Publishing House Pvt. Ltd.

JEFFERY, PATRICIA, ROGER JEFFERY and ANDREW LYON (1986) 'When Did You Last See Your Mother?: Aspects of Female Autonomy in Rural North India', in Hill, Caldwell, Hill (eds.) *The Micro-Approach to Demographic Research*, London: Kegan Paul International.

JETLY, S. (1987) 'Impact of Male Migration on Rural Females', *Economic and Political Weekly*, Vol. 22, No. 44.

JIGGINS, JANICE (1985) 'Special Problems of Female Heads of Households in Agriculture and Rural Development in Asia and the Pacific', Paper prepared for the Regional Home Economics and Social Programmes Office, Bangkok, Thailand: FAO Regional Office for Asia and the Pacific.

————— (1986) 'Women and Seasonality: Coping with Crisis and Calamity', *IDS Bulletin*, Vol. 17, No. 3.

JODHA, N.S. (1975) 'Famine and Famine Policies: Some Empirical Evidence', *Economic and Political Weekly*, Vol. 10, No. 41.

————— (1978) 'Effectiveness of Farmers' Adjustments to Risk', *Economic and Political Weekly*, Vol. XIII, No. 25.

————— (1979a) 'Intercropping in Traditional Farming Systems', Economics Programme Progress Report 3, Hyderabad: ICRISAT.

————— (1979b) 'The Processes of Desertification and the Choice of Interventions', Economics Program Progress Report 2, Hyderabad: ICRISAT.

————— (1979c) 'Some Dimensions of Traditional Farming in Semi-Arid Tropical India', Economics Program Progress Report 4, Hyderabad: ICRISAT.

————— (1981a) 'Role of Credit in Farmers' Adjustment Against Risk in Arid and Semi-Arid Tropical Areas of India', *Economic and Political Weekly*, Vol. 16, Nos. 42–43.

————— (1981b) 'Agricultural Tenancy: Fresh Evidence from Dryland Areas in India', *Economic and Political Weekly*, Vol. XVI, No. 52, Review of Agriculture.

————— (1983) 'Market Forces and Erosion of Common Property Resources', Paper presented at the International Workshop on Agricultural Markets in the Semi-Arid Tropics, Hyderabad: ICRISAT.

JODHA, N.S. (1985a) 'Population Growth and the Decline of Common Property Resources in Rajasthan', *Population and Development Review*, Vol. 11, No. 2.

————— (1985b) 'Social Research on Rural Change: Some Gaps', Paper presented at the Conference on Rural Economic Change in South Asia: Differences in Approach and in Results between Large-Scale Surveys and Intensive Micro-Studies, Bangalore, India.

————— (1986a) 'Common Property-Resources and Rural Poor in Dry Regions of India', *Economic and Political Weekly*, Vol. XXI, No. 27.

————— (1986b) 'Social Science Research on Rural Change: Some Gaps', Hyderabad: ICRISAT.

————— (1988) 'Poverty Debate in India: A Minority View', *Economic and Political Weekly*, Vol. XXIII, Nos. 45, 46, and 47.

————— (1989) 'Drought Management: The Farmers' Strategies and their Policy Implications', Paper presented at the National Workshop on Management of Agriculture and Cooperatives, Government of India.

KALPAGAM, U. (1986) 'Gender in Economics—The Indian Experience', MIDS Offprint-7, Madras: Madras Institute of Development Studies.

KANBARGI, R. and P.M. KULKARNI 'Child Labour, Schooling and Fertility in Rural Karnataka, South India', Bangalore: Population Research Centre, Institute for Social and Economic Change.

KHATU, K.K., B. JAYARAMAN and A.R. D'SOUZA (1981) *Land Use in Gujarat: Status and Strategy for Conservation*, Baroda: Operations Research Group.

KHUSRO, A.M. (1965) 'Land Reforms Since Independence', in V.B. Singh (ed.) *Economic History of India: 1857–1956*, New Delhi: Allied Publishers Ltd.

KRISHNA MURTHY, J. (1985) 'The Investigator, the Respondent and the Survey: The Problem of Getting Good Data on Women', in D. Jain and N. Banerjee (eds.) *Tyranny of the Household*, New Delhi: Shakti Books, Vikas Publishing House Pvt. Ltd.

KRISHNA, RAJ (1973) 'Unemployed in India', *Economic and Political Weekly*, Vol. VIII, No. 9.

————— (1980) 'The Economic Development of India', *Scientific America*, September.

KRISHNA RAJ, M. and V. PATEL (1981) 'Housework and the Political Economy of Women's Liberation', Paper presented at the First National Conference on Women's Studies, Bombay, India.

KRISHNAJI, N. (1980) 'Agrarian Structure and Family Formation: A Tentative Hypothesis', *Economic and Political Weekly*, Vol. XV, No. 13.

KYNCH, J. and A.K. SEN (1982) 'Indian Women: Well-Being and Survival', *Cambridge Journal of Economics*, Vol. 7.

LADEJINSKY, WOLF (1973) 'Drought in Maharashtra: Not in a Hundred Years', *Economic and Political Weekly*, Vol. VIII, No. 7.

————— (1976) 'The Green Revolution in Bihar—The Kosi Area: A Field Trip' and 'The Green Revolution in Punjab: A Field Trip', *Agricultural Development Council Reprint*, No. 28.

LEATHERMAN, THOMAS L., R.B. THOMAS and J. LOERSSEN (1988) 'Challenges to Seasonal Strategies of Rural Producers: Uncertainty and Conflict in the Adaptive Process', in R. Huss-Ashmore, J.J. Curry and R.K. Hitchcock (eds.) *Coping with Seasonal Constraints*.

LEIBENSTEIN, HARVEY (1982) 'Famine and Economic Development', in K.M. Cahill (ed.) *Famine*, Maryknoll, New York: Orbis Books.

LESLIE, JOANNE, MARGARET LYCETTE and MYRA BUVINIC (1986) 'Weathering Economic Crises: The Crucial Role of Women in Health', Washington, DC: The International Center for Research on Women.

LIPTON, M. (1983a) 'Labour and Poverty', World Bank Staff Working Paper No. 616, Washington, DC: World Bank.

————— (1983b) 'Demography and Poverty', World Bank Staff Working Paper No. 623, Washington, DC: World Bank.

————— (1983c) 'Poverty, Undernutrition and Hunger', World Bank Staff Working Papers No. 597, Washington, DC: World Bank.

————— (1984) 'Conditions of Poverty Groups and Impact on Indian Economic Development and Cultural Change: The Role of Labour', *Development and Change*, Vol. 15.

————— (1985a) 'The Poor and the Poorest: Some Interim Findings', Country Policy Department, Bank Assistance Policy Division, Washington, DC: World Bank.

————— (1985b) 'Land Assets and Rural Poverty', World Bank Staff Working Papers No. 744, Washington, DC: World Bank.

LONGHURST, RICHARD (1986) 'Household Food Strategies in Response to Seasonality and Famine', *IDS Bulletin*, Vol. 17, No. 3.

MACLACHLAN, M.D. (1983) *Why They Did Not Starve: Biocultural Adaptation in a South Indian Village*, Philadelphia: Institute for the Study of Human Issues.

MANGAHAS, MAHAR (ed.) (1978) 'Symposium on Household Economics', *Philippine Economic Journal*, No. 36, Vol. XVII, Nos. 1 and 2.

MASSIAH, JOYCELIN (1982) 'Manual on the Use of Socio–Economic Indicators of Women's Participation in Development', Paris: Division for Socio–Economic Analysis, UNESCO.

MAZUMDAR, VINA et al. (1975) 'Women in Agriculture', *Indian Farming*, 25 (8).

MAZUMDAR, VINA and HANNA PAPANEK (1984) 'Women and Household Strategies Project', UNO Report on First Regional Workshop, New Delhi: Centre for Women's Development Studies.

McALPIN, M. (1983) *Subject to Famine: Food Crisis and Economic Change in Western India, 1860–1920*, Princeton: Princeton University Press.

MEHRA, REKHA and K. SARADAMONI (1983) *Women and Rural Transformation: Two Studies*, New Delhi: Concept Publications.

MELLOR, JOHN W. and G.M. DESAI (eds.) (1986) *Agricultural Change and Rural Poverty: Variations on a Theme by Dharm Narian*, Oxford: Oxford University Press.

MENCHER, JOAN P. (1985) 'Landless Women Agricultural Laborers in India: Some Observations from Tamil Nadu, Kerala, W. Bengal', in IRRI (ed.) *Women in Rice Farming*, Los Banos, Philippines: IRRI.

————— (1986) 'South Indian Female Cultivators and Agricultural Labourers: Who Are They and What Do They Do?', Paper prepared for the Conference on Gender Issues in Farming Systems Research and Extension, Gainesville, Florida: University of Florida.

MENCHER, JOAN and D. D'AMICO (1978) 'Kerala Women as Labourers and Supervisors: Implications for Women and Development', Paper presented at

Session on WID, 10th International Congress of Anthropological and Ethnological Sciences, New Delhi, India.

MENCHER, JOAN, K. SARADAMONI and J. PANAKER (1979) 'Women in Rice Cultivation: Some Research Tools', *Studies in Family Planning*, Vol. 10, Nos. 11–12.

MESSER, ELLEN (1988) 'Seasonal Hunger and Coping Strategies: An Anthropological Discussion', in R. Huss-Ashmore, J.J. Curry, and R.K. Hitchcock (eds.) *Coping with Seasonal Constraints*.

MIES, MARIA (1980) 'Capitalist Development and Subsistence Reproduction: Rural Women in India', *Bulletin in Concerned Asian Scholars*, 12:1.

——— (1984) 'Capitalism and Subsistence: Rural Women in India', *Development*, 4.

MILLER, BARBARA (1981) *The Endangered Sex: Neglect of Female Children in Rural India*, Ithaca: Cornell University Press.

MINHAS, B.S. (1970) 'Rural Poverty, Land Distribution and Development', *Indian Economic Review*, April.

MIRACLE, MARVIN P. (1961) 'Seasonal Hunger: A Vague Concept and an Unexplored Problem', *Bulletin de l'Institut François d'Afrique Noire*, 823.

MISTRY, M.D. (1988) 'Drought Relief Work: The Other Face of the Government', Ahmedabad: DISHA.

MITRA, ASHOK (1979) *Implications of the Declining Sex Ratio in India's Population*, Delhi: Allied Publishers Ltd.

MITRA, ASHOK, SRIMANI, A.K. and L.P. PATHAK (1979) 'The Status of Women: Household and Non-Household Economic Activities', Programme of Women's Studies III, New Delhi: ICSSR.

MITRA, M. (1988) 'Women's Work and Household Survival Strategies: A Case Study of Santal Women's Lives and Work', New Delhi: Centre for Women's Development Studies.

MOOCK, JOYCE LEWINGER (ed.) (1986) *Understanding Africa's Rural Households and Farming Systems*, Boulder and London: Westview Press.

MORRIS, MORRIS D. (1974) 'What is a Famine?', *Economic and Political Weekly*, Vol. 9, No. 44.

——— (1975) 'Needed: A New Famine Policy', *Economic and Political Weekly*, Vol. 10, Nos. 5–7.

MORTIMER, MICHAEL (1989) *Adapting to Drought: Farmers, Famines and Desertification in West Africa*, Cambridge: Cambridge University Press.

MUELLER, EVA (1977) 'Design of In-Depth Employment Surveys for Human Resources Analysis in LDC', Paper presented at the annual meeting of the Population Association of America, St. Louis, Missouri.

——— (1978) 'Time Use Data', Ann Arbor: Population Studies Center, University of Michigan.

MUNROE, RUTH H., R.L. MUNROE, C. MICHELSON, A. KOEL, R. BOLTON and C. BOLTON (1983) 'Time Allocation in Four Societies', *Ethnology*, 22 (4).

MURTY, C.S. (1987) 'Influence of Socio-Economic Status on Contractual Terms of Tenancy: A Study in Two Delta Villages of Andhra Pradesh', *Economic and Political Weekly*, Vol. XXII, No. 39.

NATIONAL COUNCIL OF APPLIED ECONOMIC RESEARCH (1963) 'Techno-Economic Survey of Gujarat', New Delhi: National Council of Applied Economic Research.

NATIONAL COUNCIL OF APPLIED ECONOMIC RESEARCH (1986) 'Changes in Household Income, Interclass Mobility and Income Distribution in Rural India–A Longitudinal Study: 1970–71, 1981–82', New Delhi: National Council of Applied Economic Research.

NATIONAL INSTITUTE OF NUTRITION (1988) *Nutrition News*, Vol. 9, No. 4, Hyderabad: National Institute of Nutrition.

OUGHTON, L. (1982) 'The Maharashtra Drought of 1970–73: An Analysis of Scarcity', *Oxford Bulletin of Economics and Statistics*, Vol. 44, No. 3.

PHILLIPS, LYNN (1986) 'Gender Dynamics and Rural Household Strategies', Paper prepared for the Conference on Gender Issues in Farming System Research and Extension, Gainesville, Florida: University of Florida.

PINSTRUP-ANDERSEN, PER and M. JARAMILLO (1985) 'The Impact of Technological Change in Rice Production on Seasonal Fluctuations in Food Consumption and Calorie Deficiencies: The Case of North Arcot, India', Paper prepared for the IFPRI/FAO/AID Workshop on Seasonal Causes of Household Food Insecurity: Policy Implications and Research Needs.

QUIZON, ELIZABETH KING (1978) 'Time Allocation and Home Production in Rural Philippine Households', *Philippine Economic Journal*, No. 36, Vol. XVII, Nos. 1, 2.

RAHEJA, GLORIA GOODWIN (1988) *The Poison in the Gift: Ritual Prestation and the Dominant Caste in a North Indian Village*, Chicago: The University of Chicago Press.

RAMACHANDRAN, S. (1982) 'Method for Valuating Women's Contribution to Economic Activities', Paper presented at the Technical Seminar on Women's Work and Employment, New Delhi.

RAMAGE, COLIN S. (1977) *Great Indian Drought of 1899*, Palo Alto, California: Aspen Institute for Humanistic Studies.

RANGASWAMI, A. (1985) 'Women's Roles and Strategies during Food Crisis and Famines', Paper prepated for the International Workshop on Women's Roles in Food Self-Sufficiency and Food Strategies, Paris: ORSTOM.

RAO, HANUMANTH C.H., S.K. RAY and K. SUBBARAO (1988) *Unstable Agriculture and Droughts*, New Delhi: Vikas Publishing House Pvt. Ltd.

RATH, NILKANTHA (1985) ' "Garibi Hatao": Strategy Options', *Economic and Political Weekly*, Vol. XX, No. 6.

RAY, AMAL (1985) 'Delivery Systems for Rural Development in India: A Field View of Institutional Linkages', *Public Administration and Development*, Vol. V, No. 4.

REDDY, G.P. (1988) 'Drought and Famine: The Story of a Village in a Semi-arid Region of Andhra Pradesh', Paper presented at a Workshop on Afro-Asian Studies on Social Systems and Food Crisis, New Delhi: India International Center.

ROBERTSON, A.F. (1987) *The Dynamics of Productive Relationships: African Share Contracts in Comparative Perspective*, Cambridge: Cambridge University Press.

ROSENZWEIG, MARK R. and T. PAUL SCHULTZ (1982) 'Market Opportunities, Genetic Endowments and Intrafamily Resource Distribution: Child Survival in Rural India', *American Economic Review*, 72 (4).

RUDRA, ASHOK (1987) 'Labour Relations in Agriculture: A Study in Contrast', *Economic and Political Weekly*, Vol. XXII, No. 17.

RYAN, JAMES G. and R.D. GHODAKE (1980) 'Labor Market Behavior in Rural

Villages of South India: Effects of Season, Sex, and Socioeconomic Status', Economic Program Progress Report 14, Hyderabad: ICRISAT.

RYAN, JAMES G. and T.D. WALLACE (1985) 'Determinants of Labor Market Wages, Participation: Supply in Rural South Asia', Economics Group, Resources Management Program, Progress Report 73, Hyderabad: ICRISAT.

SARADAMONI, K. (1985) 'Declining Employment for the Labor-Increasing Involvement by Land-Owning Women', in IRRI (ed.) *Women in Rice Farming*, Los Banos, Philippines: IRRI.

—————— (1987) 'Labour, Land, and Rice Production: Women's Involvement in Three States', *Economic and Political Weekly*, Vol. XXII, No. 17, Review of Women's Studies.

SCHMINK, MARIANNE (1982) 'Women in the Urban Economy in Latin America: Women, Low-Income Households and Urban Services', Working Paper No. 1, New York: The Population Council.

—————— (1984) 'Household Economic Strategies: Review and Research Agenda', *Latin American Research Review*, Vol. 19.

SCHROEDER, RICHARD A. (1987) 'Gender Vulnerability to Drought: A Case Study of the Housa Social Environment', Natural Hazard Research, Working Paper No. 58, Madison, Wisconsin: University of Wisconsin.

SCHULTZ, T. PAUL. (1982) 'Women and Economics of the Family: Some Concepts and Issues', Paper prepared for the Rockefeller Foundation Workshop on Women, Households and Human Capital Development in Low Income Countries.

SEN, AMARTYA K. (1979) 'Issues in the Measurement of Poverty', *The Scandinavian Journal of Economics*, 81.

—————— (1981) *Poverty and Famines: An Essay on Entitlement and Deprivation*, Delhi: Oxford University Press.

—————— (1985) 'Family and Food: Sex Bias in Poverty', in P. Bardhan and T.N. Srinivasan (eds.) *Rural Poverty in South Asia*.

—————— (1985) 'Women, Technology and Sexual Division', *Trade and Development*, No. 6.

—————— (1986) 'Food, Economics and Entitlements', *Lloyds Bank Review*, April.

—————— (1987) 'Hunger and Entitlement', Research for Action, Helsinki, Finland: WIDER Institute.

SEN, GITA (1981) 'Rural Women and the Social Organization of Production: Some Conceptual Issues', in ILO (ed.) *Women in Rural Development*, Geneva: ILO.

—————— (1982) 'Women Workers and the Green Revolution', in Lourdes Beneria (ed.) *Women and Development*, New York: Praeger Publisher.

—————— (1983) 'Paddy Production, Processing and Women Workers in India—the South Versus the Northwest', Paper presented at a Conference on Females in Rice Farming Systems at IRRI, Philippines.

SHAH, A.M. and I.P. DESAI (1988) *Division and Hierarchy: An Overview of Caste in Gujarat*, Delhi: Hindustan Publishing Corporation.

SHAH, C.H. (ed.) *Agricultural Development of India: Policy and Prospects*, New Delhi: Orient Longman.

SHAH, C.H., V. SHAH and S. IYENGAR (1985) 'Agricultural Growth and Equity: Microlevel Experience', Ahmedabad: Gujarat Institute of Area Planning.

SHAH, G. (1978) 'Agricultural Labourers: Are They Bonded? Surat: Centre for Social Studies.

SHARMA, MIRIAM (1984) 'Caste, Class and Gender: Women's Role in Agriculture Production in North India', Working Papers on Women in International Development No. 357, Michigan: Michigan State University.

SHARMA, U. (1980) *Women, Work and Property in North-West India*, London: Tavistock.

SHINODA, T. (n.d.) 'Agricultural Production and Tenancy Pattern in a Village of Ahmedabad District', Mimeographed report.

SINGH, MANMOHAN (1986) 'The Quest for Equity in Development', R.R. Kale Memorial Lecture, Pune: Gokhale Institute of Politics and Economics.

SINGH R.P., N.S. JODHA and H.B. BINSWANGER (1985) 'ICRISAT Village Studies Management System (IVSDMS)', Research Management Program, Hyderabad: ICRISAT.

SINGH, R.P. and S.B. SINGH (1982) 'Features of Traditional Farming Systems in Two Villages of Gujarat', Economics Program Progress Report 35, Hyderabad: ICRISAT.

SINGH, R.V. (n.d.) *Fodder Trees of India*, New Delhi: Oxford and IBH Publishing Co.

SPOONER, BRIAN and H.S. MANN (eds.) (1982) *Desertification and Development: Drylands Ecology in Social Perspective*, London, New York: Academic Press.

SRINIVAS, M.N. (1955) 'The Social System of a Mysore Village', in M. Kim Marriott (ed.) *Village India*, Chicago: University of Chicago Press.

SRINIVAS, M.N. (1975) 'Village Studies, Participant Observation and Social Science Research in India', *Economic and Political Weekly*, Vol. 10, Nos. 33–35.

————— (1976) *The Remembered Village*, Bombay: Oxford University Press.

————— (1986) 'Notes on the Use of the Method of Participant Observation in the Study of Demographic Phenomena', in Hill, Caldwell, and Hill (eds.) *The Micro-Approach in Demographic Research*.

SRINIVAS, M.N., A.M. SHAH and E.A. RAMASWAMY (eds.) (1979) *The Field-worker and the Field: Problems and Challenges in Sociological Investigation*, Delhi: Oxford University Press.

SRINIVASAN, T.N. and P.N. BARDHAN (1974) *Poverty and Income Distribution in India*, Calcutta: Statistical Publishing Society.

STREEFLAND, PIETER H. (1987) 'Modes of Survival: Survival Strategies', Revised version of a paper for the Conference on Survival Strategies, Households and Kinship, KOTA VI, Amsterdam.

STUBBS, JEAN (1984) 'Some Thoughts on the Life Story Method in Labour History and Research on Rural Female Labour', *IDS Bulletin*, Vol. 15, No. 1.

SWAMY, DALIP S. (1976) 'Differentiation of Peasantry in India', *Economic and Political Weekly*, Vol. XI, No. 5.

SWIFT, JEREMY (1989) 'Why are Rural People Vulnerable to Famine?', *IDS Bulletin*, Vol. 20, No. 2.

TORRY, W.I. (1986a) 'Drought and the Government—Village Emergency Food Distribution System in India', *Human Organization*, 45 [1].

————— (1986b) 'Morality and Harm: Hindu Peasant Adjustments to Famines', *Social Science Information*, 25 [1].

VAUGHAM, M. (1987) *The Story of An African Famine: Gender and Famine in Twentieth Century Malawi*, Cambridge: Cambridge University Press.

VISARIA, PRAVIN (1981) 'Size of Land Holding, Living Standards and Employment in.Rural Western India, 1972–73', World Bank Staff Working Paper No. 459, Washington, DC: World Bank.
————— (1983) 'Indian Households with Female Heads: Incidence, Characteristics and Levels of Living', Paper presented at the Workshop on Women and Poverty, Calcutta: Centre for Studies in Social Science.
VISARIA, P. and L. VISARIA (1985) 'Indian Households with Female Heads: Their Incidence, Characteristics and Level of Living', in D. Jain and N. Banerjee (eds.) *Tyranny of the Household.*
VLASSOFF, CAROL (1982) 'The Status of Women in Rural India: A Village Study', *Social Action*, 32 (4).
————— (1986) 'Micro-Study of Culture and Fertility in Rural Maharashtra', in Hill, Caldwell and Hill (eds.) *The Micro-Approach in Demographic Research.*
VOLUNTARY AGENCIES OF GUJARAT (1987) 'Drought in Gujarat: Assessment and Recommendations', Paper presented at a Workshop on Drought Action, New Delhi.
VYAS, DARSHANA (1988) 'Survival Strategies in "Banni" During Drought: A Case Study of Four Villages', Paper prepared for a Seminar on Drought and Famine 1980s, Surat: Centre for Social Studies.
WADE, ROBERT (1986) 'Common Property Resource Management in South Indian Villages', in Proceedings of the Conference on Common Property Resource Management, Washington, DC: National Academy Press.
————— (1987) 'The Management of Common Property Resources: Finding a Cooperative Solution', Research Observer, Vol. 2, No. 2.
WHITE, BENJAMIN (1976) 'Problems in Estimating the Value of Work in Peasant Household Economics: An Example from Rural Java', Paper prepared for ADC–RTN Workshop on Family Labour Force Use in Agricultural Production, Hyderabad: ICRISAT.
————— (1980) 'Rural Household Studies in Anthropological Perspective', in Binswanger et al. (eds.) *Rural Household Studies in Asia.*
————— (1984) 'Measuring Time Allocation, Decision Making and Agrarian Changes Affecting Rural Women: Examples from Recent Research in Indonesia', *IDS Bulletin*, Vol. 15, No. 1.
WHITE, CHRISTINE P. and KATE YOUNG (1984) 'Research on Rural Women: Feminist Methodological Questions', *IDS Bulletin*, Vol. 15, No. 1.
WIGMS, WINATI, K. SURYANATA and B. WHITE (1980) 'Comparison of the Results of Time-Allocation Research, Using Two Different Recall Periods', Paper presented at the Workshop on Village Economy and Institutions, Los Banos, Philippines: IRRI.
WISER, W.H. (1936) *The Hindu Jajmani System*, Lucknow: Lucknow Publishing House.
WISER, WILLIAM and CHARLOTTE (1966) *Behind Mud Walls: 1930–60*, Berkeley: University of California Press.
WOLLENBERG, EVA (1986) 'An Evaluation of Methodologies Used in Time Allocation Research', Paper presented at the Conference on Gender Roles in Farming Systems Research and Extension, Gainesville, Florida: University of Florida.
WOOD, CHARLES H. (1981) 'Structural Changes and Household Strategies: A Conceptual Framework for the Study of Rural Migration', *Human Organization*, 40 (Winter).